Inside Mercedes F1

Inside Mercedes F1

Life in the Fast Lane

Matt Whyman

CROWN

NEW YORK

Published in the United States by Crown, an imprint of the Crown Publishing Group, a division of Penguin Random House LLC, New York.
crownpublishing.com

CROWN and the Crown colophon are registered trademarks of Penguin Random House LLC.

"AMG" and "Three Pointed Star in a Ring" are trademarks of Mercedes-Benz Group AG. All other logos of sponsors of the Mercedes-AMG PETRONAS F1 Team are used with the permission of their respective owners, all of whom reserve their respective rights in the same.

Library of Congress Control Number: 2024944113

Hardcover ISBN: 978-0-593-73564-0
Ebook ISBN: 978-0-593-73565-7

Printed in the United States of America on acid-free paper

Editor: Aubrey Martinson
Production editor: Liana Faughnan
Production manager: Dustin Amick
Copy editor: Kevin Clift
Proofreaders: Chris Fortunato and Tess Rossi
Publicists: Mary Moates and Lindsay Cook
Marketer: Mason Eng

9 8 7 6 5 4 3 2 1

First Edition

CONTENTS

CONTENTS

PREFACE

Right now, this desert circuit under the stars is the last place anyone in the team wants to be.

The timer has just run out on the qualifying session that determines the grid order for tomorrow's race, the first in Formula 1's 2023 season. At the back of the garage, here at the Bahrain International Circuit, it feels as if the air is running out fast. All around, personnel are vacating the space as quickly as they can. The mechanics rush to meet the cars as they return to the pit lane while the engineers make their way out to a briefing room to work out the next steps. Everyone, it seems, from the technicians to the team physio, has suddenly found a pressing reason to be elsewhere. Within less than a minute, just one individual from the team remains.

Toto Wolff, the Austrian billionaire, part owner of the Mercedes-AMG PETRONAS F1 Team, CEO and Team Principal, is seated on a high stool with his back to me. The boss, as he's informally known here, is positioned at the bridge of the engineers' station: a central island that divides the garage into two bays. In terms of motor racing real estate, the confined space within this live working environment is at a premium. Sixty minutes earlier, with the session just under way and the garage teeming with people, I had been ushered in to stand before a tool cabinet just a few feet behind Wolff and then quietly advised not to move. As a result, I don't believe he's aware that I'm here. Nor does this feel like the right time to even clear my throat.

Wolff is six foot five inches tall and in good shape for a man in his early fifties. Usually, this helps him to present an outer confidence. Just then, I am alone in seeing a rare chink in that armor. The neckline of his dark hair is just low enough to brush the collar of his white team shirt, below which the fabric is pulled tight by slumped shoulder blades as Wolff stares into the monitor before him.

This is the captain of a ship. Having set eyes on the passage ahead, it's his heart that has just sunk.

Wolff hasn't moved since the twenty driver name tags and lap times on his monitor's leaderboard window locked into order. As the 2023 racing calendar gets started, it's the first competitive test of performance across the field. The result is painfully revealing on several levels. In a foreboding show of strength, the two-time F1 world champion, Max Verstappen, has just placed his Red Bull car on pole (the front of the grid in a position known as P1) with some ease. Trailing in at P6 and P7 respectively, Mercedes F1 drivers George Russell and Lewis Hamilton are down on the Dutch driver by over half a second. It might seem little more than the time between successive heartbeats but it represents a seemingly insurmountable gulf. As one team member tells me later, bridging that gap could take "at least six months of car development time."

Alone in front of his data screen, Wolff is faced by the reality of the situation, which has him by the throat. That Aston Martin's Fernando Alonso has surprised everyone to claim P5 behind the two Ferraris and the second Red Bull adds to the jugular squeeze. As an engine supplier to the Aston Martin team, as well as several others on the grid, Mercedes have just been outclassed by a customer. He could be confronted by the numbers or simply staring at a reflection of his own soul, for this moment can mean many things. Without a doubt, it's an existential horror for Wolff and one made harder to bear by the history of Mercedes since their return to the sport as a team in 2010. After all, this is the racing outfit that has won a record-breaking eight consecutive World Constructors' Championships from 2014–2021. It's also helped power superstar driver Lewis Hamilton to match Michael Schumacher's record of seven World Drivers' titles. That the previous season saw Mercedes F1 misfire with a car that no longer raced from the front was considered by some to be a long-overdue leveling. For Toto Wolff, a visceral perfectionist, the experience was both painful and deeply challenging. For all the talk of resilience as a key component of this team, often by Wolff when things were going well, it presented an opportunity to see if Mercedes F1 really could grow stronger and wiser from this uncharacteristic year. Wolff duly sharpened his saber, emboldening his troops to bring a car to the 2023 title fight that would dispatch both critics and competitors.

Throughout the preceding winter months between race seasons, governed by strict restrictions surrounding on-track testing, the team believed they could see light at the end of the wind tunnel. As the new car evolved from concept to a carbon fiber and titanium challenger, all the simulations pointed toward another race winner. In a confident mood, Mercedes F1 livestreamed the launch of the 2023 car under gleaming spotlights and the proud gaze of Wolff and his two drivers. Here was a legendary team signaling that they were back on the front foot. *Trust us. We have the pedigree. This year is ours for the taking.*

As the brake dust settles on the new season's opening qualifying round, despite all the talk and expectation, Mercedes F1 find themselves painfully exposed.

*

A few weeks before the cars had made their track debut, I found myself presented with a rare opportunity to be embedded with the Mercedes F1 team. Over eighteen months, I would be witnessing their efforts to stage a comeback. The time frame on the table straddled two racing seasons because behind every F1 squad is a dual narrative. At the front end is the trackside drama that plays out at each race weekend around the world from early spring to late autumn. Netflix's *Formula 1: Drive to Survive* had made the sport more accessible to fans than ever before, but this was an opportunity to go deeper with one team not just in the paddock but also back at base. For just as the racing gets under way in one season, work begins on the design, production, and build of the car for the following year. It's an intense project involving thousands of people, seemingly overwhelming at times, and culminating in a frenzy of activity over the winter months. In chronicling both sides of the story, including the opportunity to see the evolution of the 2024 car, Mercedes F1 were offering me unprecedented access.

We want you to push us, came the call to arms in the invitation from Mercedes F1, *and we will push you.*

I interpreted this to mean that I would be encouraged to peer into places that until now had been off limits. Such a pledge of transparency appealed to me. Frankly, if Mercedes F1 wanted to present me with a select view of life on the inside, it would be very difficult to maintain across such a prolonged period. As well as seeking to put the previous season behind them, this was also a chance to shine a light on the fact that a racing outfit like Mercedes F1 is about much more than those who sit at the head of the table: namely two drivers and a team boss. As the sport had also moved on from erecting screens in front of the cars in the pit garage, it seemed an opportune moment to offer new insight by applying the same principle to the wider organization. Above all, there exist entire ranks of talented men and women behind the scenes whose efforts often go unrecognized. Directly and indirectly, to borrow a favorite line from Toto Wolff himself, everyone contributes their own millisecond of performance.

Standing in the Mercedes F1 garage a short while later, in the aftermath of qualifying for the Bahrain Grand Prix, I am witness to the team boss silently absorbing what the session has revealed. After a long year in the wilderness, and a fight back at the factory to deliver a competitive car for this season, Toto Wolff has just witnessed a heartfelt collective effort fall catastrophically short. I don't judge him for seemingly forgetting to blink and breathe. This team he has led for ten years is woven into the fabric of his identity like the sponsors' names on his team shirt.

The performance deficit to the front of the grid isn't just about what it means for the championship ahead, even if it is unthinkable at this moment. For Mercedes F1 have also been set on laying to rest a profound sense of injustice that marked the climax of the 2021 season in Abu Dhabi, when human error by the race director robbed Hamilton of the chance to become the most successful F1 driver of all time. The episode, which was caused by a failure to correctly implement the rules following a safety car period (a deployment that slows and compacts the field while a track hazard is cleared), handed Red Bull's Max Verstappen a last-lap advantage over race leader Hamilton. While the Fédération Internationale de l'Automobile (FIA), the sport's governing body, would go on to uphold the result, having agreed to tighten procedures in the future, it was widely considered to be the greatest miscarriage in motorsport history. Despite Mercedes F1's struggles throughout the subsequent season, in contrast to Red Bull, who strengthened their hand by winning both the Drivers' and the Constructors' World Championships, the experience crystallized into a motivating force. It kept the fire burning as Wolff emboldened his team to deliver a car for 2023 that would right so many wrongs.

And now we've arrived at what should be a blazing turning point in the team's fortunes, only for such hopes for the season ahead to be snuffed out by their rivals.

In the pit lane outside the garage, personnel from rival teams sweep one way and the other. Media crews, marshals, medics, and officials jostle among them. Collectively, they move to a soundtrack provided by public speaker announcements, the cheering and whistling from fans in the grandstand on the opposite side of the track, and the beating blades of the camera helicopter overhead. Largely hidden from sight by the engineers' island, Wolff seems oblivious to it all. In a moment from now, he'll surface from his thoughts, roll up his sleeves to just below the elbow and become the public face of the team. Until then, he must come to terms with the fact that reality has just overtaken his expectations.

I had half expected my tenancy to be cut short. Instead, Mercedes F1 recognized that a team in adversity revealed more about its true nature than a racing outfit that simply won everything. So, rather than a handshake and a goodbye, I was issued with team gear for the season to help establish trust with the trackside personnel. Equipped with my notebook and voice recorder, and now with a long, challenging season ahead as a backdrop, I was free to get to know not just the drivers but also the mechanics, engineers, technicians, analysts, and strategists, the trainers and supporting staff, as well as those who handled external interests: from celebrity guests and commercial partners to journalists seeking a scoop. I would travel with the team, share meals, stay at the same hotels, and transfer to and from each circuit alongside them. In the same way, I would become a familiar face at the Mercedes F1 factory, charting the development of the car for the subsequent season from concept to design, manufacture, production, and what had to be a change in fortune.

In sharing life with the key players at races around the world and back at base, I had open access to one of the greatest sports teams in history. The 100-strong race crew facing twenty-three grand prix races in that season is effectively just a visible front end. The design, development, and build of each year's World Championship challenger takes place at the Mercedes F1 operational headquarters just inside the ring road around the market town of Brackley in Northamptonshire. Then there's Mercedes-AMG High Performance Powertrains (HPP), the team's engine development center in nearby Brixworth. Here, HPP designs, manufactures, and supplies Mercedes F1 and several customer teams with state-of-the-art hybrid power units (combining turbocharged combustion engines with energy harvesting systems). The team refer to both sites as factories. In reality, they're immaculate production, commercial, marketing, communications, and administrative complexes populated by a highly skilled workforce of more than 2,000 people. All of whom devote their professional lives to the existence of just two cars on the track.

Collectively, these men and women would help me to paint a portrait of an elite racing team in extremis. Following a year that was never meant to be repeated, but across a more revealing season than any golden age, exactly how would Mercedes F1 rise to the challenge? They had the resources and expertise, but could the mindset, hunger, and desire endure? Would this be a lesson in humility, composure, and even renewal, or a slow-motion act of self-destruction? No team had faced this kind of immense pressure before, a weight of expectation applied to itself as much as from external forces. If it didn't result in a transformation, this time it could prove crushing.

Inevitably, in joining any close-knit group, some individuals proved harder to crack than others. I understood why Toto Wolff would become my greatest challenge. A joint equal shareholder in the team, alongside the Mercedes-Benz Group and the chemical multinational INEOS, this man at the heart of Mercedes F1 remained a warm and generous host throughout. It's just the story foretold on that Bahrain track that tormented him. If anything, that moment of raw vulnerability in the garage revealed Wolff's core character to me. For a man committed to performance excellence, that first qualifying result was a devastating blow. It could have floored him. Instead, over the course of my time on this F1 front line, Wolff seemed to absorb the pain and then trust in his team to keep pushing to make it bearable.

Across an elite motor racing organization, everything moves in high gear. It doesn't just need to be sustained over a nine-month season visiting twenty countries across five continents, but also throughout the winter months before the cycle starts again. To be successful in Formula 1, a team of this caliber have to channel their energy in one direction only. Ultimately, winning is the goal. In competition with nine other teams, Mercedes F1 are in a fight for engineering, mechanical, aerodynamic, and driving perfection. The margins are minuscule, measured in milliseconds. When it arrives, victory can be translated into the pride that justifies the blood, sweat, and sacrifice, and financially on a sliding scale from a commercial prize pool worth more than a billion dollars. Without that unremitting drive, and with so much at stake, a team won't just stall but implode.

What Mercedes F1 faced now was a process. It would be one that began with squeezing every atom of performance from another underwhelming car and tilted headlong toward the creation of a challenger that could embody the brilliance Wolff craved. In doing so, he demanded that his team live by their values, apply critical thinking to where they had gone wrong, and then redouble their efforts to get back on track. As that moment of realization arrived for Wolff, at a circuit far from home, I had no need for him to put it into words. From the Team Principal's body language alone, he had just witnessed a tragedy. And yet I had time on my side to discover if he could transform it into a tale of redemption.

At heart, I found myself watching a man on the wrong end of a winning streak truly put his resilience to the test, and then seek to galvanize every member of the motor-racing powerhouse he'd built to come back wiser, stronger, and faster. Mercedes F1 might be represented by two high-performance cars, in a ruthless and demanding combination of sport and precision engineering, but at every level of Wolff's racing team that driving force is human. Which is what this book is all about.

CHAPTER ONE

SHOCK & AWE

The Bahrain Grand Prix
Bahrain International Circuit, Sakhir
March 3–5, 2023

Six days before the opening race weekend of the season, a fore-telling had occurred at the Mercedes F1 factory in Brackley. It presented itself to key personnel on a crisp Sunday morning as bright and clear as a crystal ball. The prediction concerned the car for the forthcoming season. Nobody liked what they saw.

This glimpse into the future involved no dark arts, just data from the three days of on-track testing permitted to all teams. The assessment had taken place at the same circuit in Bahrain where Toto Wolff's ambition to launch a championship contender would ultimately run out of road. Until then, as the trackside engineers convened to pick over their findings—having just returned from the Gulf island state on a red-eye flight—a shard of time was still available to unlock performance from that year's new car. According to the simulations, the W14 had the potential to be at one with the track in terms of better handling and ultimately faster lap times. The team just needed to conjure it from the car in order to reshape their destiny.

I arrived at the Mercedes F1 factory in good time for the post-testing debrief. This isn't your conventional manufacturing plant.

The team's base is more like a sprawling tech campus comprising trim and functional buildings and a tree-lined avenue that takes visitors across a bridge over a river to the main operations center. In a race to be the fastest on the track, Mercedes F1 can't afford to be a nine-to-five operation. Apart from two mandatory annual shutdowns that apply to every team in the sport—literally freezing all work for a fortnight in the summer and again at Christmas—the factory is open day and night. So, despite the fact that dawn had only just broken on this traditional day of rest, I checked in with a lobby receptionist looking like he was midway through his shift. Here, visitors like me take a lanyard and then pretend to be cool about the enormous wall cabinet of trophies. It's a reminder, if one is needed, that this is the headquarters of one of the most successful teams in Formula 1. I also found it impossible to ignore the fact that an actual racing car is on display in the seating area. The bodywork is sleek and predominantly black—part of a commitment to promoting diversity and fighting racism. Toward the rear of the car the livery fades to silver, a signature color for Mercedes throughout their history in motorsport. Indeed, the current F1 team are also known as the Silver Arrows. Look closely at the front wing and tiny chips and scratches incurred at high speed reveal themselves like scars from the heat of battle. In the silence and stillness of the lobby, at odds with its natural environment on the track, the car seemed like some kind of engineering taxidermy.

The car in question is the Mercedes-AMG F1 W12 E Performance, commonly abbreviated to the W12.* Like fine wines,

---

* The full naming convention combines the team's German automotive heritage (the "W" standing for "wagen," which means "car" in the home country of Mercedes-Benz) with a numbering system that began with 01 in 1926. The current Mercedes F1 team adapted the system with a number reset and the insertion of "F1" in front of the "W" to distinguish the modern era of

there have been plenty of vintage years since the current Mercedes F1 team returned to the sport in 2010 with the W01. While the W12 counts among them, this one also comes with a finish that is still hard for many to swallow. That the nose sported a #44 decal—Lewis Hamilton's iconic race number—spelled out to me that this is in fact an artifact from motorsport history: the 2021 challenger in which Hamilton had been denied the World Drivers' Championship under such controversial circumstances.

It only takes me a moment, before I am invited to join the meeting upstairs, to recognize that the car is on display lest the team forget.

For such a significant prize to be snatched away on the last lap of the final race of that season had floored Mercedes F1. In 2022, it was just as painful for the team to find that the successor to the W12 was unable to match the performance of Red Bull and also Ferrari. For the Silver Arrows as much as the fans, the W13 just served as a reminder that Formula 1 is a car development competition as much as a battle on the track. Now the new season beckoned. With every team set to pick over their findings from the three-day testing session, the race was effectively under way.

My first impression was that I'd walked into some advanced war chamber, a clinically white space accommodating a boardroom table that had to be twenty meters in length. From slots in the table's surface, monitors were in the process of rising soundlessly in front of every seat. The generals, represented by some two dozen engineers and car-critical personnel, had gathered on arrival to refuel at the coffee trolley. They had come a long way to be here, after all. Even without the caffeine hit, however, this

---

cars. In recent years, a new "E Performance" technology label has been added in recognition of the work by the team's Brixworth division.

group, in team regulation travel wear (a casual combination of white T-shirt and sneakers, gray sweater and blue joggers), seemed to be strikingly alert. In Formula 1, time waits for no team. These are people well-versed in hopping continents and then putting in a solid shift at the factory. With just a week to go before the season start, every available second could make a difference to performance.

Among the major players, I recognized Technical Director Mike Elliott and Andrew Shovlin, the team's Trackside Engineering Director known to everyone (quite possibly including his own family) as "Shov." As well as the group gathered in this room, another ten or so names and faces popped up in the video-conference window that appeared on our monitors. It was only as the meeting convened—on the hour and with no preamble—that I detected some anxiety behind such focus among those present.

"Where we've ended up is not acceptable," said an opening voice from so far down the other end of the table that I couldn't see who was behind it. The view is quickly echoed by those who address the room in turn.

"It wasn't long ago that we were kings of winter testing," said Peter Bonnington ruefully. He is better known as Bono, Lewis Hamilton's Race Engineer. "It feels like we've slipped."

With every contribution over the next forty-five minutes, effectively a summary of performance from the testing session presented by a different group head, the data on the screen changed. From lap-time telemetry to tire-wear analytics, each pictogram or tracer chart highlighted different characteristics of the W14. With only fractional differences between teammates Lewis Hamilton and George Russell, but notable shortfalls compared to key rivals like Red Bull and Ferrari, the overall picture provided little scope for interpretation.

Throughout, Shov steered the meeting in his efficient and

pragmatic style; a voice of calm but with an awareness that improvements had to be found.

"Are we, as leaders, holding standards high enough?" he asked at one point.

It's a rhetorical question, but one met by an uncomfortable pause. In less than a week, these engineers would fly back to Bahrain for the first grand prix of the season. Until then, as they saw things, there was still time to overcome obstacles. In a race of their own, it would begin with identifying why the performance was not forthcoming and then working out how to wrest it from the car. Around the table, I sensed people begin to shuffle as if turning their thoughts to the onerous task at hand. It was only when Shov seemed set to wind up the meeting that a voice cut in to address the room remotely.

"This is just not good enough."

The Austrian accent instantly identified the contributor on the videoconference link. If anyone had been set to breathe out, on hearing Toto Wolff they promptly put that on hold.

"We need to feel a certain degree of embarrassment here."

The boss sounded tense and frustrated. The car was central to his concern but what also needled Wolff was the fact that as an engine supplier to several teams on the grid, Mercedes were being outperformed by a customer. If Aston Martin delivered on the promise they had just shown in testing . . . and here he paused, to let those in the room play this out for themselves. Then, as if returning to a more comfortable space, Wolff went on to remind his team that they possessed everything necessary—the values, knowledge, expertise, and resources—to build a race-winning car.

"We blame the problem not the person," he finished, stressing a collective responsibility that included himself, "but nevertheless . . . come *on*!"

*

5

At the Bahrain International Circuit, surrounded by desert scrub, the swipe gates to the paddock stand as a portal between two worlds. The outside area is open to fans, with 36,000 in attendance on this first race day of the season. It's only mid-morning but the grandstands are filling up and already one of the first support races is under way. The banshee howl of Porsche cars can be heard from afar. I can't see the track as I follow the walkways, signposts, and a tunnel under the home straight to my destination, but the noise commands attention. In the same way, I hear the argument by F1's governing body that the presence of the sport in a country with questionable human rights records—one of several on the racing calendar—encourages opportunities for engagement and dialogue. In my short stay here, however, I only find this in the grassroots outreach efforts by some of the teams to engage with minority groups, and most visibly the rainbow design that decorates Lewis Hamilton's helmet this weekend. It's a bold personal statement in support of an oppressed LGBTQ+ community in the region, and indeed the Mercedes F1 driver argues that the sport should be doing more to make a tangible difference.

Such is Hamilton's profile, along with his fellow competitors, that I find crowds gathered behind crush barriers flanking the paddock entrance. They're here to see their heroes or key team personnel transformed into familiar faces thanks to the phenomenal global success of *Drive to Survive*. It's just one example of the huge upswing in attention that F1 has experienced since the American giant Liberty Media purchased the commercial rights to the sport in 2017 for $4.6 billion. As sport and entertainment come together on this global scale, with money as the driving force, inevitably it becomes tangled in politics.

Here in Bahrain, the majority of fans are wearing team merchandise in the form of T-shirts and caps. Strikingly, there's no strong sense of the tribal loyalty more commonly found outside soccer grounds. I negotiate my way around families and groups of friends sporting a mix and match of gear from every team in the competition: Mercedes F1, Red Bull, Ferrari, Williams, McLaren, AlphaTauri, Haas, Alfa Romeo, Alpine, and Aston Martin. It's an atmosphere of shared excitement, finishing as I approach the paddock with the kind of uncompromising security checks you'd expect at an airport. Collecting my bag from the X-ray scanner, I press my lanyard to a reader on the pillar at this closely guarded gateway. In response, my mugshot appears on the screen above it. Paddock passes are a precious commodity, and it has taken some red tape cutting for me to reach this moment. With a click of internal locks retracting, the turnstile light flicks from red to green and I am free to cross the threshold into F1's inner sanctum.

At once, the mismatch of team clothing settles into something altogether more uniform.

There are ten teams on the grid. Each one dresses their trackside personnel in regulation gear. The colors define them as much as the sponsors' logos, from Ferrari's iconic "rosso corsa," or racing red, to the lawn tennis greens of Aston Martin, and the sky blues of Williams to McLaren's papaya orange. Mercedes F1 adopt a high contrast, black and white approach with flashes of silver and turquoise. Everything from the choice of pants or shorts to the collared shirts, polo tops, sweaters, and jackets is designed by team partner Tommy Hilfiger, with sneakers provided by team supplier Puma. Although I feel a bit like I'm in cosplay on my first race weekend, I notice how people in the same team gear nod and smile in passing. Yes, we're walking billboards but there's a unifying element at play here. I also register that across the teams there exists a great deal of mutual respect. Given that everyone here is on the same road around the world for ten months each year, I feel like I have just joined a troupe in a traveling circus.

At every circuit on the F1 calendar, the most important feature of the paddock is the pit. This is a long row of motor racing stables that feed into the pit lane where the cars are meticulously prepared for race day. Teams line up according to the outcome of the previous season's constructors' fight, with Red Bull taking the top spot closest to the pit lane entrance where Mercedes F1 had presided since winning in 2014. This year, as a reflection of an arduous 2022 for the team, the Silver Arrows occupy the third garage along with Ferrari sandwiched in between. With creative use of portable paneling, teams can also partition the available space to suit their requirements. While the two cars representing each team take prime real estate at the front, a garage often allows for additional areas to the side and rear to serve as engineering meeting rooms, technician stations, workshops, and storage facilities.

Toward the back of the pit, a narrow corridor leads to the paddock's central artery: a bustling open-air promenade that connects everything from media pens to team hospitality suites. With upward of 1,000 people inside what is effectively a gated community—the majority working flat out to deliver on their team's objectives—it's not one for the claustrophobic. From press conferences to media interviews, as well as each team's commercial engagements and promotional events to connect with spectators and promote the sport, I find myself inside a hive of activity within which every bee must display the correct credentials around their neck.

A strict timetable governs the events and activities that take place at each race weekend—both on and off the track—overseen rigidly by the sport's referee or ruling body, the FIA. In the world of F1, that weekend starts early and generally extends to four days. Proceedings kick off with a media day. This had taken place on Thursday here in Bahrain and saw leading figures from all the teams engage in press conferences and interviews. At this season opener, Friday comprised two hour-long preparatory sessions on the track. In Free Practice 1 (FP1), the teams and their drivers used the sixty minutes available to explore car configurations such as aerodynamics, suspension, brake settings, engine modes, and fuel loads. Often known as the setup, the aim here is for the teams to tune or "dial" their cars' handling capabilities into the track.

Tires are central to this process. With a choice to be made by every team, it can inform the heart of a tactical plan and make or break their race.

In Formula 1, the Italian manufacturer Pirelli has been the sole supplier since 2011. The race tires it manufactures and provides are very different from road car treads. They're a giant eighteen inches in diameter and precision engineered according to strict technical specifications. For the 2023 season, Pirelli has produced eight different rubber compounds. Six are known as slick tires for racing in dry conditions. Categorized as C0 to C5,* these are engineered to range in durability and performance. Two more compounds, the intermediates and full wets, are reserved for rainy conditions.

For each race weekend, Pirelli makes just three compounds from the C0 to C5 range available to the teams. These are simply referred to as hard, medium, and soft. Every team receives the same allocation of thirteen sets,† which consists of two lots of hards, three mediums, and eight sets of softs per car. Ultimately, each car must run two different compounds during a dry race (with wet-weather tires on hand if required).

---

* C0 is the more durable tire compound with the least grip, while the C5 is the softest with the most traction. Generally, C5 is the fastest in the range but quickest to wear out.
† For race weekends featuring Sprint events, the tire allocation is slightly tweaked.

Tires are effectively the interface between the car and the track. Like any relationship, it's complicated. Understanding how to bring out the best in them, however, can bring happiness to both driver and team.

In FP1, Mercedes F1 and their rivals had their first chance to assess how the cars performed on the tire selection available. This weekend, it's C1 to C3, which are more suited to the abrasive quality of the Bahrain track surface. Factors such as temperature or a car's particular aerodynamic characteristics can also influence how quickly they warm up sufficiently or "switch on" for optimum grip as well as determining the rate of degradation. With so many variables to consider, no team could afford to waste a second of this first Friday session in devising a tire strategy while establishing the base setup for their cars.

Later, following a comprehensive debriefing between the drivers and engineers, Free Practice 2 (FP2) provided the teams with an opportunity for further exploration and refinement. As every team is permitted to run a different program in each session, it's hard to see precisely how a car is performing relative to the rest of the field. Nevertheless, as Technical Director Mike Elliott began to sense how the teams stacked up, he conceded that it presented "an uncomfortable picture." Both Mercedes F1 cars had only been capable of delivering midpack lap times, with Red Bull comfortably leading the field and Ferrari performing strongly. Even if the team had conjured some improvement since the post-testing debrief, it wasn't enough. Hamilton and Russell both reported issues with rear sliding, which chews up tires and costs precious milliseconds, while Aston Martin's Fernando Alonso topped the time sheet to turn Toto Wolff's worst-case scenario into an inescapable truth.

That is the stark reality of where we are at, lamented Elliott in his dispatch to the factory at the end of the day, as it began to dawn on the team that the W14 wasn't just suffering from teething trouble but something more fundamental in design. *We will need to be honest about the fact that we have not done a good enough job over the winter, and need to quickly figure out why.*

Saturday morning opened with the third and final free practice session (FP3). Overnight, armed with the data collected from the track, the team's simulation engineers back at the factory—working with the former F1 driver Anthony Davidson—had sought to evolve and improve the weekend's car setup. There would be no magic bullet for Mercedes F1, however, but a reckoning as a hazy dusk settled over the circuit ahead of qualifying. In this one-hour session, divided into three knockout rounds (Q1, Q2, and Q3) of diminishing durations, drivers compete to set the fastest lap times to determine the starting grid for the race. For Red Bull, as well as Ferrari and Aston Martin, the results brought only confidence and high hopes, and not just for this first grand prix of the year. Car development is an unforgiving race in its own right. It waits for nobody. If any team falls behind, they must work to reclaim that lost ground and then also catch up with those who have continued to push ahead. It meant that late that night, as the paddock slowly emptied, Mercedes F1 found themselves facing a season that had just become even more challenging.

"Composure is the keyword of the weekend," says Bradley Lord, Chief Communications Officer, ahead of the race. Since qualifying, both the team and the media are asking the same question: why has the W14 fallen short of expectation and what can be done about it? In response, as a Team Principal who is quite evidently reeling in the face of the car's performance so soon after the curtain lifted on the season, Toto Wolff is on record as saying the concept will be scrapped. "I'm just not quite clear how we define 'concept,'" cautions Lord, the man responsible for steadying Mercedes F1 in the face of narrative turbulence generated by the press. Ultimately, Lord is seeking to avoid any kind of misinterpretation while the team considers its direction with the car. It adds some importance to the information sheet his communications team had handed out to the assembled media earlier in the race weekend when the W14 was first wheeled into the pit lane for closer inspection. Russell's car—identifiable by his #63 race number—had been selected as the Mercedes F1 representative for this mandatory showcase that applies to all the teams, along with the issue of a printed summary of the main updates.

Here at the debut race of the season, and especially in the wake of last night's qualifying outcome, the W14 attracts a great deal of attention. While much of this is down to the shortfall in performance, the main focus settles upon one visible aspect of the car that sets it apart from its competitors. While every rival challenger sports sidepods, a bodywork feature to shape and sculpt airflow, Mercedes F1 have continued with a move from the previous year in which they all but departed from them completely. The "zeropods," as they became known, look as if a vacuum has been created inside traditional pods, which somehow pulled them in. If an F1 car could inhale and hold its breath, that's what is going on here. It looks magnificent, but appearance counts for nothing when it comes to results.

That Mercedes F1 failed to challenge for the championship in the preceding season has left fans and observers baffled. In 2022, the W13 claimed just a single grand prix victory. A far cry from their dominant form that defined an era, why would they continue down the same design path? Of course, there is a great deal of complex aerodynamics and mechanical engineering at work here. The zeropods are simply one feature of an innovative design that was intended to win championships. It's just that they're so visible—or invisible—they've become the smoking gun.

12

The team back Wolff's assertion that something has to change. It takes courage to admit to failure this early in the season, but the inevitable pain is the only way to make progress. Until the engineers are able to make an informed decision about the precise shape and direction of the car, however, it falls to the Mercedes F1 communications team to anchor the story in facts from the here and now.

While one of the cars attracts further press scrutiny in the pit lane, the two Mercedes F1 drivers are preparing to go on show in a different way. Back in the paddock promenade, I fall in with Lewis Hamilton and a small entourage as he heads for the swipe gates. With his long braids pulled back into a hair tie, and wearing stonewashed jeans, a white team shirt, and sunglasses, he's a unique mix of racing driver and rock star. Above all, Hamilton's achievements define him; not just the seven drivers' crowns but also the fact that a mixed-race kid from a humble background north of London tore through a sport at a time when privilege, connections, and financial backing propelled so many drivers. On the other side of the gate, Hamilton will be collected by minibus and escorted a short distance inside the circuit to a stage behind the main grandstand. There, thousands of fans wait for their F1 heroes to step out from the wings to wave and take part in a noisy, adrenalized Q&A session. Every driver on the grid will make an appearance. It's just one part of a packed daily engagement schedule they're required to keep across the weekend, from interactions with media and fans to an audience with strings of partner guests. All such commitments must be squeezed in between the serious business of engineering and strategy meetings before ultimately strapping themselves into the motor racing equivalent of a rocket ship and shooting for the Moon.

The contrast in demands placed upon the drivers is stark, and the reason why veterans like Hamilton aim to be as efficient as they can with their time and energy. He moves briskly, chaperoned by team members but still greeting fans and posing for selfies on the move. Two minibuses await us, as does Hamilton's teammate, George Russell. The young British racing star is chatting to a colleague while the film crew from *Drive to Survive* work from a discreet distance and eavesdrop with the aid of a boom microphone as long as a fly fishing rod. As Hamilton and his people climb inside one minibus, I join Russell's group in the vehicle behind. I barely have time to settle into my seat before we swing around somewhat overdramatically on to an access road. Russell glances up from his phone. He swaps a side-eye with me and then a quiet smile in the wake of the maneuver. I can't help but feel sorry for the poor guy behind the wheel of the minibus, under pressure from the mere presence of his passenger.

"I'm just texting my nephew," says Russell, who briefly returns his attention to his phone. "It's his birthday."

"Is he a fan?" I ask.

"Not like my niece," he says, giving me his full attention now. "I gave her my cap after I won the Brazilian Grand Prix last year. She wore it to school and literally had to be ordered to take it off her head."

It takes me a moment to equate the slender, relaxed passenger with the extremely fast and determined former Williams driver who took his first top step of the podium in his maiden season for Mercedes F1. In this short escape from the paddock, in between engagements, George Russell is just a proud uncle.

Inevitably, as we follow a service lane inside the track perimeter, talk inside the minivan turns to the race. Here, possibly because we've only just met, the F1 driver presents careful soundbites. We're focused on "extracting the maximum from the present package," he says, and though I've no doubt that he means it, there must be some frustration. After three years at Williams, with his sights set on this dream seat, Russell joined Mercedes F1 at the start of the 2022 season. His arrival coincided with a big change in technical regulations governing the cars, which occurs every few years and can effectively serve as a reset across the teams. The current regulations, in force until the end of the 2025 season, placed a focus on ground effect. In aerodynamic terms, this is all about generating a large proportion of the car's downward force (often called downforce) by creating a suction action between the vehicle floor and the surface of the track.

On paper, the current technical regulations aim to enhance grip and cornering ability, and ultimately encourage closer racing. In reality, it's proven to be a complex challenge for every team and with varying levels of success. While Red Bull's interpretation of the central changes resulted in a 2022 championship-winning car, other teams including Mercedes F1 experienced a bumpier ride. The effect, known as "porpoising," was caused by the airflow underneath the car stalling and then reengaging in rapid succession. As well as affecting handling, the bouncing could be felt quite violently by drivers in cars engineered to run so close to the ground. It prompted tweaks to the regulations by the FIA for safety purposes but ultimately compromised the performance of this once unbeatable team.

Following a raft of updates to the car throughout that year, the team's fortunes were sweetened by a single win in Brazil—and maiden F1 victory—for Russell. Occurring late in the season, it was one that went some way to persuading Mercedes F1 to keep pursuing the same design path for 2023. By nailing this aspect of the regulations that had proved so challenging, they believed it would unlock performance from the car to put them in contention for the title. Without a doubt, the start of this season has been a shock to the system, and yet the 25-year-old Norfolk-born driver maintains a positive front. There's an inherent calmness about him that comes into play just then, in fact, when an urgent call comes through for the minivan to turn around. As the driver brakes, the vehicle carrying Lewis Hamilton speeds by in the opposite direction.

"Security have found a suspicious package in front of the stage," says the team member who took the instruction. "Someone's probably forgotten their bag but they're evacuating the area."

In my rookie F1 weekend with the team, this is drama I hadn't anticipated. No doubt it's disappointing for Russell and his teammate—for I later come to witness how the pair carry so much energy from the fans into the race—but it also means he can tick another engagement off the list. As our minivan driver tries and fails to spin the vehicle around in one hit, only to be forced into a flustered three-point turn, Russell turns his attention to the remaining items on his agenda before the noise around him must shut down for the event that matters most.

In the countdown to the race, as a giant red sun bows out on the day, all color drains from the surrounding desertscape. At the same time, under powerful illuminations, the track takes center stage. Grandstands, circuit buildings, and palm trees also light up against the darkening sky in washes of violet and powder blue. Even the paddock undergoes an evolution, for it strikes me that the VIPs invited inside this microcosm of the Formula 1 world have become significantly more glamorous. There are more dresses and unnecessary sunglasses on display, blazers and faces waiting to be recognized. It feels like an occasion in the making, even if many guests present seem more preoccupied with being seen than settling in to watch the imminent action on the track.

Inside the Mercedes F1 garage, we're into what the team call the preflight launch procedure. Having picked up a headset from a recessed wall rack, one that also displays the signature red baseball cap of the late racing legend and Mercedes F1 mentor Niki Lauda, I take my place just back from the central island. On each side of the garage, with both cars without wheels and up on trolley jacks, the two drivers are just clambering into their cockpits. In their black overalls and colorful race helmets—volt blue and bright yellow for Russell and Hamilton respectively—the pair now seem set apart from the people around them; team players but preparing to go it alone like astronauts in the capsule.

As the drivers sink into their race seats, a dozen mechanics crawl around the cars and under the chassis. This time, they're wearing fire-retardant suits in readiness for their dual role as pit crew, with helmets of their own to hand. At any time during the course of this fifty-seven-lap race, a car can enter the pit lane and stop within box markings outside their team garage. Even at a restricted speed, it's still a fast-moving projectile with a blade for a front wing and combustible race fuel onboard. One tire change is mandatory in dry conditions, which is all but guaranteed in this part of the world, but equally a driver could pit for fresh rubber, repairs, or mechanical adjustments, any of which the pit crew must perform within seconds where possible. At this moment, however, these personnel are focused on priming the cars for the grid. The tires are fitted with a pneumatic shriek of wheel guns and then steering wheels locked in place once Hamilton and Russell are strapped into position. Throughout, a row of LED lights on the tail of each car traces steadily one way and the other. They signal that the pit speed limiter is active, but on the back of these beasts they possess a sentient, predatory quality.

"Two minutes . . ."

The smell of solvents, race fuel, and burnt rubber is intense. So too is the focus displayed not just by the mechanics as they hurry to finish preparing the car but also the performance engineers, strategists, and technicians at their stations. They gaze intently at the data on their screens—as do the two drivers courtesy of the dual drop-down monitors resting on the bridge of their cockpits. While the cars are in the garage, all communication with the drivers is conducted via an encrypted, hardwire connection. The umbilical, as it's known, allows Hamilton and Russell to speak freely with their teams. On the track, every exchange between the driver and his Race Engineer is open season. Potentially, it can be shared by Formula 1 on the official broadcast feed. Being in such close competition, all the teams account for this with strict radio protocols. From the viewers' point of view, whenever the camera is focused on the drivers in their cars in the garage, they appear to be just brooding in silence. In reality, as I listen into the two channels via my headset, both Hamilton and Russell engage in intense fine-tuning talk with the engineers on their respective sides of the garage.

Can we afford half a turn more wing?

Bringing brake balance forward in that corner will keep temperature out of the rear tires . . .

Large wall-mounted screens on each side of the garage display the TV coverage that goes around the world. An overhead shot from the helicopter shows packed grandstands before the director cuts to a close-up of fans, who take a moment to register themselves on the big screens dotted around the circuit. It's somewhat disconcerting when one of F1's designated camera operators in the pit lane moves into the Mercedes F1 garage to capture the moment Toto Wolff arrives. I watch the feed on the wall as he takes his position just in front of me accompanied by his wingmen and advisers, Bradley Lord and reserve driver Mick Schumacher. Around the world, millions of fans are tuning in to watch this first race of the season. From inside the garage, everything looks familiar from the footage I'm used to seeing on TV. It's just the sensory assault is off the scale.

On the screen, a Boeing Dreamliner performs an unnervingly low flyby over the circuit. It explains the thunderous rumble as well as the shadow that has just swept over the fans in the grandstand facing the garage. Next, the broadcast feed cuts to the pit lane, where the first cars slip from their stalls to begin the installation lap. Ultimately, the field will come round to line up in two rows of staggered boxes on the home straight that reflect qualifying order, where the final section of prerace programming takes place. The grid walk is a fifteen-minute window of opportunity for broadcasters to pick out race personnel and notable figures invited onto the track for their last-minute thoughts and predictions. As for the drivers, they will continue the steady retreat into their own minds. Finally, following a warm-up lap that brings the cars back into position, the red lights will go out on the starting gantry and the entire purpose of existence for those behind the wheel will be reduced to a single objective.

"Fire up!"

Back in the team garage, as rival cars continue to stream into the pit lane, the two race engineers pull the trigger at the same time. The chainsaw roar when the engines start is monumental. I feel it in my chest. Dropping off the jacks, both cars squat on their haunches. As the ground shakes to the foundations, the mechanics whip away the tire blankets like conjurors at the big reveal. At this moment, only an act of magic could propel the W14 ahead of its competitors. Even so, there is a determination at play here to push for performance excellence. It's evident in everything from the choreographic execution with which the mechanics clear the car to the unblinking concentration of Shov and his three colleagues across the pit lane on the stand facing the wall. For a racing outfit on the back foot, even with two monster engines growling in neutral, the forward drive is relentless. Ultimately, it's the only way to win. Then, with military coordination and a jolt into gear, the din intensifies before each car snaps and squeals into the pit lane heading for the grid. Even the temperature drops in the wake of these blazing chargers, leaving empty spaces along with the hopes and expectations of the entire Mercedes F1 team.

CHAPTER TWO

ARE YOU EXPERIENCED?

The Miami Grand Prix
Miami International Autodrome, Miami
May 5–7, 2023

"What's up, Miami?" LL Cool J swaggers onto a section of the grid that now looks more like a catwalk. He's accompanied by the strains of a live orchestra conducted by another iconic artist, will.i.am. "Lemme introduce you to the twenty best drivers in the world!"

In the USA, Formula 1 is enjoying its day in the sun.

As a reflection of the sport's rising popularity, a trinity of race weekends will take place across the country in 2023. Miami is first off the line in May, just ahead of hurricane season, followed in October by the now well-established race in Austin, Texas. Then we have this year's headline act: the inaugural, much-hyped November showstopper in Las Vegas.

In what is just its second year in existence, the Florida fixture has established itself as the good-time grand prix. Blessed with the kind of weather that AI might return when asked to paint a picture of a superficially happy place, Miami is a living playground. It boasts pristine beaches and palm trees, clusters of sleek glass skyscrapers and classic art deco buildings in pastels that would look out of character anywhere else in the world. Every bar seems to spill revelers out into the streets, while the aromas from open-fronted restaurants serve as a reminder that a melting pot of cultures exist here: from Cuba and the Caribbean to Latin America and beyond. Collectively, Miami's spirit is infectiously upbeat, all of which draws people who know how to party to this race weekend.

The city's Hard Rock Stadium is the Swiss army knife of sporting and entertainment spectaculars. It's home to NFL stalwarts the Miami Dolphins, but regularly flexes and reconfigures to host everything from Super Bowls to superstar concerts by the likes of Taylor Swift, the Rolling Stones, and Beyoncé. The complex has a seating capacity of 65,326 and boasts parking spaces for just over 26,000 vehicles. This final fact might seem somewhat mundane, and yet it's key to the reason why Formula 1 stages a takeover for one weekend in the racing calendar. For what is effectively a vast surface area—along with several access roads—is transformed into a high-speed street racing circuit: the Miami International Autodrome.

The stadium seating is empty for this event, overlooking a pitch that now serves as the race paddock. On a vast carpet of fake grass, the teams have set up their respective stalls. As if by a wave of the F1 wand, these temporary, boilerplate cabins have undergone a transformation. Each one is now uniquely identifiable in team colors and branding, and furnished inside to promote a sense of high-end comfort and belonging. There is room to breathe here, in contrast to the cramped walkway behind the pit, even if the steep-sided seating tiers around this rectangle of plastic greenery create a cauldron of heat.

We're deep into the afternoon on Friday, the first day of the race's track sessions that sees the cars on track. Inside the Mercedes F1 headquarters, small parties of guests enjoy food, drink and chatter topped by high hopes because George Russell and Lewis Hamilton have just finished FP1 in P1 and P2 respectively. It's a strong start, they agree, and perhaps a sign that the team have found traction at last. As glasses are charged people barely notice those figures in white team shirts who arrive from the garage after the session and head quietly for a discreet passage behind the bar counter.

For this makeshift structure isn't just a hospitality suite—with the chefs squeezed into a kitchen under canvas to the rear—but also a backroom working environment for the engineers and drivers.

"The problem with our car is that you don't know what to expect from one moment to the next."

Shov has just opened the driver debrief following FP1. Like his colleagues around the table, the Trackside Engineering Director is wearing a headset as this meeting connects a small army responsible for the car's performance both trackside and back in Brackley and Brixworth. Unlike the suite's main area, there are no soft furnishings, potted plants, or artworks on display back here. It's really just a space formed by a series of temporary partition walls that's crammed with office tables and chairs, open laptops, coffee cups, cables, power banks, and trackside personnel. Lewis Hamilton, George Russell, and Toto Wolff sit among them, team members like everyone else, and seek to tune out from the chatter front of house.

In order to address weaknesses and build on strengths, the driver debrief is a constructive and forensic inquisition that takes place after every session. Despite the fact that Russell and Hamilton have topped the time sheets, Shov has purposely opened with a note of caution pitched as pragmatism. Even when the team are on a roll, the car continues to present significant challenges.

In this case, at what is the fifth race of the season, Shov has also seen enough to recognize that the W14's primary characteristic is unpredictability. There have been flashes of promise—just like today—notably a P2 podium finish for Hamilton at Melbourne back in early April. The setup that enables the cars to sing, however, is both highly track-specific and infernally hard to find. Such a frustrating hunt largely determined the team's fortunes at the last race in Baku, Azerbaijan, with a P6 for Hamilton and P8 for Russell. Even when the car is primed so the drivers can mine its full potential, the slightest variable only has to shift to undo their hard work. Anything from a change in track temperature to turbulent air in traffic or tricky tire wear can render a decent setup redundant. All of which combines to deliver a volatile platform and persuaded Shov to kick off the debrief with a giant caveat.

It's the fans, however—just like much of the media—who focus on the car's current form rather than the potential the team hope to unlock from it. Earlier in the week, when the social media team dropped a series of undeniably sleek images of the W14 for use as backgrounds, one wag commented: "Even the wallpaper made my phone slow."

At present, Mercedes F1 are "a long way from where they want to be." Which is, frankly, a place currently occupied by Max Verstappen in a runaway Red Bull. It's a phrase the team have begun to deploy in their public statements and press releases as if asking fans to keep the faith. It would be unfair to suggest that the once invincible Mercedes F1 have taken their foot off the gas. The competitive drive is still present, even if it's currently manifest in a sense of profound frustration both trackside and back at the factory. What's become apparent, two months into the season, is that the team has taken a wrong turn. And in a sport that demands every player moves at full throttle, there can be no going back.

What's harder to swallow is that Mercedes F1 ran with a similar design the previous season, even though it produced just one race win for Russell in Brazil. So, what possessed the team to press on with an evolution of the same concept? A great deal came down to data. When the engineers peered at the numbers, they saw patterns emerging in the shape of a rocket ship. It's just much of the data in question was coming from simulations.

Even though the outcome on the track through the previous year had largely failed to match what the computers predicted, that modeling still sang like a siren to the engineers. That late-season win for Russell in Brazil had only served to amplify the call. If they could just iron out the bumps encountered on a design path that had otherwise made the 2022 car such a handful, so they believed, it could put them in contention for the title.

Instead, after a start to the season that would have been unthinkable to the team over the winter, Mercedes F1 find themselves far from where they want to be for a deeply uncomfortable reason.

The W14 is no kingmaker. It's obstinate, unruly and cantankerous.

Already this weekend in Miami, Wolff has been moved to call it "a diva." A weak rear end is the car's worst feature, contrasted by an overly sharp front that makes it so hard for Hamilton and Russell to trust it in corners. There are times when a setup brings stability, but that's a rarity rather than a reliable feature. For a racing outfit that prides itself on the fact that every single team member pulls together as one, frankly the W14 should be on notice. Its attitude stinks. Even if the performance is in there, it's useless if the car won't consistently release it.

"We outsmarted ourselves," one senior race team member admitted to me earlier in summing up just what went wrong.

In 2021, Formula 1 introduced a cost cap. This aimed to bring some sense of financial equality to a paddock populated by big fish such as Ferrari, Red Bull, and Mercedes F1, as well as minnows like Haas and Williams. Had they found themselves in their current situation preceding the cap, the team possessed the resources to rush out an entirely new car. With a mighty push at the factory, it could have been ready within a matter of a few races. Now, with budget restrictions in place, all the team can do for the rest of the season is wrestle with the current challenger and seek to refine it. Yes, an upgrade package is in the works. Everyone hopes the significant changes this should bring to the floor, front suspension, and sidepods will help to at least settle the car. Then it can be brought up to speed throughout the rest of the season. It's just nobody is prepared to sit back and wait.

This weekend, Mercedes F1 have arrived in Miami determined to squeeze every last drop of performance from the car. It might have delivered in FP1, but the race team know from recent experience that all manner of variables from track temperature to gusting winds can cause the W14 to slip from their control. Despite the strong outing, the debrief is all about room for improvement. Both Hamilton and Russell contribute to the conversation using the language of the track. One after the other, each driver takes his team through a meticulous breakdown of each lap. Russell is fiercely analytical, noting details like "vibrations through the pedal with light pressure through Turns 4 and 6" and "front limitations at Turn 17," while Hamilton's feedback comes from a more intimate, emotional place when he talks about how "power to the brake feels like the car is pushing." Combined, their critique of every corner phase is staggeringly comprehensive. It also serves to illustrate that being a Formula 1 driver isn't just about extracting the maximum from their car at any given time. It also requires both drivers to read and record every handling characteristic while tearing around a track at speeds that can top 320 kilometers per hour. The engineers have access to data from sophisticated telemetry systems. Where Hamilton and

Russell come into their own is in supplementing that understanding with insight from a human perspective. In effect, they're living sensors. Combining feedback from man and machine, the team can begin to pinpoint tweaks to the setup.

Come FP2, later that afternoon, it seems that the car has picked up on Shov's earlier remarks about its behavior and duly doubled down. Despite some fine-tuning, both Hamilton and Russell drop off the pace to finish P7 and P15 respectively. The 5.41-kilometer track loops the stadium grounds in a series of long sections and tight, unintuitive turns. The layout is designed to test the drivers, but in a session that takes place in cooler conditions Mercedes F1 struggle with their tires. In order for the rubber compounds to activate, they require heat. This softens the tire surface, making it stickier and hungry for grip. Thanks to all manner of factors from aerodynamics to suspension and downforce, however, some cars find it harder to generate and retain the optimal temperature in their tires than others. When it comes to establishing a setup for an F1 car that connects with the characteristics of a track, race engineers talk about working within an "operating window," When it comes to the W14, however, it seems that window is so narrow that every effort to find it misses the mark.

"Our cars are just very sensitive," Shov remarks before the team leave the circuit for the day. "We need to think on our feet in the next session, react to the drivers' comments, and work out what we can change in the limited time we have."

Tires aren't the only thing that Mercedes F1 work hard to switch on this race weekend. *Partner activation* is a term used frequently here. When Senior Media Manager Adam McDaid drops it into conversation on the way into the paddock the next morning, he looks fleetingly abashed when I ask for the plain English translation.

"It's easy to get caught up in the buzzwords," he says, raising his voice to be heard over the waspish drone from the cars in a support race. "Basically, it's about delivering the full Mercedes Grand Prix experience to our partner guests."

In the paddock or the walkway behind the garages I find myself making way for hosts from every team escorting small tour parties. Some are dressed up like they're in search of a red carpet. Others just look like normal, wide-eyed F1 fans in their race caps and team T-shirts. What unites them is the color of their lanyard passes. One glimpse means they're permitted inside this secure inner sanctum by special invitation. Often, it forms part of a reciprocal arrangement between a race team and the sponsors. Or partner guests as they're more delicately called in this world.

Sponsorship has long been the fuel in the tank for motorsport. Any money that a team could get their hands on was poured into the design and build of a racing car. Through the eyes of Russell Braithwaite, the team's Chief Financial Officer, the introduction of the cost cap has transformed the business model behind Mercedes F1. Rather than viewing the budgetary limit as an obstacle, effectively closing the performance money pits of old, Braithwaite considers it to be a liberation.

"With the cost cap came entrepreneurial change and financial sustainability," he says, on setting out how a combination of a significant share of the F1 prize pot, combined with sustained appetite from sponsors, has turned a racing team into an independent organization that provides a return to its three equal shareholders: Mercedes-Benz, Toto Wolff, and INEOS. "Lap time is still the primary currency," Braithwaite stresses. "It's just the cap has changed the mindset of the engineers into engineering efficiency. With a finite spend they need to optimize it, and that's transformed the way we work."

Faced with an income stream that can't all be put into the car,

Mercedes F1 have effectively reinvented what it means to be a race team. From the supply of gearboxes and rear suspension to customer teams running HPP power units (currently Aston Martin, McLaren, and Williams) and the creation of an applied science division that has made innovative advances in engineering and aerodynamics, the Silver Arrows have sought to establish an operation that doesn't just bring a return on the track.

"We're on a journey to make Mercedes F1 a real independent organization," says Braithwaite. "It's just everything we do needs to fit together with performance."

In recent years, such a drive by the team has changed the nature of their relationship with sponsors. Braithwaite explains that it's evolved beyond persuading organizations with a marketing spend to pay to see their brand name plastered across the car. Now, it's framed as the start of a meaningful and mutually rewarding relationship, in which the injection of financial lifeblood into a high-performance race team can see a tangible return for backers in terms of profile, prestige, and even sales. It can also bring them into the Mercedes F1 court at key races around the world. If you're a major business player who recognizes the value of F1, this can be priceless.

Traditionally, partner guests who attend a grand prix as part of the package are hosted in the F1 Paddock Club. This is Formula 1's corporate hospitality arm, which teams can buy into as a surrogate host. It usually takes the form of an exclusive space where VIPs, from corporate representatives to anyone prepared to pay a premium, can wine, dine, and view the race in heightened luxury. From here, many can also enjoy a range of guided excursions by their host teams to the paddock, pit lane, and garage. As the popularity of the sport continues to climb, however, Mercedes F1 have found demand for Paddock Club tickets pressing on availability. This year's Miami GP is a case in point, which is why

Mercedes F1 partner guests can expect to enjoy the trappings of an additional experience that specifically embodies the spirit of the team as much as the race weekend.

The Mercedes F1 Miami Club overlooks Turn 5. It's arguably one of the best vantage points on the circuit to watch the cars thread the midpoint of a high-speed three-corner section. This is no ordinary stand, however, with folding plastic seats and burger wrappers littering concrete steps. In what feels like an open-sided beach club transplanted to a motor racing circuit, guests are invited to enjoy two elegantly styled and furnished lounge levels. Several weeks earlier, the structure didn't exist. Such is the demand from the team's sponsors that it's been purpose-built for the occasion, and completed with an expansive, high-walled garden terrace. Fueled by an endless supply of tantalizing food and drink, this is an opportunity for guests to live the high life and sample the spirit of both the team and host city.

Across the race weekend, they also enjoy an audience with their racing heroes.

George Russell has just finished addressing an enthusiastic gathering in the Miami Club's garden. There, the F1 star has shared his hopes for the race and the season ahead. Afterward, I'm keen to discover more about the Mercedes F1 experience from a driver's perspective. As we find a place to talk, I find him to be composed and forward-focused. Indeed, on settling at a table away from the throng, Russell politely asks to swap places so he can take the corner seat.

"I like to . . . look out," he says with a half-smile and drifts his hand around the space.

Just two years earlier, in his third season for Williams, Russell could expect to find very little behind him. The team were struggling both on and off the track. Although Russell possessed the skill to effectively outdrive his car, he would regularly finish last.

"When you're at the back, you're not really proving anything," he says of a time that was both formative and frustrating. "I didn't have the chance to truly shine or achieve what I wanted."

Up until this point, Russell had come far since discovering a passion for karting as a seven-year-old from King's Lynn in Norfolk. With support from his family, who he is quick to credit as he pursued a career in motorsport, the young driver developed into a formidable talent. Notably, he won the 2017 GP3 Series and 2018 Formula 2 Championship as a rookie in both seasons. In that time, Toto Wolff recognized Russell's potential and took him under his wing as part of the Mercedes junior program: an initiative aimed at nurturing drivers with the potential to become F1 stars of the future.

George Russell's big break would come in 2019, after Mercedes F1 negotiated a deal with Williams. On earning the seat, he hoped to blaze a trail. Instead, in what would become a prescient turn of events, Russell's arrival coincided with a downturn in the fortunes of the Oxfordshire-based racing outfit.

"I signed with the team when they finished fifth in the Constructors' Championship," he says. "They went on to finish last in four of the next five seasons, and almost went bankrupt."

Channeling his frustrations, all Russell could do was seek to push his car to the limit while watching his rivals pull away on the track. Then Covid struck, turning motorsport upside down as much as any other aspect of modern life. For an F1 driver determined to prove his worth, however, it also provided an opportunity to deliver Russell from the back to the front.

"Suddenly I've got this dream chance to join Mercedes," he says, after Wolff forged a deal with Williams for a single race weekend loan of their driver. Hamilton had just tested positive for the virus ahead of the 2020 Sakhir Grand Prix, and his seat needed filling at short notice. "It was my thirty-seventh race in F1," he recounts in illustrating the step up he faced. "I hadn't scored a single point and was finishing last every weekend."

Without a doubt, the pressure on Russell was intense. Nevertheless, he rose to the challenge. Staged at the Bahrain International Circuit, but utilizing the outer loop, the young driver topped the time sheets in both FP1 and FP2, while qualifying just twenty milliseconds behind pole-sitter and temporary teammate, Valtteri Bottas.

"Suddenly, I've jumped cars and I lead the whole race," says Russell, having described the moment he snatched P1 at the first turn. He speaks with some pride about what could have been a fairy-tale win had it not been for a muddled pit stop beyond his control and then a puncture later in the race that curtailed a valiant comeback. The Williams driver finished in P9, and yet Russell had perhaps claimed a higher victory in proving that he was worthy of a permanent seat with Mercedes F1. "Toto always believed in me, and I think there were also a number of engineers who always believed in me," he says, "but others needed convincing because I was still a young kid."

While thankful for the opportunity to prove himself in a championship-winning car, Russell points out that race weekend shone a light on what he considers to be a "flaw" in the sport.

"I was the same driver as I had been before. And I was exactly the same driver a week later when I was out in Q1," he says bluntly.

Formula 1 is determined not just by drivers but also engineers who design superior machines. One car has the potential to leave another in the dust, but much also depends upon the racecraft and courage of the individual behind the wheel. While Russell had seized a rare opportunity to showcase his talents by stepping in for one of motorsport's living legends, his return to making the best of an underperforming car also worked in his favor. For when the call-up came to replace Bottas for the 2022 season, as teammate to Hamilton, Russell joined Mercedes F1 as a new set of technical regulations came into force that encouraged ground effect aerodynamics.

"I knew there were no guarantees. We were going into the biggest rule change that the sport had seen for a long time, and all the teams faced problems," he says of the bouncing effect that plagued the cars in the early stages of that season. "It's just Red Bull designed a car that had substantially fewer problems than ours. With a good base from the off, they could focus on developing and building."

Here, Russell's formative F1 experience in facing adversity meant he knew what was required of him to help the team improve. Listening to the #63 driver in a debrief as he breaks down a lap of the track is "where he earns his money," as one team member put it this weekend. Taking the engineer through each turn and straight, he's clear and articulate in describing the precise characteristic of every snap and vibration. When I remark that it's not the first skill that springs to mind when assessing a driver, Russell surprises me with an admission that his efforts to communicate clearly are the result of overcoming another obstacle.

"I used to mumble so badly that I saw a speech therapist," he reveals of his childhood years. "From that time on, I've always focused on my words. When I started racing as a kid in Europe I had an Italian mechanic. His only English was "espresso two sugars." So I also learned to be quite clear and pronounced with my descriptions so he'd understand me. Now, I could be speaking to a hundred people at a time. Everything we say in an engineering meeting is written down [by an AI voice-to-text translator]. I don't want anything to be misinterpreted, so I try to be pinpoint clear."

In debriefs, both Russell and Hamilton tend to focus on the

negative issues with their car. It might sound like they have nothing positive to share, but ultimately their focus is on areas for improvement. In the same way, no matter what's happened on the track, Russell seeks to keep his emotions out of the frame. "The way I see it, the best feedback I can give will allow me to achieve my goals, and the whole team's goals, sooner. Whereas if I have a bad day in the office, and speak hotheadedly," he continues, "it doesn't really bring anything constructive to the team. Potentially, it can point you in the wrong direction."

That Russell is a decent communicator is one thing. It's on another level entirely considering that he absorbed the details he conveys while throwing his car around the track.

"I have a marker button to help me," he says, describing what sounds like the equivalent of dropping a Post-it note on the track. "If I feel something, like a bad upshift or hopping into a particular turn, I'll click the marker. That draws a line on the data, and then we'll discuss it afterward."

Even with his solitary memory aid, Russell still faces a sensory challenge and especially when faced with the growing complexity of a contemporary F1 racing car.

"There's so much to think about like tire temperatures, the gap to the driver ahead, wind direction and speed, oversteer, understeer . . ." Russell trails off there, but it's clear the list could go on for some time. "We also have new gadgets on the car," he says, having referenced the buttons and dials on his steering wheels that impact on different aspects of the car's handling. "These are things that have been invented by the team. As of six months ago, I didn't know what they did. They were just an idea in somebody's head. Then they get designed and built, and we drive with them in the simulator. So I need to learn what they are and what they do, and then describe to the team how it affects the car."

Russell speaks from a place of calm assurance. He's undoubtedly a talented young driver. Even so, he's had to earn that confidence in his rise to a Mercedes F1 seat through hard work and an absolute commitment to being at the top of his game. It would also seem necessary when stepping up to race alongside his seven-times world champion teammate. While recognizing Hamilton's spectacular achievements in the sport, Russell remains focused on what is required of him.

"I back myself," he says frankly. "When I walk into the garage, put on my helmet, and step into the car, it makes no difference who is alongside me." In the same breath, however, Russell makes it quite clear that it matters on the track. "I want to be ahead of Lewis. I think I've proved I'm on his level but I want to be above it. His prior successes don't change any of that."

George Russell talks like an outright racer. His fierce ambition is no different to any other driver on the grid. In some ways, it's a requirement in this uncompromising sport. Throughout our conversation, he stresses his desire to be in the fight for a World Championship, but the car just isn't there. In understanding how he stays motivated, Russell invites me to consider Michael Schumacher's career.

"You see this great titan, with seven titles to his name, but it was only when I got to Formula 1 that I realized he spent five years at Ferrari before winning his first championship with them."

Russell frequently refers to the collective effort. He recognizes his place within a team but confesses that with over 2,000 personnel at Brackley and Brixworth it can be challenging to stay connected with everyone. Ultimately, he has to stay laser-focused on his role as a driver.

"There are definitely some people that I wish I could see more often. But then if I try and put in the time with every single individual, I'm not going to be able to spend as much time working on the simulator." Russell pauses here, and then summons an outlook that helps him to do his job with the same commitment as everyone else in the Mercedes F1 team back home. "We're all competitive, and we all want to be quickest," he says. "When everyone sits down on a Sunday afternoon to watch a race, that's all they care about."

At this level of motorsport, the complex aerodynamic and engineering puzzles can be maddening. Just as a solution to a problem presents itself, other factors can creep in that continue to hold a car back. In Miami this weekend, teams in almost every garage face a string of challenges in a bid to establish the optimal setup for their cars. If that afternoon's FP3 is an exploration, a turning and gusty wind proves unsettling for all the cars on the circuit. Mercedes F1 have additional concerns, after Shov and his engineers decided to run slightly different handling setups for Hamilton and Russell. In theory, this is a neat way to pinpoint an issue. As the timer runs out on the sixty minutes on the track, however, both drivers continue to experience the same difficulties with grip. The car turns just fine. It just doesn't have the balance or back end to support the exit.

In the debrief, during which Russell suffers a momentary lapse in his otherwise mighty reaction skills by spilling coffee across his keypad, the team continue to interrogate the tracer charts and data sheets intensively. Traditionally, when a car isn't handling well, any issues repeat in broadly the same way on every lap. In this case, even with an unpredictable wind not helping matters, the performance problems seem somewhat random.

"We're left with a headache in terms of finalizing our setup direction," rues Shov as they turn their attention to the upcoming session to decide the grid. "There's no clear and obvious path to tread."

If the W14 remains an enigma for the team at this grand prix, the weekend is by no means a lost cause. With just a few hours to go before the grid is determined for the race, both drivers remain locked in dialogue with their engineers. Hamilton and Russell might sit on opposite sides of the table to each other, but they're here to pull as one to persuade the car to join them.

Even when that fails to materialize in qualifying—a frustrating session cut short by a red flag* in the closing minutes—the drivers are back to don headsets with their engineers and strategists to pick apart the session with the same resolve to make Sunday's race count. When Toto Wolff talks about resilience, as he does to a packed press conference staged in the hospitality suite on the other side of the partition wall, it's in evidence in the tone and course of the debrief taking place around these tables.

"You have a great opportunity to move forward in the race," Shov tells Russell, after a Ferrari-shaped spin into the wall by Charles Leclerc halted the session and prevented the younger Mercedes F1 driver from seeking to improve from P6 on the grid. Then Shov turns his attention to Hamilton, forced to settle for P13 having been caught out by congestion as cars jostled for space. "You have a tougher task," he admits, "but we've seen many times what you can do when you're out of position."

Here, Russell follows up with his own bid to lift chins.

"I want to acknowledge all the effort everyone is putting in. For whatever reason, it's not coming to us. But yeah," he says to finish, sounding down but far from out, "tomorrow's a new day."

Come race morning, the epicenter of this weekend's circuit is an oasis of calm. While the tangle of freeways around the Hard Rock

---

* A red flag is used in Formula 1 to halt a race, qualifying, or practice session—temporarily or permanently—due to hazardous conditions or an emergency that renders the track unsafe for continued competition.

Stadium are host to incoming traffic, and the first fans begin to parade through the main gates, the paddock with its temporary structures feels more like the sunlit grounds for a village fete. It's peppered with personnel, most of whom are here to fuel on caffeine before the lights go out on the start of their day. Aware that this weekend's circuit will soon be rammed, I head out to explore the public campus area.

Away from the team hospitality suites and the partner guest champagne bars, I'm interested in finding out how the experience compares on the other side of the track.

Crossing a covered bridge, I find a series of pleasant, winding public walkways. Food and drink stands stud each side, along with an array of entertainment opportunities at every turn. Beyond the fan zone, effectively a concert stage on which the drivers make appearances throughout the race weekend, I pass driving simulators as well as stalls selling everything from team merchandise to mojitos. The marina section is quite something, with occupied yachts embedded in a vinyl floor made to look like water, and the deckchairs in the beach area are filling up fast. I stop to admire a replica racing car, in hot pink and aquamarine livery, seemingly hovering amid fountains in the center of a pool, and then step aside when I realize it's a prime selfie spot. People are here to have fun. Clearing the frame for a couple, it takes me a moment to orientate myself in order to spot the catch fencing bordering the track.

An F1 race will take place here later today, but in this space that could be a theme park it almost feels like a sideshow.

Whether you're arriving on foot or by helicopter, entertainment is the name of the game for this second year of the Miami Grand Prix. For the motorsport purist, it must feel like a turn for the worse. Such a vibe might not sit well in Europe, where a dry hot dog and a warm beer on a mound is racing heaven for so many. Here, it's just how things are done.

"The racing is the same as it is at any grand prix," Adam McDaid points out later. "What's different is the packaging, and that's tailored to wherever we are in the world."

By midday, with another support race spinning around the stadium circuit, the enthusiasm has risen like the mercury in the thermometer. With the public grandstands and private clubs heaving, this grand prix party is well and truly under way.

Back in the F1 paddock, stratospherically high-end celebrities seem to have converged at the same time. Jeff Bezos and Elon Musk are strolling around like prospective house buyers. I've also passed Vin Diesel basking in the sunshine and attention. Meanwhile, the Mercedes F1 team are preparing to welcome Roger Federer, Shakira, and Tom Cruise as special guests. Some visits are carefully choreographed, as evident in one of the team's many working group chats about everything from arrival timings to conditions imposed by certain stars as to how they should be portrayed by the team's roving content creators. It can sound controlling to the point of absurdity (*"Do not make it feel all about X . . . solo shot of X in garage not fine"*) and yet the paddock is a media tinderbox. One picture or clip open to misinterpretation could ignite a story that trends around the world. It could even become bigger than the race weekend itself. As a result, the team are happy to accommodate any such requests for the sake of the sport as much as for their guests.

"A lot of people who come here have everything they need on earth, and yet it has to feel like a unique, once-in-a-lifetime experience." Sarah Morgan is Head of Hospitality and Events for Mercedes F1. She's part of the team responsible for the Miami Club and looks after the VIPs throughout each grand prix weekend. "Some can show up with a surprise entourage of fifteen, all of whom want to sit down and eat. But we never say no. We also bring in regular fans and allow the media and even other teams to use the suite," she adds. "Our home should feel like your home. That's just how Toto wants it to be."

Undoubtedly, the Mercedes F1 Team Principal would like nothing more than to complete the experience for his guests with a stellar performance on the track. It comes as little comfort to any team, but when a driver starts behind his expected grid slot they can afford to roll the tactical dice. Working with his race strategy engineers, Lewis Hamilton opts to begin on the hard tires. The popular opening choice is medium, which George Russell favors in starting up ahead on the third row. The harder compound is a fraction of a second slower in pace but more durable and consistent. This pushes back the need for fresh tires and potentially allows the car to capitalize on the track as competitors pit earlier. There are risks with any tire decision, of course. In this case, it effectively means the cars around Hamilton on the faster medium tires will start with an advantage and the #44 driver could initially drop further down the pack.

This is just one of multiple factors for the race team to consider in their final briefing as it stretches into lunch. In the corridor behind the back room, the catering staff lay out a buffet. From time to time, engineers break out to load up a plate, grab a can of water, and return to their desks to eat as they work. Meanwhile, outside the stadium in the Miami Club garden, partner guests mingle with champagne flutes in hand. People have dressed for the occasion and chatter happily in the shade created by awnings and gazebos softened by decorative foliage. A classic Mercedes F1 car on a plinth serves as the garden's centerpiece, overlooked by a DJ with her eyes closed and arms aloft. Lost in her laid-back groove, she's stationed on a balcony at the back of a huge, two-story structure that serves as the Miami Club's track viewing gallery. Upstairs, the bars on both levels offer not just drinks but sorbets, cakes, and gastronomic delicacies served on dainty plates.

As well as the hospitality staff shuttling food and drink, the team's partner managers mingle with the throng. Some are here to personally chaperone their guests. Others host prospective partners. These are individuals or company representatives interested in sponsoring Mercedes F1, and we're in a key market. For Miami isn't just a fun-time city but an important business hub. It means there are major players here, and so it makes commercial sense for the team to maximize the opportunities available off the track as much as on it.

The Miami Club is an attractive place to be, with unparalleled views of the racing on both the big screens beside the bar or from the balconies overlooking the track. But it's more than just elevated entertainment. This is a networking opportunity, for Mercedes F1 and their partner guests as well as a chance to show interested parties what they're missing out on. In this view, like fast-moving share prices, the performance of the cars on the track becomes even more critical. Without a doubt, the team can call upon its legacy for the stock to stay high, but there is pressure to get back into contention. In this cost cap era of F1, it isn't just driver and championship points at stake for the teams but their value to investors. Which is why Sarah Morgan and her hospitality team must keep delivering an unbeatable package.

At this time more than ever, it has to be a *winning* experience.

Throughout the race calendar, Mercedes F1 seek to facilitate this strategically important opportunity to mix business with pleasure. Not every grand prix weekend merits a dedicated space such as this, but here at the Miami Club Morgan and her team have incorporated a taster of what's to come in the form of a bespoke room that feels like a retro speakeasy. It's a darker, glitzy, high-stakes affair called the Vegas Club, which promises to be even bigger in scale than this one when F1 visits Sin City in

November. Such are the planning demands of her work that Morgan is also in the process of chartering a 298-passenger super-yacht for Mercedes F1 to host partner guests during the 2024 Monaco Grand Prix.

As attention turns to activity on the grid, guests in the Miami Club begin to gravitate to the cushioned seating at the front of the gallery. Some take to the sofas for the screen at the back and the chance to take in the bigger picture. To accompany the un-rivaled view of the track, several overhead monitors provide the official broadcast feed. Here, commentary is provided in-house. It's achingly professional, with a focus on the Silver Arrows, but also tellingly pitched at guests with no prior knowledge of the sport. Everything from downforce to tire choice is explained in advance to make the experience as accessible as possible, for the rules and regulations can be daunting.

Then there are features particular to this grand prix weekend that need no explanation.

On the grid, backed by symphonic strains and now cheerlead-ers twirling pom-poms, LL Cool J looks up and around at the grandstand.

"This is the greatest spectacle in motorsports," he intones into his microphone ahead of the big delivery. "This is *Formula 1!*"

As collaborations go, and with his little baton in one hand, will.i.am looks more like he's guiding a taxiing aircraft than con-ducting an orchestra for his fellow rap star, but the intent is there. Having paused in his introduction for dramatic effect, and then quietly consulted the notes on his cue cards, LL Cool J proceeds to invite each driver out by name from behind a curtain. "He grew up right here in Miami. A local boy done good. Let's give it up for Logan Saaaargeant!"

For fans who like to consume their sport with a large side order of entertainment, the sequence that follows seems like a suitably dramatic way to meet the characters set to tell a fast-moving story for the next ninety minutes. For many others, including Russell, who later questions if stepping out in turn and then standing around in the full glare of the sun is the best use of the drivers' critical preparation time, it's kind of cheesy. Personally, I can't stop watching even though I feel that I should look away to stop my cringe muscles from going into spasm. If I'm being generous I would echo Hamilton's view that any attempt to modernize F1 has to be a positive move. I just hope this one is a work in progress.

Despite dividing opinion, each driver introduction is delivered with showbiz-levels of bombast. It certainly goes down well with the spectators in the grandstands as much as with those in the Miami Club, who clap, whoop, and cheer enthusiastically when the Mercedes F1 duo make their entrance. A short while later, everyone is on their feet for the start of the race itself, which is never less than breathtaking to witness first hand. At any grand prix track around the world, whether you're watching from a patch of dirt or in pampered luxury, the Jurassic roar, power, and sheer grace of the cars commands attention.

So far this season, Red Bull have dominated. It's a reign that's likely to continue until teams such as Mercedes F1 can tap as deeply into that same alchemical well of ground effect performance buried in the sport's current technical regulations. For now, as Max Verstappen focuses on outshining his teammate, Sergio Pérez, the real drama can be found among the pack that follows.

Starting on different tire strategies to each other, in P6 and P13 respectively, Russell and Hamilton make steady progress as the race develops. Overlooking both the exit and entrance of the corners that bookend Turn 5, the Miami Club guests watch a column of guided missiles on wheels seemingly defy the laws of traction.

One after the other, punching through the air, they swing through the same line within a margin measured in millimeters. Only when a car turns to prey for the predator behind do those lines deviate to become attacking or defensive. As those high-speed battles play out, people switch their attention from the track to the screen for a minute or so in a bid to keep up with the action until it comes full circle.

Over the course of almost ninety minutes, before Verstappen takes the checkered flag, some remain glued to the leaderboard. Others, meanwhile, seem entranced by what is effectively just a fleeting section of the race below them represented by the sensory trio of speed, sound, and fury. On the track, Russell's early focus is on conserving his medium tires while maintaining position in a close field. On pitting for the harder compound, it's notable that one of the two cars he passes to finish P4 is the Ferrari of Carlos Sainz, who is running a similar strategy. Having also bided his time to maximize the life of his opening choice of hard tire, Hamilton claims the advantage when switching to fresh mediums to carve his way through the field to an impressive P6. For Mercedes F1 fans, it's an encouraging result after a trying weekend. While the outcome is "a long way from where they want to be," it keeps the team in touching distance of second-placed Aston Martin in this early stage of the Constructors' Championship. That afternoon, I leave people recharging their glasses at the Miami Club. For these partner guests, at the close of a race weekend that has brought them into the Mercedes F1 embrace, it's not the result they're celebrating as much as the experience.

In the back room of the Mercedes F1 hospitality suite, while Max Verstappen sprays champagne from the top of the podium with his teammate, Sergio Pérez, in second and Aston Martin's Fernando Alonso in third, a postrace debrief is already under way.

Only Hamilton and Russell are absent, having been called at random for doping tests. This is standard procedure, troubling nobody. As for the mood around the table, there is a palpable air of relief that the cars complied with the drivers when it mattered most. Having proven to be stubborn when running on the ragged edge in a single qualifying lap, both had come alive in the sustained demands of the race. From an engineering point of view, there is a great deal to be done to understand the precise factors at play. With upgrades promising to settle the car and open the operating window, it can wait until the team are home. For now, this final debrief of the weekend feels more like housekeeping before work resumes back at the factory, and a chance for Shov to put the race into perspective.

"Miami has been a lesson in perseverance," he says. "Today's rewards weren't our ultimate aim, but we can be proud of the spirit we've shown."

When George Russell appears, greeted by applause, he pointedly fist bumps everyone present to thank them for their work this weekend. Lewis Hamilton isn't far behind, and shows his appreciation in exactly the same way. Both drivers seem invigorated despite the rigors of a race in which they had to pick off opponents one by one. Having seen how much focus and work went into the preparations, and as Toto Wolff reminds everyone—on finding a moment away from the media to join the closing phase of the meeting—this really does feel like a collective effort.

"Two years ago, we wouldn't have been as pleased with a P4 and a P6 as we are today," he concedes, before encouraging everyone to look forward to the next race in the hope that the upgrades can establish a new baseline.

It's not winning talk. The Red Bulls are too far up the track for that, but Wolff's words are intended to demonstrate that he too has faith in the process. Finding himself in another season without a championship-winning car is agonizing for him. Even if the path proves to be long and challenging, Wolff leads as if to suggest that a return to contention will open up so long as his team remain fully committed to the charge. As Team Principal he has no other choice.

With the race complete, almost everyone across all teams in the paddock demonstrates a racer's instinct to complete their work as swiftly and efficiently as possible. Not everyone from the Mercedes F1 team will be leaving Miami this evening. The mechanics work late to strip the car and dismantle the garage, just as Sarah Morgan remains on the front line of hospitality until the last VIP departs. As for the Miami Club, it's going to be a few days before the build crew take down the structure and leave the site as they found it. For those whose work at the circuit is over, there's a flight to be caught. As Florida's late light settles into blankets of lilac and flamingo pink, I travel with a group of engineers and technicians in the convoy of minivans and rental cars that take us to the airport. Along the way, I am reminded that the high-performance standards Toto Wolff expects from the team are rewarded on many levels. In this case, we pull in at a hotel on the outskirts of the airport. There, I learn that rooms have been booked for us to freshen up before checking in.

"That's a nice touch," I say to Aleix Casanovas, George Russell's performance coach. He had just started advising me on how to minimize jet lag like the drivers (something about strategic light exposure) but this stop leaves me in the dark.

"Let's go!" At once, Casanovas scrambles to slide open the side door like a stopwatch has just started.

As it turns out, I discover that we really don't have much time. Mercedes F1 have block-booked four rooms so that approximately twenty team members can shower and change in less than fifteen minutes. As people assemble into groups in the lobby, I join one in case I'm left like the last to be picked for soccer. For everyone here, this is just a regular aspect of life on the road for a racing team. As a newcomer it's deeply awkward, especially as my fleeting roommates chat happily as they strip down, take turns in the shower using the same small, complimentary bar of soap, and then emerge to throw on their team travel gear. Despite such strong initiation vibes, it's all been part of my Mercedes F1 experience at the Miami Grand Prix. It also feels good to have washed away the weekend as we regroup outside in the twilight to the sound of cicadas and aircraft as they heave into the air.

CHAPTER THREE

SPINNING SPANNERS

The Spanish Grand Prix
Circuit de Barcelona-Catalunya, Barcelona
June 2–4, 2023

Stepping out of Barcelona airport, ahead of the Spanish Grand Prix, I find Toto Wolff's chauffeur waiting to collect me. We're heading into the eighth race on the calendar—but the seventh to take place after Italy's Emilia-Romagna Grand Prix was canceled in the wake of catastrophic flooding in the region—and I have yet to sit down with the Mercedes F1 Team Principal. I've observed him from just feet away inside the garage, and in both strategy meetings and driver debriefs. We greet each other in passing, and yet at race weekends I've never seen Wolff with a spare second to himself. I've also been advised that an appropriate time and place will arise for the two of us to explore what this team represents to him.

Reading between the lines, I believe this mystery moment will materialize when the team are on a firmer footing.

In Wolff's shoes, I would be equally wary of finding a writer in the mix at a time when Mercedes F1 are facing a performance shortfall of their own making. After a decent finish in Miami, Lewis Hamilton claimed P4 and George Russell P5 at Monaco. These are respectable results in view of the challenges presented by the current car, and yet we're talking about a team that were once imperious.

By Toto Wolff's standards, it's not good enough.

I can see in his face what this drop in form means to him. Wolff is a commanding presence, but this season he strikes me as someone who also longs to experience a peaceful night's sleep. In some ways, it's a physical manifestation of his uncompromising commitment to return Mercedes F1 to the front of the grid. As team boss, he embodies the pain that everyone feels having worked so hard. Now he must entreat them to double down on their efforts to get back on track, and that demands his full focus and attention. I reflect on this from the back seat of the SUV as Wolff's driver cuts through the city's rush-hour traffic with smooth assertiveness. I know my ride comes from a place of courtesy, but Wolff is a formidable figure with a master plan, and I have yet to properly meet him. Inevitably, it feels like I've just been swept up in a Bond movie sequence.

"What's he really like?" I ask Martin Koch, my man in full Mercedes team gear behind the wheel.

"Toto?" he asks, and with one glance I realize this is someone who knows how to read a rearview mirror. "Very nice."

If there's one thing Wolff respects, it's loyalty. From what Koch tells me about his career as a Team Principal chauffeur, which began twenty-three years earlier with the Jordan Grand Prix squad before settling happily behind this wheel, he's earned that right to be trusted. So, instead we talk for some time about his favorite race ("Montreal has a lovely shabby chic vibe") and the most challenging for him ("when we raced in India, the traffic was madness"). He's a personable guy, though I imagine quietly relieved when we pull into the forecourt of the hotel where many team personnel are staying for the weekend.

Judging by the small crowd of people in F1 caps and T-shirts now eyeballing our car as we approach, I'm guessing this is also home to some key players in the race ahead.

"I won't wind down the window," I say as they point camera phones in our direction, and Koch laughs a little too hard for my liking.

"I hope you meet Toto this weekend," he says a moment later, having climbed out of the car to retrieve my luggage from the trunk. I shake his hand to thank him for the ride, and this time it feels like he's addressing me off duty. "You'll like him."

The Spanish Grand Prix takes place in early June at the Circuit de Barcelona-Catalunya. Located some 30 kilometers outside the city, the track boasts a long, 4,000-capacity grandstand on the home straight that's shaped like a breaking wave. Approaching the venue, across a landscape that mixes bucolic agricultural holdings with light industrial estates, it's a skyline feature.

From the grandstand seats, fans can look down into the pit lane behind the wall on the opposite side of the track. They also have a great view into the team garages, each one the motorsport equivalent of a stable for a pair of pedigree stallions. Inside the Mercedes F1 stalls, I find the man in charge of a twenty-six-strong crew in the process of assembling both chargers. This is Matt Deane, the team's Chief Mechanic. It falls to him to have the cars primed for the race weekend, which is light-years from what first drew him to tinkering under hoods. For when Deane was just fourteen years old, it struck him as something that could be fun even if it got his father into trouble.

"My dad bought and sold cars in his spare time," this trim and smartly turned out team veteran tells me when I ask how his journey here began. "One day, he and my uncle were respraying an old Triumph Stag with cellulose paint. I went down to see them in the garage beside our house only to find them staggering around, slurring their words and giggling for no reason. I ran back to tell Mum something was wrong with them, and she just went: 'Oh, the silly buggers! They haven't been wearing their masks!'"

Inspired by his dad's passion for cars, Deane first settled on the idea of becoming a regular mechanic for domestic road cars. In his early teenage years, he found casual work after school and on weekends at his hometown garage near Silverstone, where his mother was employed as a bookkeeper. There, he checked oil and tire pressures, swept the floors, emptied garbage cans, and washed up coffee cups for the mechanics he hoped to join on a permanent basis.

"I just thought it would be great," says Deane. "All I wanted to do was work at the local garage and live a nice, quiet life. So, once I'd finished my GCSEs I asked the boss if I could become an apprentice. I think he felt I should be more ambitious, because he told me to go up the road to Silverstone and find work as a race mechanic."

A cottage industry of motorsport has always existed on the outskirts of Northamptonshire's iconic circuit. Equipped with a CV and written reference from his boss at the garage, Deane landed an apprenticeship with a small Formula 3 outfit run by the Australian entrepreneur Alan Docking. There, through his late teenage years, he would come to learn the tools of his trade doing something he really enjoyed. It was often a good laugh as well, which is what had first attracted him to the role as a youngster.

Then, one afternoon in April 1992, Matt Deane learned that being a race mechanic also came with a huge responsibility.

"We went racing at Thruxton [a fast-flowing circuit in Hampshire] with a young Dutch driver called Marcel Albers. He was a little older than me, but we became friends," he begins. "That weekend, we'd had to swap his engine. We worked quickly to get it done. He got out on to the track OK, but then during the race he was involved in an accident. It was a big shunt. The car turned upside down. Tragically, Marcel was killed."

Deane pauses for a moment. He's outwardly composed, but even after all this time it's clearly not something he finds easy to share.

"I was asked to go and help the marshals retrieve the car," he continues. "I just remember the ambulances at the scene and the sound of the breathing apparatus as the medics worked in vain on my friend. I was only nineteen, and his death had a huge effect on me. In my head, I started questioning if mechanical failure was responsible, or something I had done because we'd been working so fast. Even though it was ruled that his death was due to a racing incident, it left me feeling like I couldn't do it anymore."

Deane has invited me to join him for this conversation in the back of one of the team's race trucks. Stationed behind the garage, this one is effectively a mobile parts department with steps to a front door, a corridor between two floor-to-ceiling walls of trays and cases, plus an alcove at the back that serves as his office. It's really just a plush swivel chair and fitted desk, big enough for a laptop and a cup of coffee, but offers space for Deane to think and plan. The door also seals us from all external noise. Just then, it allows me to reflect on how dangerous this sport can be.

"After the crash," he tells me, "I came really close to packing it in."

It was his team boss, Alan Docking, who recognized both the impact of the tragedy on Deane and also his potential as a calm, diligent, and efficient individual to become a great race mechanic. With both factors in mind, Docking duly offered the young man an alternative way to process his grief.

"Before he died, Marcel had been restoring a vintage motor-bike," says Deane. "It was super rare. A 1975 MV Agusta 750S that he had planned to do up and give to his dad. The bike was just in a pile of parts in the corner of the team workshop, and so Alan suggested I skip the next few races and make that my project."

Taking him up on the offer, Deane threw himself into the restoration. At a time before the internet made sourcing parts simple, he found himself joining owners' clubs and visiting automotive museums in a bid to bring the MV back to life. On completion, Deane presented the bike to Marcel's father.

"He was in bits, but it helped us both," he says. "Because after that, I got back into being a race mechanic."

Matt Deane is still hugely grateful to Alan Docking for the kindness and faith he showed in keeping his career on the road. In 2005, after thirteen years working his way from Formula 3 to Formula 1, he joined British American Racing (BAR), the Honda-partnered constructor that would ultimately morph into the Mercedes-AMG PETRONAS F1 Team five years later.

"There was more movement in those days," he says, referring to a time of plentiful work opportunities for mechanics when teams were permitted to run a spare car. For Deane, it opened up a pathway that would take him from Number One Mechanic, with responsibility for a car, to the top post in the garage.

"Becoming Chief Mechanic was a learning experience," he says. "You're in charge of a crew, but as a mechanic nobody teaches you to become a manager. You just tighten up nuts and bolts, do the wiring correctly and make sure you don't trap an O-ring when fitting a hose. All that stuff is detailed in assembly drawings. It's easy. I'd been spinning spanners for so long it came naturally. But then I had to deal with people. They can be introverted, extroverted, or just difficult, and I had to figure out how to bring out the best in them all."

Matt Deane is a considerate guy. In the truck, he was quick to haul out a flight case so that I could sit as we talked. He's also helpful when members of his crew pop in with questions about the cars or impending meetings. Nobody seems intimidated by him, which Deane tells me is an old-school way of running a garage, and yet everyone shows respect as much as camaraderie. I tell him he must be doing something right.

"It's about taking a step back," he says, "and making sure they have everything they need to do their jobs to the best of their abilities."

Later that morning, ahead of FP1, I watch Deane at work with his crew. Quietly patrolling each car in different states of assembly, he's an observant presence whose pale blue eyes switch from one mechanic to the next. He's about to turn fifty, but is as fit and alert as a man half his age thanks in part to a passion for running. As a measure of his diligence, he glances regularly at a timer display on the wall counting down to the first practice session. The track won't go live for another ninety minutes, and yet Deane checks so frequently it's as if he's covering off the possibility that time might race ahead.

In that window, the Mercedes F1 Chief Mechanic is also responsible for making sure one of the cars is ready to be wheeled out for the show-and-tell presentation. Reporters, photographers, and television crews are already gathered behind a cordon in the pit lane in front of the garage. Such is the level of expectation and hope that the team can return to their former dominance that this year's first update package has reached almost mythological status. After the cancellation of the Emilia-Romagna Grand Prix, where the cars had been scheduled to run the improved floor, suspension, and sidepods, followed by the tight, twisting streets of Monaco that allowed just a limited test, this weekend is the first real opportunity to make an assessment. As a result, this standard showcase has attracted a sizable crowd. When George Russell's W14 is maneuvered out into the Mediterranean sunshine, Deane stands back from the media scrum. I ask how he feels about people getting so close to the car, but he shrugs and tells me he's already thinking about a task that follows that could make or break a race.

"We do about sixty practice pit stops every race weekend," he says. "As mechanics, we can build a car and do everything correctly. We make sure every nut and bolt is tightened and every wire connected as it should be. But when that car hits the pit box for a tire change, the pressure on the pit crew is immense." For Deane, it's not just a mechanical process but psychological. "We have to get it right," he adds.

Pit stops are crucial in Formula 1 and also mandatory. At some point in the race a team's car will enter the pit lane, at a speed often limited to a not inconsiderable 80 kph—depending on the circuit—and then come to a halt in the pit box outside the team garage. There, working in perfect synchronization, it's on those mechanics in the role of the pit crew to jack the car and swap all four tires as swiftly as possible so the driver can exit and return to the track. They may also have to adjust the front wing flaps to tweak aero handling or even replace a damaged front wing. Time isn't just precious here. It's race-critical.

This season, from the moment a car arrives in the box and then screeches away, Red Bull and Ferrari have been putting in pit stops that average at around 2.10 seconds. Mercedes F1 trail them by a few hundredths of a second. In motor racing terms, that's significant. It's also something the team have been aggressively investigating in a bid to improve, and their findings point not to the pit crew but their tools.

"It's our wheel locking mechanism," Deane says, collecting a wheel gun from the floor. I find myself looking at a cross between a power drill and grenade launcher. It's intended to fit over the wheel nut and spin it on or off at high speed. The issue, as Deane outlines, is with a safety retention measure designed to keep the wheel on the axle. When the gun goes on to the wheel nut, it depresses the mechanism, known as a pawl. If an attempt is made to withdraw the gun before the wheel, however, the pawl can jam. It means the gun has to be pushed back on again to free it, sometimes using brute force. As a result, the crew have to approach each stop with less haste to achieve more speed, but it's clearly galling. Even if the procedure goes smoothly, it's still milliseconds slower than some rival teams who have devised a locking mechanism that doesn't jam when the wheel is removed too quickly. As each wheel change requires three mechanics, one on the gun, one to remove the old wheel, and one to fit the replacement, the choreographic demands are already intense.

In a bid to find a few hundredths of a second, it's an example of the intense scrutiny that all Formula 1 teams must apply to every detail of their race. Recently, the team's design department has been tasked with creating a new wheel retention mechanism. Until that comes to fruition, it falls to Deane and his crew to shoot for maximum pit stop efficiency with the current pawl. There's only a very small chance that it can jam, but it's an additional pressure that he tells me they're currently feeling. "We had a slight issue with it at the last race in Monaco," he says. "So that's in the back of everybody's minds."

Once the car's showcasing is complete, I join the press pack to watch the pit stop practice. Deane prepares to oversee the whole operation. He stands at the head of the pit box with a control unit in one hand. This operates the traffic light system—replacing the traditional "lollipop" stop/go sign on the end of a stick—which signals to the driver when they're good to floor the accelerator once more. From checking his crew are clear of the car and the pit lane free from traffic, there's a huge amount of sensory input for Deane to process quickly while making safety a priority.

"I use my ears as much as my eyes," he tells me. "Above all I want to hear the sound of four wheel guns going on at the same time."

With a mechanic in the cockpit for the purposes of practice, looking curiously small without a helmet, two of his colleagues push the car from behind so it rolls into the pit box. The stand-in driver behind the wheel brakes hard and a twenty-strong pit crew pounce. As well as three mechanics on each tire, there's a front and rear jack, and another four on hand to steady the car when it's off the ground, adjust front wing flaps, and clean mirrors or radiator ducts. A further three stand by to replace the car's nose if needed. All of them wear fire suits and heavy gloves. It's a brutally physical and breathtakingly fast maneuver marked by the collective dual shriek of wheel guns: once to spin off the old wheel and another to lock the new one into place. With a thud as the four wheel-off operators swing the old tires clear, the car is back on the tarmac with fresh treads on each axle.

"One point nine seconds," says the technician at a mobile control station in front of the garage. Beside him, and behind a pair of dark glasses, George Russell looks on with interest. It's a decent result for a manual "push in," with the measurement in a live session extending by a few hundredths to include the driver's response time in exiting the pit box. Rather than pursue the fastest time, and risk a jammed pawl, the key has to be consistency.

"Let's go again," says Deane.

Under a midday sun, which leaves everyone sweating from exertion inside their helmets, the crew perform one pit stop after another. The margin between each drill is measurable by one or two hundredths of a second. Even if I wanted to pinpoint that potential sticking point the team are aiming to overcome with a new pawl design, it's simply too quick to see. It's clearly on Deane's mind, however, because before the car is trolleyed back into the garage he works with one of the wheel teams to refine their technique. His aim is to minimize the potential for error but concedes that most pit crew mechanics master their roles by learning from mistakes.

"When it happens, some of the boys will look at the social media response and really beat themselves up about it," he says, before acknowledging it's one more reason why he talks to them all across a race weekend. Ultimately, it's in the interests of the team that everyone in the garage is able to grow stronger from any slipup rather than stew about it.

Then again, Deane tells me, sometimes a member of the pit crew can struggle with the pressure of expectation. In such cases, if it's causing problems then it's on the Chief Mechanic to replace them for the sake of maximizing performance. "It goes down like a cup of cold sick," says Deane, who has nevertheless learned to use psychological tools as constructively and effectively as any ratchet. "The team always comes first, but I make sure they get the opportunity to earn their position back again."

With FP1 looming, the garage floor space around each car slowly fills with personnel. Engineers begin to occupy their positions around the island workstation, which is headed, from a high stool at the rear, by Toto Wolff. He is soon joined by Bradley Lord, while partner guests—including several international soccer players in attendance this weekend—look on from the two viewing galleries at the back of the garage. Over the weekend, the *Drive to Survive* film crew are shadowing the team. This amounts to a guy with a shoulder-mounted camera who seems to smell drama breaking, and a sound man with an extendable boom mic that can catch people unawares. Despite the scrutiny and increasingly cramped environment, Matt Deane and his crew are focused solely on their work to ensure both cars are ready for Hamilton and Russell. Wearing shorts and black team polo tops, in contrast to the engineers in white long-sleeved shirts and pants, the mechanics never stand still. The practical demands on them are relentless. Despite so much going on around them, however, they remain as laser-focused as their data-driven counterparts on preparing the cars to maximize the hour when the track goes live.

Back in the parts truck, after a steep learning curve of a session, Matt Deane summons a team job list on his laptop. Following the drivers' debrief, the engineers will begin to send the first of a raft of setup changes for Deane and his mechanics to implement. For now, he reflects on how his role comes with pastoral responsibilities. Most of his crew are only in their late twenties to midthirties, and the pressure on them can be relentless.

"Well, I have to make sure they get on the right flights," he says, laughing, and then tells me that a spot in any F1 garage tends to suit younger mechanics because they're away from home for so much of the year. As they settle down and start families, Deane explains, the prospect of living out of suitcases quickly loses its appeal.

"Some do it for three years and realize it's not for them. Others are lifers who have very strong partners at home," he says, counting himself among that number as a husband and proud father of two. "It's also a trust thing," he adds. "We're working in the garage until ten o'clock at night, but if we're in Monaco everyone assumes we're partying on yachts or going to nightclubs. It's just not like that, but I've known lads whose girlfriends are phoning the whole time, constantly checking up on them, and it can cause a big problem."

For those mechanics who struggle to balance life on the road with home, says Deane, or simply outgrow the travel demands, a more settled, conventional but equally rewarding future often awaits them at the factory. "There's always opportunities for people to go back, and we would never discourage that," he says. "It's also useful to have a link back at the factory to ex–race team members. Those guys know what we expect, which is good."

There's a great deal to process when observing a team of Mercedes F1 mechanics working in high gear. The intense activity coupled with the shriek of wheel guns and smell of fuel and solvents is a heady mix. I'm also struck by just what a male-dominated profession it continues to be. This weekend, covering for a colleague, Spares Coordinator Georgia Parslow is the only woman working in the garage. It's a broadly similar picture along the length of the pit lane, in fact, where any female presence speaks volumes about the state of play. Deane tells me this is an issue that the sport is seeking to address.

"The drive to attract women into engineering has been very successful," he says. "We're following that example by actively encouraging more female mechanics into our apprentice scheme." For all his evident enthusiasm to instigate that change, Deane recognizes that the current lack of female visibility in the F1 garages is an uncomfortable barrier. "We're in a chicken and egg situation," he concedes. "It takes time for any mechanic to gain the experience they need to work at this level. Once our female apprentices come through, it won't be long before girls see them on TV and think, *I can do that!* But it's only then that we'll see the upswing."

When it comes to recruiting for the Mercedes F1 garage, Deane looks to the lower racing formulas. There, he explains, mechanics haven't just learned how to use the tools of their trade like extensions of their own limbs, which he considers to be a minimum requirement. With tighter budgets behind their cars, they also come to him with a built-in resourcefulness. "They might have had to manufacture something in the fabrication or machine shop to make their job easier," he says. "That sort of thing gets my attention."

With setup change requests beginning to pop onto the job list, Deane folds his laptop and transfers back to the garage. A detail of mechanics is assigned to each car, and by extension each one is responsible for a certain field, from the front and rear end to the engine, gearbox, and hydraulics. With the tasks distributed and a busy period ahead for everyone if the cars are to be ready in time for the second practice session, Deane stops briefly at the keyboard in front of Toto's monitors. From there, he summons the Spotify desktop application and selects a playlist. As the Chemical Brothers crash through the garage sound system, it's the pit crew's long-standing Rear Jack Operator, Karl Fanson, who rolls his eyes and crosses the floor to find my ear. "Matt's stuck in the '90s," he says. "It's this or thrash metal."

For the next few hours, to a soundtrack featuring rallying songs that most of these guys would have been too young to remember when they were first released, the Chief Mechanic and self-appointed garage DJ works at full throttle with his team. The engineers have requested a comprehensive suspension change on Hamilton's W14, and there is some question as to whether it'll be ready for FP2. With Russell's car close to completion, several mechanics from that side of the garage cross the floor to help out. Throughout, I observe from the same spot allotted to me from the first race of the season and take notes from there. It's a few feet back from Toto's stool, with just enough room to clear the way for passing tire trolleys. At one point I am tempted to take myself to the comfortable seats behind each car that are reserved for the drivers. It just feels wrong, however, given how hard everyone is working. Even though there's nobody else in the garage but the mechanics and me, I stay on my feet.

Just then, work stops momentarily as Deane peers into the gearbox with a pen torch. A young mechanic peers over his shoulder, looking like the culprit at the scene of a crime. Seemingly satisfied by what he finds, Deane swaps a few words and then brings his laptop across to the work surface behind me.

"That's one of our newer lads," he tells me while clearing tasks from the job list. "I happened to see a little washer ping off as he unscrewed a bolt. He saw it, too, but with time pressing he's not chased it down." Deane pauses for a moment to scroll through the list. "Turns out it had dropped right through to the floor. But it could so easily have been catastrophic."

I glance across at the mechanic in question. He's back working on the car but I feel for him. While he must be chewing himself up on the inside at the fact that his boss had busted him, Deane handled it in a way that put the car first while ensuring that he'll never make the same mistake again.

"He's still learning," he says in what has been a stark reminder that at this level of motorsport there can be no room for corner-cutting.

Deane has exacting standards, but rather than demand it he encourages his team to uphold it for themselves. He's constantly checking that they understand what's required of them, ensuring they're not overloaded, and then trusts them with the space to deliver. Ultimately, every member of his team must earn the right to be here and from that comes a source of pride. As we talk, the first engineers arrive in the garage ahead of second practice. Minutes later, as the influx of white shirts begins to outnumber the black tops sported by the garage crew, I spot a tall, dark-haired figure among them who then looms large behind Deane.

It's Toto Wolff, who catches my eye as if to ask for a few words with his Chief Mechanic.

FP1 had been somewhat testing for the team, and that's evident in Wolff's expression. It may not be an ideal time, but I prepare to at least introduce myself and see where it leads. In that same moment, a muff-clad microphone lowers into view just between us. I blink on registering the bigger picture, namely the *Drive to Survive* camera guy beside the team boss alongside the sound man with the boom hoisted over his head. I intend to work on Wolff to gain his trust, but not in front of millions, and instinctively retreat from the frame so that he can speak with Deane.

In FP2, the engineers focused on running the cars with high and low fuel loads while continuing to explore the potential of the upgrade package. A P8 finish for Russell and P11 for Hamilton prompted some F1 pundits to question if the package would deliver, but there's a brighter story breaking within the team. At breakfast the next morning, word is that the overnight work in the simulator back at the factory—equipped with Friday's setup data and reserve driver Mick Schumacher behind the wheel—has unlocked good performance gains. Nobody is under the illusion that the days of Red Bull dominance are done, but the news serves as a rallying call for the team.

"It's going to be another long day," says Matt Deane when I find him in the garage. He's sounding remarkably cheerful given the long list of setup changes on his laptop that he has to scroll through to reach the end. Both racing cars are basically just carcasses, with tubes curling out of them like they've been intubated for surgery. His mechanics swarm around the vehicles. Wearing thin black nitrile gloves, they carry out tasks in double-quick time to the sound of "Two Tribes" by Frankie Goes To Hollywood. "We were late back to the hotel last night," he says. "Just time for a beer and tapas before bed, but this evening's going to be different. After qualifying is finished, we're planning on running a lap of the track and you're welcome to join us. I've put up a list on the fridge round the back. You just need to write your name down and your projected pace. One of the engineers is working with an AI program to devise a staggered start time so we all cross the line at exactly the same time for a photo finish."

The deployment of performance technology to optimize a casual jog around the track sounds about as Mercedes F1 as it gets. And I'm in.

Deane smiles to himself as he consults the job list one more time. Having spent time in the garage, I appreciate that the Chief Mechanic can only deliver in his role if his team operate as a tight unit under pressure. If this was a high-end kitchen, the head chef would be red in the face and throwing plates to instill the discipline and pace required to get results, but Deane's exacting, holistic approach seems to be equally effective and plays to his character. I've seen him relating to his mechanics not just as a leader but a colleague and also a mentor. It's hard to pull off, but I sense he achieves it by balancing high expectations with genuine care for their welfare.

So when it comes to something like an exercise in bringing everyone together, he knows these guys are both smart and cynical enough to see right through a conventional, corporate approach.

"I've sat in presentations where people propose building bridges out of crates or something," Deane tells me, "but to be honest the best team-building happens at the circuit. Last season, in Austria, both cars went into the wall during qualifying. One of them needed a completely new chassis, and we worked on it until two in the morning. We were up against it, but everyone got on with the job. We had the music going and it was just a really good moment of camaraderie."

As the sound of an engine firing makes further talk impossible, I drop into a room at the back of the garage to find the list for this evening's postqualifying run. With no time during race weekends to break for lunch, this is where the mechanics come to grab drinks and snacks. Most have added their names, along with some impressive pace projections. In Deane's finely engineered exercise, they'll all be winners when they cross the finish line in lockstep.

It isn't just the Chief Mechanic who plays a unifying role in the garage. Following the debrief after every session on the track, from practice to the race itself, Lewis Hamilton and George Russell make a point of returning to personally thank the mechanics for their efforts. They stop for a few minutes to chat, laugh, and joke. It doesn't look like a requirement. Both drivers clearly enjoy the company of the crew they rely upon for so much.

"It makes a huge difference," agrees Deane, who has run cars for a roll call of contemporary racing greats, including Rubens Barrichello and Jenson Button after BAR became the Honda F1 Racing Team in 2006. Three years later, following a management buyout after Honda's shock withdrawal from the sport, and with Mercedes-Benz as engine supplier, the newly created Brawn GP propelled Button and the team to an extraordinary 2009 championship-winning season. Matt Deane would subsequently go on to serve Nico Rosberg and Michael Schumacher from 2010 when Mercedes took over the team on their return to Formula 1 as a constructor for the first time in over half a century. While he rates the current drivers highly for the relationship they've built with his mechanics, Deane considers Schumacher to be the one who led the way.

"The first time I met Michael," he recalls, when the German first signed for the team, "he showed up on a freezing cold morning in this massive sheepskin coat. He introduced himself to everyone and learned their names straightaway. He was a cool guy that everyone liked. Michael remembered birthdays and had this great trick on nights out after race weekends where he would get everyone drunk but somehow remain sober himself." Deane illustrates his point by mischievously tossing an imaginary drink over his shoulder. "One year, during the summer shutdown, he even invited us all out to his ranch house on the shore of Lake Geneva to go skydiving. He was just a real team player," he says to finish, and for a moment that memory seems to hang in the air.

Later, just ahead of the third and final practice, I return to my spot in a crowded garage. This time there seem to be more camera crews, engineers, and partner guests present, and generally less space for everyone, yet the mechanics remain completely undeterred. Russell is in his car early, talking over the radio to Marcus Dudley, his Race Engineer. "Can I adjust my wing mirror," he asks, having just discovered it's a new fitting. "Or will that affect the aerodynamics?" Dudley consents to the request, and at once a mechanic is in attendance with an Allen T-Key to make what will be a minimal shift.

On the other side of the garage, looking like some battle android in his racing overalls and helmet, Lewis Hamilton has just stepped up onto the floor scales. This is mandatory for all drivers to be sure their weight,* combined with the car, meets the 798 kilogram minimum. Having passed the check in the presence of an FIA representative, Hamilton nods at his mechanics on crossing to a small stepladder that allows him to access the cockpit. As he squeezes in, which always leaves me feeling claustrophobic, Deane's team continue to flit around the car like courtiers locking a knight into his suit of armor. The Chief Mechanic watches over them without interfering. He might be experienced enough to know how to perform under stress, and cut no corners, but potentially for the sake of this race weekend he has to be sure that every member of his team can also handle it.

In the closing minutes before the track goes live, a sense of expectation intensifies within the garage. Thanks to gathering storm clouds over the circuit, there is quite literally a charge in the air. Both cars are primed for takeoff. All personnel are in their

---

* The FIA states that the driver weight must be a minimum of 80 kg, to not disadvantage taller drivers; most come in under this number and so ballast is often used in the car to comply.

positions, while the guests look on in awe. Including one, I notice from the corner of my eye, who has just made himself comfortable in the plush seat behind Hamilton's car.

"Who is that?" the driver asks over his radio, sounding like F1's Papa Bear. "The guy in my mirror."

At once, having registered the question in their earpieces, both mechanics and engineers side-eye the unsuspecting guest.

"Pass," replies Bono, from his race engineer's station, and I give silent thanks that I had earlier trusted my instinct not to park myself there.

Heading into this last practice session, all eyes are on the weather radar screens. Unlike in a race, when anything from a shower to a downpour can create strategic opportunities, nobody wants it to fall in this session. "There'll be nothing to learn," reasons Shov, and the Trackside Engineering Director goes on to explain that a wet track can only compromise performance and by extension the setup program.

It means that when the clock starts on the sixty minutes available to all teams, both Mercedes F1 cars snap out of the garage toward the pit lane exit. Having brought the tires up to temperature on a precisely timed out lap, Hamilton and Russell punch into P2 and P3 respectively. It's an encouraging start to the session, even though Verstappen remains dominant by half a second. With so many variables in the mix, however, from tire choice to fuel loads as each team pursues a different program for the session, what matters here is process more than position.

So, when Logan Sargeant's Williams car scythes into the gravel on the final turn, triggering a red flag, it feels like the session has just been frustrated on an avoidable front. This is compounded when the storm finally breaks overhead. By the time the flag turns green once again, rain is bouncing off the pit lane surface so violently that it creates a low-level mist. Back in the garage, Hamilton is out of his car. He consults with Wolff for some time and then, with phone in hand, somewhat pointedly takes to his chair at the back of the garage.

"I've never seen him use it before," observes one mechanic with a quiet smile.

As time ticks away toward the close of the practice session, Russell remains in his cockpit. He's still wearing his helmet, unwilling to stand down. Over the radio, he sounds audibly frustrated. "It's not going to get any drier," the young driver says. "Let's get out so I can feel it."

With just minutes to go before the session ends, a sudden break in the rain sees Russell's wish granted. Along with Hamilton, and just a handful of competitors, he takes to the track as if to catch up on lost time. Having put in hours behind the wheel of the sim overnight back in Brackley, Mick Schumacher is now present in the garage at Toto Wolff's side. Judging by the performance gains despite the restricted session—which sees Hamilton finish in P3 and Russell in P6—his work this weekend has been invaluable.

"That felt pretty decent," says Russell as the session draws to an end, and indeed as the sunshine returns it leaves a sense of optimism behind.

"Mechanically, everything went fine," says Deane, which speaks volumes about his priorities here, before notifying his team via their earpieces to prepare a car for another pit stop practice.

Having spent time in the garage this weekend, I can appreciate why the Chief Mechanic limits his attention to the smooth running of the car. Everything beyond that is out of his hands, and yet when his responsibilities come into play—in the garage or the pit lane—it can prove critical. "Can you imagine the pressure Deano and his crew must have been under at the final race of 2016 when Lewis and Nico were in the same title fight?" one team member later observes. "Had a pit stop gone wrong for either car, it could've determined the Drivers' Championship."

I dwell on this during qualifying. While the mechanics appear to stand down when the cars exit the garage, in reality they must be ready for them to return at a moment's notice. This comes close to happening in the final, somewhat chaotic moments of Q2 when a timing miscommunication from the pit wall sees the two Mercedes tangle with each other at high speed on the home straight. The contact produces a squall of shattered carbon fiber bodywork and forces Hamilton onto the grass. At once, Deane and several of his mechanics rush to prepare a spare nose for Russell's car. Even though the timer promptly runs out on the young driver's chances of joining Hamilton in the final shoot-out, leaving him with work to do from P12 in Sunday's race, it's clear that both drivers rely on their garage crew to react both rapidly and decisively to unpredictable situations.

I catch up with Deane just after qualifying, in which Hamilton claimed P5 and then advanced another place after Alpine's Pierre Gasly incurred a grid penalty for impeding another driver. With Russell's result in mind, following the unfortunate tangling of the two cars, it's been a mixed result for the team. In terms of how the garage has performed under the Chief Mechanic's watch, however, some weight has lifted from his shoulders. Behind him, Spotify is back up on Wolff's master screen and we both have to raise our voices to be heard over yet more vintage bangers.

"So now we're in parc fermé," Deane says, referring to a period of time during a race weekend in which the FIA may inspect the cars but work on them is heavily restricted. On each side of the garage, under the watch of scrutineers with clipboards, several mechanics are carrying out permitted tasks such as bleeding brakes and draining oil. Another is pushing a floor polisher across an already spotless surface as if in search of one stray dust mote.

Deane directs my attention to his laptop, where he's busy dropping close-up photographs of various parts of George Russell's car into a form. "We're also permitted to carry out damage repairs before we put the covers on the cars for the night," he says, and there's evidently work to do after Russell and his teammate tripped over each other during qualifying. "I just have to submit an approval list to the FIA by 7 p.m. Then we can go running," he adds.

Toward the end of each day at a race weekend, a horn blares over the pit lane. It marks the moment that the track is no longer live, which means paddock personnel with the right lanyards are free to venture out on foot to unwind after a long day. Apart from slow-moving sweeper trucks or safety vehicles, there's no need to look over your shoulder on stepping onto the asphalt. The sense of danger that hangs over the track when cars are racing is gone. But not forgotten.

As arranged, I return in my running gear to find a very different atmosphere in the garage. Each car has been stripped of wheels and blanketed under dust sheets like museum pieces out of season. The mechanics have vanished. The music switched off. Just one figure remains in the space. I find him at a worktable. Now wearing sneakers, shorts, and a T-shirt, he's simultaneously jabbing at the calculator app on his phone and scrawling on a sheet of paper. The Chief Mechanic appears a little embarrassed to see me.

"That AI program the engineer was using to work out the staggered times? Turns out it's produced a complete work of fiction." Deane shakes his head as if caught between despair and derision. "He's had three days to sort it, and the best he can come up with expects our slowest runner to put in a 3.30-minute-kilometer pace. Most runners couldn't keep that up for more than a hundred meters, let alone a lap of the track. So I've binned it off and worked it out the old-fashioned way." Deane shows me his calculations, which basically amount to a list of digits, with several rows crossed out, and a rough grouping of names. It's not very Mercedes F1. "We're always resourceful," he remarks with a smile before inviting me to follow him out of the garage to a gap in the high fencing between the pit lane and the home straight.

The first thing I notice is the grand piano straddling the start line. A pianist plays variations of the same refrain, seemingly oblivious to her incongruous surroundings. It's something to do with the race day ceremonials, a rehearsal no doubt, but a reminder of how unreal this all seems. We join the mechanics on the verge. They're limbering up in the shade from the late sun, but mostly focusing on ribbing the poor engineer for stumbling over his own technology. He's laughing along with everyone else but looks like he's dying a little on the inside.

"Ready, go . . ."

From the start line, we set off in small groups at intervals of a minute or so. It seems to be a finger-in-the-wind exercise in terms of making sure each group has time to scoop up the one in front so that everyone finishes as one. Mindful of my conversation about it with Matt Deane, I'm also aware that's not the point of the exercise.

I'm in the middle of the pack with the first mechanic on Russell's car and front right wheel gun man Stuart Green (known as "Flannel," after once wiping his face with a used rag from the garage that caused an allergic reaction) and his front left wheel-off colleague John Taylor. None of us can see the pack in front. "They'll be finished before we reach Turn 1," I hear one of them grumble. With some serious catching up to do, that's where the chat ends.

Unsurprisingly for F1 personnel, the pace is way faster than predicted. The aim might be to catch the group in front, but equally nobody wants to feel like they could be overtaken. Just to add to the challenge, the elevation around the track is formidable. From Turn 2 to 4, we embark on a climb that seems to wind around endlessly. When we finally crest to begin a drop down to 5, my heart is hammering hard. It comes as a relief to be running downhill. In a Formula 1 car, however, such a change in track profile combines with the turns to create an unrelenting ride with considerable G-forces. It's hard to appreciate the ups and downs from an armchair in front of the TV, or even from the grandstands. I'm not entering this corner at 100 kph and then swooping into a further descent toward the next turn at double that speed, but even on foot I have a newfound respect for the demands placed upon the drivers by the full shape of the circuit.

By the time we arrive in the closing section, where a popular, sweeping final turn has been restored for this year's race, any chance of the high speed it affords the cars has completely left my legs. While Flannel has fallen behind, Taylor has dropped me for the home straight. So far we have collected just one guy from an earlier group. I glance behind me. Runners from other teams are out for a jog, a far cry from the 320 kph that the drivers can touch on this long straight. In 2021, Max Verstappen set the race lap record at this 4.6-kilometer circuit in a fraction over seventy-six seconds. A glance at my watch tells me we're going to cross the finish line well over the twenty-minute mark. I see no sign of the final but fastest group that set off after us and which includes the event's architect. The trouble is I've reached the closing 200 meters, running alongside the grandstand where a few last spectators clap and cheer, and there's no way I'm going to stop in front of them all and wait for Deane and his group to catch up. The team's photographer is in attendance at the finish line, but any chance of capturing a mass finish fell apart long ago.

A moment later, having taken the checkered flag in my mind, I'm in a hot mess on the tarmac alongside a handful of mechanics.

We're fighting for breath, bumping fists and basically just having a good time as our number slowly grows. Where I had been on nodding terms with most of them in the garage, this exercise has broken down barriers that would otherwise have taken much longer to dismantle. For the mechanics, it's been a great way to blow off steam ahead of what will be the most important day of their race weekend. Through my eyes, a corporate team-building exercise just wouldn't come close to achieving the same result.

"What happened there, then?" asks Deane as he crosses the line, and I don't suppose I'm alone in feeling a little embarrassed that I had let my racing instinct get the better of me. He rests his hands on his knees as several of his crew clap him on the back. Without having to ask, I know he's achieved the result he wanted. "We'll get it right this season," he says.

With both cars on the grid, in the closing minutes before lights out on the Spanish Grand Prix, sunshine floods the entrance to the garage. With Toto Wolff at the bridgehead of the engineers' island, the Mercedes F1 personnel seem to bring their own light. They appear energized today, based on the steady evolution in performance over the race weekend. The boss, meanwhile, studies a weather radar on the screen in front of him. He's perched on his high stool with both legs crossed at the ankle, in sneakers and no socks, and with one foot twitching restlessly.

The F1 TV feed, broadcast onto screens around the garage, provides a live view of the conditions that are clearly concerning Wolff. It switches between establishing shots from different points on the circuit, and the menacing thunderclouds that loom over-head. One camera captures spits of lightning, which could be from a different track given that the pit lane outside the garage is basking in sunshine. "It's the calm before the storm," says Lewis Hamilton's Performance Engineer, Michael Sansoni.

Just then, having left the two W14 chargers primed on the grid, the mechanics return to the garage. In each space vacated by the cars, they find a row of chairs have been set out for them. Here, wearing their protective pit crew outfits, they'll watch the race on the side screens just like millions of people at home. The only difference is that with little warning they'll have to spring into action to play their role in the outcome. Matt Deane returns from the grid, wheeling a tool trolley into a recess at the side of the garage. He makes his way across to me, glancing at the weather radar still commanding Wolff's attention. I lift one headphone away from my ear to speak to the Chief Mechanic and ask if he thinks it will rain.

"We're always prepared for the worst," he says, gesturing at the intermediate tires on a trolley that are currently keeping warm under heated blankets. Then he tells me they ran through another pit stop practice earlier. "Just to calm the nerves so the lads feel settled."

As the mechanics now occupying the seats settle in for the start of the race, now transformed into the pit crew, everyone looks quite relaxed. They're sitting shoulder to shoulder, visors up, chatting and joking as the cars begin their formation lap. Deane tells me that given the crew have worked so hard all weekend this moment requires some vigilance.

"The race gives them space to think about other things," he says. "They can start to turn their minds toward other jobs to be done, but I need them ready to react." He taps the mouthpiece attached to his radio device. "So I'll talk to them regularly over their earpieces. We also have water and snacks on hand to keep up their blood sugars."

The team's determination to maximize performance is played out by the drivers from the moment the cars launch at the lights. In the opening turns, Lewis Hamilton spots an opportunity to steal third place from McLaren's Lando Norris, while George Russell makes an almighty start to storm from twelfth to seventh. Toto Wolff and the race engineers barely blink as they study the live data from the cars now streaming across their screens, leaving it to the pit crew to cheer and applaud every move.

"Be ready for a safety car," Deane reminds them over the radio. He's standing at the entrance to the garage, well aware that the race has yet to settle down.

Running first stints on soft tires, both cars come in one lap after the other to switch to the more durable and longer-running medium compound. Hamilton is first into the pit box, leaving 3.0 seconds later, and no doubt Deane will be yearning for the new wheel retention mechanism after what had been one sticky tire transition. When Russell follows, the crew recover to see him off in 2.6 seconds. Shortly afterward, as other cars peel off into the pits, Hamilton and Russell find themselves holding station in second and third place respectively. Verstappen is long gone up the road, which is no surprise to anyone, and it leaves Russell to manage the gap behind him to Sergio Pérez and speed toward the first double podium of the season for Mercedes F1.

On the final lap, following Deane's verbal nod over the radio, the mechanics rush from the garage to see the cars home. "Keep your feet on the ground," he warns them, mindful of a recent safety directive from the FIA to stop crew from climbing up the pit wall fencing. The last thing the team needs is a penalty in a race that has just elevated them to second place in the Constructors' Championship.

While the pit crew respect their Chief Mechanic's reminder, those left in the garage erupt in jubilation once both cars are over the line. From the engineers and technicians to the team members who have steadily filled the back of the garage throughout the race, they hug and punch the air with unbridled joy. Yet more world-class soccer players look on from the viewing gallery, but there isn't much about the art of celebrating that they can teach the team here. Wolff remains at his high stool, crowded by cameras from every angle. This time I join the sudden exodus from the garage in the rush to meet the cars as they pull into parc fermé under the podium.

I am about two seconds too late in getting out into the pit lane, where I find myself swept along in a sea of paddock personnel and VIPs. When the surge comes to a halt, I'm too far back to spot the drivers as they climb out of their cars. On the big screen, the Mercedes F1 mechanics have claimed pole position behind the belt barrier that keeps the crowd from the cars. Clearly they reserved some pace from their lap of the track to sprint there from the pit wall in order to welcome Hamilton and Russell home. Still, like everyone around me, I have a great view of the pair when they appear on the balcony several minutes later.

Together with Max Verstappen, celebrating his fifth win of the season and an unbroken streak for Red Bull, the Mercedes F1 drivers unleash a spray of champagne across each other and over the crowd below. The cheering, applause, and whistling is widespread and intense—not just all around me but from the grandstand on the other side of the home straight—and it's underscored by the constant thrum of the TV helicopter overhead. I glance around to see team members who had earlier been watching the race unfold in quiet concentration now looking like they've come undone at the emotional seams.

Keen to catch up with the team's Chief Mechanic, I extract myself from the throng. On my way back to the garage, weaving between media crews, paddock personnel, and race guests, I reflect on just how much this must mean to Mercedes F1. For a team that until recently fought for nothing less than a win, only to find themselves lacking throughout much of the previous season and unthinkably into this one, today's outcome is important. It isn't a victory but a move in the right direction. The question is whether this is a track-specific result for the W14 or a sign that the team have unlocked sustainable performance at last. With gigabytes of data from the race weekend, the engineers and analysts will be hard at work back at the factory next week in a bid to understand it. For now, however, they've earned this moment of celebration.

"I'm happy that we got that result on merit," says Deane back in the garage. With the guests departed to toast the team's success, he's retreated to the front row of the viewing gallery. Still on his feet, but with some space to himself, he's supporting his laptop with one hand while consulting the job list. "But mostly I'm happy that we did our job." For someone who played a key role in the race, it's a humble response.

"There was a time when we were just winning, winning, winning," he says. "It reached a point where I'd walk down the pit lane feeling bad for the other teams. I didn't know where to look. I've been around long enough to know how it feels to be in their shoes, whereas some of the boys who joined in those championship years had no idea how tough that can be. So now I want to keep a sense of balance in the garage because we're only as good as our last race."

As we talk, those mechanics who stayed behind with Deane have begun to pack up. They've swapped their overalls for luminous team T-shirts, which is a safety precaution as the pit lane is about to fill with forklifts and freight containers. It'll be some while yet before the cars are returned to their stalls to be picked apart to the chassis and prepared for transport to the next race. In that time, both Hamilton and Russell will drop in to the garage to recognize the contribution that the Chief Mechanic and his crew have made to this weekend. His crew will still be here, in fact, long after the engineers have rushed to catch the evening flight home. Deane tells me that most of them won't head for the airport until later on Monday, but most have plans on their return.

"We enjoy our time off," he says. "Some of the boys are into projects like house renovation. It means they'll be in the DIY store on Tuesday when it's not too busy. We'll all be back in the factory on Friday, preparing for the next race, and that suits us all. In this job we get to travel around the world and work with some of the best technology, but right now I'm looking forward to going home and doing the school run."

For those in the paddock with family, such domestic normality must be quite a precious thing. For Deane, after the demands of a race weekend, it's a chance to get back to the quiet life he had imagined for himself when he first set out to become a mechanic at the village garage. I draw breath to ask him about his young son, as I've been told he's a budding F1 commentator, but for a second time this weekend I see the team boss approach with purpose. This time, however, having just broken free from a media interview in the pit lane, Toto Wolff strides toward us both with his shirt sleeves rolled to the elbows and a smile that's been missing since the start of the season. All the tension has left his jaw and with it that sense of guardedness. Frankly, he looks reborn.

"Great job!" he says to Deane, pumping his hand and then mine as we finally make our introduction at what feels like exactly the right time.

CHAPTER FOUR

NIGHT RUN

The British Grand Prix
Silverstone Circuit, Silverstone
July 7–9, 2023

"I'll be downstairs . . . in my dark cave."

Mick Schumacher is about to go motor racing. For this opening stint in the cockpit, he's wearing a T-shirt and shorts. He also keeps his mobile phone with him should he need to kill time on the grid or in the gravel. It all looks very casual, and yet what Schumacher is about to do behind the wheel as the Mercedes F1 reserve driver could determine how the team deliver at this weekend's British Grand Prix.

It's approaching five o'clock on Friday afternoon. I've just joined the 24-year-old German and several performance engineers in a window-free industrial building on the Mercedes F1 campus in Brackley. This is home to the simulator. In a motorsport with strict limitations on preseason testing and race weekend practice, on the track and in the wind tunnel, the virtual world has become a critical tool for gathering data. The team have invested millions of pounds in the current build, which became operational in 2020. The technology is both highly developed and closely protected in pursuit of a competitive edge.

Here, the simulator can be used to assist in car development through the year, which includes testing designs and components without expensive manufacturing commitments. It also allows drivers to get into the rhythm of an upcoming track in the season and assist in preparing a baseline setup for the car.

Then there's the contribution that the sim team can make during a race weekend. Tonight, with data gathered from FP1 and FP2 at Silverstone, Schumacher and his engineers will run simulations based on briefs from the trackside team in a bid to fine-tune performance or even make serious gains. Given the overnight transformation in car handling between FP2 and FP3 at the Spanish GP earlier in the season, the work carried out inside this two-story metal box can yield tangible results on the track. I am just one of a handful of outsiders who have been permitted to view the simulator in operation. As a measure of the technology hidden away here, Mercedes F1 recently hosted a knowledge-sharing delegation from NASA.

So when I climbed the industrial stairs from the lobby to the control room a few minutes earlier, to be faced with what looks like the bridge of a starship, I couldn't ignore the battered, old racing rig tucked away at the back. Comprising an old karting seat and steering wheel, bolted onto a paint-chipped steel bench and facing a bank of three computer monitors, it looks like the kind of thing your best mate might have knocked together in the spare room for a more immersive video game experience. Race Simulation Engineer Zhaoming Li has just buzzed me into the building. He notes me watching Schumacher head for a side door rather than the rig and reads my mind immediately.

"Sometimes we use that seat to calibrate settings," he says before crossing the floor to a gallery window at the front of the room. A blind covers the glass on the other side. Li flicks a switch. The blind begins to lift theatrically. "The sim work takes place in here."

In preparing for a race weekend, as well as providing development support throughout the year, F1 teams can call upon two virtual tools. One is effectively a sophisticated computer software system that does all the driving. Among many functions, this lap simulator can work with data imported from the performance of a real race car on a specific circuit to produce an optimized setup. At the touch of a button, the program sends the theoretical vehicle around hundreds of thousands of virtual laps. It's a process that can be performed quickly, and with several versions running simultaneously, to explore how different setups compare. The insight returned by the simulator can be invaluable and provides the engineers with options to shape design or inform setup decisions.

There is one thing that this box of tricks is unable to nail, however, and that's the behavior of a human in the cockpit. While the lap simulator can identify the limit of adhesion as the car takes a corner in terms of pure physics, it simply cannot compute how an F1 driver would handle it in the moment. At speeds testing courage, skill, and instinct, that lone individual also has to factor in dynamic racing situations such as a rival car challenge or sudden wind gust. So what might seem like an optimal line through a corner on paper could see the vehicle hit the wall on tarmac. There are just too many factors to consider that lie beyond the scope of what the lap simulator can replicate, and much of this comes down to how the car *feels*.

Ultimately, a computer-simulated lap lacks a critical component, which is where Mick Schumacher's work begins this evening. I'm here to witness him at work behind the wheel of the "driver-in-loop" simulator (DiL), which places a human being at the heart of the system. "We call this Sim Six," says Li on introducing me to the Mercedes F1 team's latest incarnation.

Through the control room window, as the blind lifts, I find

myself looking down into a deep chamber. On the floor, in almost willfully low light, I make out some kind of giant mechanical maw. Tall digital screens envelop the space, reaching upward of three meters to just below my vantage point. In surround vision, they display one dark blue loading page, and this provides the prime illumination as Schumacher appears below me. It's only when he proceeds to climb into the throat of the contraption that I make sense of the scene. If I didn't know this was a race simulator, I'd be bracing myself for Mick to spin up some new kind of energy source.

"It's our new motion platform," he tells me as Schumacher straps himself into what I now see is a cockpit. It's the halo device that threw me. Normally fixed into position, serving as it does as a critical safety feature to protect the driver, this one is hinged at the back like a jet fighter canopy. As Schumacher lowers it into place, and the screens light up with a digital replica of the Silverstone track, I see him at the heart of his virtual world. I can appreciate that the cockpit is mounted on something very sophisticated, but the whole apparatus is sitting in such a pool of darkness that I can't fully make it out. Even if I hoped that my eyes might adjust, however, Li then closes the blinds. Evidently I have seen enough.

"The previous platform performed three degrees of freedom," he tells me as we move to his station. "This one is capable of all six."

Aware that I'm facing an engineer who lives and breathes pure physics, I admit that I might need some help here beyond recognizing that Sim Five must have moved forward and backward, left and right, and then up and down. "Now we have pitch, yaw, and roll." With one hand, Li demonstrates the movement of a ship or an aircraft in turbulent conditions.

Judging by the size of the chamber, scale is key for the driver to feel as if they're behind the wheel of a real racing car. That can't be achieved with the likes of the fixed seat calibration rig in the control room, which served as one of the first simulators used by the team some fifteen years earlier. Today, the experience is far more immersive—delivering a close approximation of how it feels when the driver is on the track—and yet Li explains that the DiL doesn't set out to match the same sensory assault.

"In this simulated environment, which will never match the reality of a full-size racetrack, the motion it can create is still capable of making things too intense for the drivers. So we purposely dial it back a little."

With the simulator running at less than full throttle, does that take away from the realism? "It's fine for our aims," says Li. "We're not trying to send the drivers on a roller coaster here. We just want to provide them with a sense of what they'd normally experience on track rather than the real thing so they can read how the car feels. We also don't want them to get physically tired," he adds, in explaining why the platform doesn't force the driver to wrestle with the car, "because that can affect performance and means they're less consistent."

As the sim engineers run through the opening procedures before Schumacher begins his late shift, I take a moment to appreciate their objectives. If the DiL is capable of replicating much of the racing experience, it only really focuses on key elements. This largely comes down to the vehicle and the track, and the relationship between them. Essentially, it's all about balance, and this is where every effort is made to match reality. Mick is buckled into a replica monocoque, which is the survival cell designed to protect the driver in the event of a crash. The steering wheel and the foot pedals are also real, as are Mick's gloves and helmet. Everything under the hood, however, is pure data. Li shows me a folder on his screen that stores digital renderings of all the mechanical and aerodynamic components of a real racing car. The fact that he gives up scrolling through the list reflects the exhaustive attention to detail. Then there's the circuit. The virtual version of Silverstone is no approximation. It's constructed from a laser scan of the track that gathers measurements to create a 3D model. The scan can also reproduce the shape of every camber, curb, and bump to an astonishing degree of accuracy, though Li cautions that circuit owners often carry out resurfacing work without notice. "We can also control track and ambient temperature as well as wind direction and speed," he adds, as Schumacher sits on the grid and awaits instructions from above. "Silverstone is a former airfield, so the wind can be different at every turn. It can affect the handling of the car, and so we take the meteorological data from today and feed it all into the sim."

"How about rain?" I ask, aware that the forecast is mixed for this race weekend.

Li considers my question for a moment. "It doesn't change the physics," he says. "We could create a mathematical model that reproduces rain, but it provides no useful performance data."

Just as wet weather offers no tangible learning for the sim engineers, and also the trackside team when it comes to optimizing the car setup, a photorealistic environment is also surplus to requirements. Here in the control room, the sim engineering team face banks of wall-mounted screens. All but one present data. Nobody pays much attention to the screen that shows the driver's view of the circuit. At present, the car is stationary at the exit into Silverstone's Wellington Straight. I recognize the section on account of the bridge across the track, but the graphics remind me of the kind of quality that video gamers enjoyed about five years earlier. Then there is the rendering of the car itself. Disconcertingly, it's comprised of just the front tires and the steering wheel. All three components simply float there, disconnected from each other and moving only when Schumacher begins to drive. It looks very basic, and yet all the engineers require is a visual confirmation that the car is in motion. They don't need to see a virtual model of Schumacher wrestling with the wheel to know he's hit the corner apex, or glints of sunlight from his helmet to fuel the impression of movement. The engine growl is present, but it's a simplistic version that serves as just another cue for the driver. Everything they need is in the telemetry, from lap times to tire temperature and degradation, fuel load and cornering speed. As Schumacher puts in the first installation laps, a stream of data begins to fill the screens that matter.

"Mick, we're looking for a lap of 1:29.2."

Running the evening's proceedings is Performance and Simulation Engineer Russell Paddon. Having provided the reserve driver with his target time over the comms channel, Paddon returns to inputting commands from his keyboard.

"That's a very precise time," I say to Li, keeping my voice down now that the session has begun.

"We're going for correlation," he says, which is a term I often hear from the team's engineers.

"So the virtual car has to replicate the performance of the real car, right?"

Li registers my summary like a diplomat trying to hide a touch of heartburn. "Even if we put in the same car setup and weather conditions, there's always going to be a little bit of difference. We can see that in the data, and also the feedback from the driver. So in order to achieve the closest correlation we tune the car a little."

As we talk, Schumacher puts in a lap that's just a few hundredths of a second off the target time. Over the next few laps, that gap closes. It's a striking measure of his skill and precision behind the wheel. Li tells me that dedicated sim drivers can often outpace their F1 colleagues. It's just they lack the same sense of respect for the track as there are no consequences should they crash, and this is a critical quality when it comes to refining the setup for a real car. As we talk, a communication between Paddon and his driver in the chamber leads to a tweak to the setup. It's enough for Schumacher to enter a narrow performance window that achieves the desired lap time and provides agreement among his team that the DiL car is correlated to its real-life counterpart. To the best of their abilities, Paddon and his team have matched the aerodynamic and mechanical setup as well as the characteristics of the power unit delivery. Even so, it doesn't suggest to me that within this window Schumacher is on the ragged edge. When I share this with Li, he tells me it's purposely no hot lap.

"In order for us to get good quality data, we need a lap time that's repeatable. The driver still has to push," he stresses, "but there's no need to go for the lap record. This evening, we've taken one of Lewis's lap times from FP2 that we know the sim driver can put in consistently. It means the data will reflect any setup changes we make while the driver can report on how that feels."

Earlier, Li tells me, Schumacher had studied cockpit footage from the lap in question in order to replicate the same line as Hamilton. With data gathered from the car's sensors in that session transferred to the simulator, every effort is made by the sim team to bring the virtual car in lockstep with reality in what Paddon calls "a continuous loop."

Before the real work begins, the sim team break to tune into the driver debrief taking place back at the track. Gathered in the engineering room behind the garage, a dozen kilometers northwest of where we're currently holed up, Lewis Hamilton, George Russell, and their engineers chew through the findings from FP2. In silence, we listen in live via radio headsets as once again, Hamilton reports that his main issue is with the back of the car. He cannot find the grip he expects, which is forcing him to "tiptoe" round corners to prevent sliding. "We're doing all these changes," he says, "but it's having no effect on the rear end."

Shov is next to speak. Effectively chairing the debrief in his role as Trackside Engineering Director, he flags up the fact that even with the ongoing shortcomings the car balance favors long runs, which bodes well for Sunday. The challenge, Shov proposes, is in bringing the tires up to temperature for a single lap. This has implications for qualifying and grid order going into the race.

Toto Wolff is also present at the Silverstone debrief. He delivers a call to arms in understanding just how to light up the rubber compound to deliver when it matters most. "We need to be meticulous in analyzing the data tonight in Brackley," he says to finish and, as that concludes the meeting, I begin to appreciate just how much responsibility the sim team carry on their shoulders.

As Paddon and his colleagues await a detailed brief from the trackside engineers, we leave the building to grab a bite to eat from the canteen. It's quiet outside, and yet even in this early evening hour the barrier across the entrance to the Mercedes F1 campus is rarely down for long. Personnel come and go through day and night. In pursuit of the competitive edge, there's always work to be done.

As we make our way to the main building, I fall in with Mick Schumacher. Inevitably, his surname brings a weight of expectation. As the son of racing legend and former Mercedes driver Michael Schumacher, it's impossible not to look at Mick and see his father. They share the same strong jawline, commanding eyes, and endearing smile. That Mick has chosen to follow in his father's footsteps by pursuing an F1 career just adds to my intrigue about his character.

Despite entering this top tier having become F2 world champion in 2020, his path hasn't been without setbacks. The German driver joined Mercedes F1 as reserve driver this season, following a testing two years of racing for the Haas F1 Team. There are many in the sport, including Wolff, who feel that Schumacher deserved more support in order to shine. As we talk about the sim session ahead, and his expectations for this evening, I find a young man who has strived to grow stronger for the experience. He's endearingly polite and attentive, humble and perhaps a little shy, but determined to show that he's worthy of an F1 race seat. Over supper I note that he has just a modest helping of pasta in front of him and wonder if that's because he's thinking ahead.

"Is motion sickness an issue for you in the simulator?" I ask.

"For sure," Schumacher replies in fluent English with a continental edge. "If the visuals are even slightly out it can have an effect. I always try to take regular breaks, and just get outside so I can ground myself."

On the return to the simulator building, Li tells me that one former Mercedes F1 driver more than any other struggled with the vestibular demands placed upon them in a virtual driving environment. "Michael couldn't even watch other drivers in the sim without feeling ill," he says. "Sometimes a driver who is perfectly all right with movement in real life can be sensitive to motion cueing, especially if we overdo it." To illustrate the complexity of the human brain as much as our mastery of technology, Li goes on to refer to the early days of Sim Six before the team dialed down the inputs. "The drivers reported feeling disorientated," he says, "and that's when some were getting sick."

In Sim Six, the Mercedes F1 team have created a virtual racing environment that closely matches the real thing in all but one cue: velocity. Unless the sim is physically moving at more than 350 kph it simply can't be synthesized, and when that data is missing from our internal motion sensors it can quickly derail a driver. As a result, Sim Six only comes into its own when running a subdued version of reality. Then, the driver can cope with the missing sensory element, and is free to focus on what really matters here.

"It's snappy and unpredictable," says Mick Schumacher once the session is under way, having just been asked over the comms channel to report on how the car feels after his opening four laps, "with mid to exit understeer."

Driver feedback is the one thing the lap simulator cannot provide, but when communicated effectively to the sim engineers from the DiL it can translate to improved performance. Like Russell and Hamilton, Schumacher's use of language is clear and precise. He also echoes their findings from the first two practice sessions that revealed a lack of trust in the back end of the car. For Russell Paddon and his colleagues, it equips them with the information they need to make tweaks to the virtual car setup. It doesn't require a team of mechanics to execute the changes before Schumacher is reporting improvements. Just a few keystrokes.

Tonight, the sim team have been specifically tasked with testing whether out lap speed—and the impact it has on tire temperatures—has a bearing on the push lap, which the team must maximize in qualifying tomorrow. Working into the night, in blocks of six laps, Schumacher and the sim team explore a series of scenarios. Each time, they play with factors such as the speed of the out lap, ride height, and track temperature in a bid to understand how to prime the tires for that all-important qualifying hot lap. As well as this specific brief from the trackside engineers, Paddon and his colleagues explore tweaks to the car to refine balance and handling. "We don't tell Mick what changes we've made," he tells me in between blocks, as Schumacher's virtual car is reset on the track once more several turns from the start/finish line. "We want him to pick up on the difference it makes."

The process of watching sector times on the screen and listening to the driver feedback is mesmerizing. It's an exercise in performance optimization that takes place while the real cars lie under covers in the garage. Every hour or so, Schumacher takes a break and joins us in the control room for a debrief. Toward midnight, he's completed well over 100 laps of the virtual track, which is twice the distance that Hamilton and Russell will drive in the race itself. Driver fatigue is a factor they need to take into consideration, Li tells me, as Mick studies the timing screens while stretching his arms and rolling his shoulders. It's here that Paddon tells him that he can enjoy an extended break. When Schumacher asks him why, the Performance and Simulation Engineer provides an explanation I did not see coming.

"So, have you heard of the Millennium Bug?"

"No," says Schumacher with a shrug, which just reminds me how young he is. Paddon provides a brief summary of the infamous late-twentieth-century concern. At the time, a widespread belief existed that the coding in computer networks around the world would fail to cope with the four-digit calendar change that marked the transition from 1999 to 2000. Even though it came to nothing, the sim engineer spends an enjoyable few minutes educating Schumacher while laughing at the anxiety it caused at the time.

"Anyway, the sim has its own version," he drops in to finish. "If we run a stint through midnight, the system crashes."

The young German driver's expression switches from amusement to disbelief. "Really?"

"So we run the sim from four servers downstairs," says Paddon, having assured him there's a simple work-around. "That covers the ECU [the engine], the car, the tires, and the motion platform. There is a fifth, which runs the track, but it's provided by an external client. At midnight, if we're using the sim, something occurs with the track time stamp, which means it stops talking to our servers."

The reboot takes us from the closing minutes of Friday into Saturday, which is long enough for the jokes to run their course in the control room. Then Mick Schumacher is back in the chamber for the final push. He's there for another two hours, the human plug-in within a multimillion-pound computer that simply cannot replicate his role. By the time we're done, leaving Paddon to write up his recommendations for the trackside engineers to consider over breakfast, the young German seems understandably appreciative of the fresh air that awaits him outside.

Theoretically speaking, Schumacher has just raced close to 600 kilometers—or roughly two grand prix distances. In doing so, the sim team have learned that slowing the out lap by a specified time, combined with a change in the ride height measured in millimeters, will bring the tires to a temperature for qualifying that maximizes grip and ultimately performance. As we part company outside the sim building, I tell Schumacher that I hope he isn't too wired to sleep and then watch him head to his car.

Before he even reaches the barrier, it'll be the farthest he's driven all night.

When I next catch up with the Mercedes F1 reserve driver, on the morning before the race, he's just finished listening in to the drivers' briefing. The day before, from FP3 through to qualifying, Schumacher watched both Hamilton and Russell report improvements in car performance having acted on the recommendations from the sim. Despite punching home lap times that seemed out of reach to the team on Friday, the top ten shoot-out placed Mercedes F1 at the back of a tight bunch of front-runners. Frustratingly for the team, there are just two-tenths of a second between the McLaren of Lando Norris on P2 and P6, where Russell finds himself, with Hamilton one place behind. Since Barcelona, where both drivers made it onto the podium steps, it's been a testing time for the team. A P3 finish for Hamilton in Canada provided further confidence in the upgrades, despite the misery of a DNF (did not finish) for Russell following a brush with the wall and subsequent brake issues. In keeping with the maddeningly unpredictable character of the W14, however, the subsequent race in Austria saw both cars off the pace and draining confidence from the drivers in corners. Here at Silverstone, it means there is work to be done from lights out if the pair are to deliver in front of a record-breaking weekend attendance of 480,000 F1 fans.

In true British fashion, the mixed weather forecast means many spectators are wearing variations of summer wear under transparent ponchos. Nothing can dampen their spirit, however. Outside the gates to the paddock, the incoming drivers and even team personnel are greeted with big-hearted enthusiasm by fans. In his supporting role, and no doubt because his family name invokes such huge passion in motorsport, Mick Schumacher has found himself mobbed whenever he's out in public. In view of the attention, his elevated background and the contribution he's made to performance this weekend, it's refreshing to find him so down-to-earth. He stands to greet me when I find him in the paddock, and invites me to join him for coffee. As one team member observed earlier, such grounding must come down to "good parenting."

"I was a crazy kid," laughs Schumacher when I ask if he's always been this way. At first, I think he's suggesting that he had an appetite for trouble. Then he credits one person for this trait, and immediately I realize he's talking about thrill seeking. "Everything my dad did, I did," he says. "I started karting aged three. I was six when I first went scuba diving. Age ten I was skydiving."

While he may have struggled with the race simulator, Michael

Schumacher's achievements on the track are unsurpassed. With seven Formula 1 World Drivers' Championship titles to his name, matched only by Lewis Hamilton, Mick's father is universally regarded as motor racing royalty. Having closed a record-breaking F1 career racing for Jordan, Benetton and Ferrari in 2006, Schumacher came out of retirement in 2010 to join the Mercedes F1 team in their return to the pinnacle of motorsport. He raced for the Silver Arrows for the next three seasons before bowing out with a career total of ninety-one wins and a reputation as one of the greatest drivers in the sport's history. Michael Schumacher's name is also synonymous with tragedy, after a skiing accident in 2013—when Mick was just fourteen—left him with a serious brain injury and retirement from public life into the protective embrace of his family. A decade later, on reminiscing about his own pathway into motorsport, Mick talks about him not as an F1 legend but a loving and nurturing father.

"My dad was always very open to me trying out whatever I wanted to do," he says, "and racing is all I wanted to do because I enjoyed it the most. He was really supportive, and a lot of fun, but could also be challenging. One time in a karting race I braked very late going into a corner and gained a lot of time. When I told him about it, he said: 'Yes, but you should have braked like that in *every* corner!'"

A familiar gleam comes into Mick's eyes as he says this, and it's easy to imagine his father conveying such an uncompromising message behind the jokey delivery. At the same time, quite possibly aware that Mick had set his sights on a pathway that would inevitably bring attention and expectation, Michael frequently tested his son's commitment to the sport.

"Whenever he felt like I wasn't taking it seriously, he would say: 'Mick, would you rather go and play soccer with your friends? If so, we don't need to do all of this.' I insisted that I wanted to race, and he said: 'OK, then let's do it properly.' So we started doing more European karting, and I was getting better. Then my dad had his accident. I started racing in the Formula classes the year after, and from then I had to do it all on my own. But I definitely learned a lot of technical points from him that I still use today, as well as from his coaching, and I've always been very resilient. Whenever I got hurt I would jump back on." Schumacher pauses there for a moment. "I'm still like that, in fact," he adds, and I can't help thinking he's mindful of his early release from Haas and the fact that it led him to the reserve seat with Mercedes F1.

With the support races in action, the paddock can be a noisy place. At times, I find myself leaning in to hear Schumacher. He's softly spoken and yet there is a passion behind everything he says, like when I ask what he's learned since joining the team.

"The biggest one for me, both personally and as a racing driver, is seeing that everyone is human," he says. "Last season, I was concerned that I was the only driver to have insecurities. I was afraid to make mistakes, and in that situation it's easy to stop taking risks, and then you fall back. What's really impressive with Mercedes F1 is that you're allowed to make mistakes. You just have to learn from them. I feel that sense of not being scared to try something is really positive, and if anyone is struggling there's always someone who steps up. Toto plays a big role here. He's able to display that sense of calm. It shows good leadership."

Naturally, Mick Schumacher would rather be racing this season than sitting on the sidelines. He remains laser-focused on earning a seat, and speaks about it with a conviction I find both heartfelt and admirable. For now, he recognizes that his experience as the Mercedes F1 reserve can still help him to grow. Schumacher's sim work is highly rated by the drivers and engineers. He's primed to step in should Hamilton or Russell suffer illness or injury, while

Wolff keeps him close by during races because he values his driver insight and expertise. Ultimately, this time will be the making of "young Mick"—as he's known by many in the team—wherever the road might take him.

That afternoon, if support from the crowd dictates the outcome of the race, Mercedes F1 should be clear winners, alongside McLaren. There is patriotism at play here, not just for Lando Norris, George Russell, and Lewis Hamilton, all of whom are close enough to the front of the grid to trouble the dominant Red Bulls, but also the fact that both teams are British-based. On the opening lap, when Norris briefly takes the lead from Verstappen into Turn 1, the extended roar from the grandstands and grass verges is the loudest I've heard at any circuit all season. Later, as the field reshapes following a safety car and the opportunity to pit, the crowd strike up once more as Hamilton thrills in his attempt to take down the resurgent McLaren. His tires might go off before he can strike, but the determination is there to earn him third place with Russell earning decent points in fifth.

"For us to get on the podium is huge," says Hamilton after the race, having delighted in looking out as a sea of race fans filled the home straight in a bid to celebrate with their heroes. Mercedes F1 have also just strengthened their second-place position in the Constructors' Championship. It's easy to forget the challenges presented by this year's car, but I've witnessed firsthand how they've gone without sleep to get here. Despite the fruits of the overnight sim work, however, and the efforts both trackside and in the factory, Hamilton echoes the sentiments of the team when he registers that there's still a great deal to be done. "As soon as we can improve the rear end we will be on our way," he says, flagging up his central issue with the car that has dogged him all season. "We just need to hold on to the good bits and add a few others."

CHAPTER FIVE

THE SHOW ON THE ROAD

The Belgian Grand Prix
Circuit de Spa-Francorchamps, Spa-Francorchamps
July 28–30, 2023

"This is where I keep the naked man."

I'm standing alongside Tobias Genrich, the man responsible for the Mercedes F1 motor home. He's just opened a discreet door under the stairs from the ground floor to show me the extent of the hidden wiring. I expected to see bundles of cables and circuit breakers. Instead, having clearly popped into this narrow void to change into his work clothes, an electrician in a state of undress and embarrassment blinks back at us. I share his surprise, whereas my seemingly unflappable guide doesn't miss a beat before restoring his privacy with an apology for the interruption. Dealing with the unexpected is a quality that is central to his role, in fact. Representing the logistics supplier DB Schenker, which supports the team through the European leg of the F1 calendar, Genrich heads up the motor home crew. Across nine races, he's tasked with overseeing the transportation, construction, and disassembly of the team's trackside HQ.

It's midweek and we're in Belgium for the final grand prix before the summer break. Set amid the forested slopes of the Ardennes, the Circuit de Spa-Francorchamps (simply known as

Spa) is the longest track on the 2023 calendar. A nose over seven kilometers long, it ticks all the right boxes for motor racing fans by stringing together high-speed straights with testing elevation changes and dramatic, sweeping turns. Even the paddock is on an incline, which adds to the challenge faced by Genrich.

When the sliding entrance doors open on Thursday, the first official day of the race weekend, the Mercedes F1 motor home will feel like a permanent structure. Every team boasts one, geared to host not just trackside personnel but also VIP guests, which duly transforms the paddock into a kind of motor racing million-aires' row. From Ferrari's bold red-and-black striped edifice to Red Bull's open-plan, timber-clad "energy station" that seems purpose-built for postpodium parties, each motor home displays a well-defined character. The Mercedes F1 three-story facility is no exception. In graphite gray and silver, the glass-fronted structure aims to embody the spirit of the team. Even in a state of assembly, the motor home is sleek, light, and airy.

For now, however, the paddock is just a construction site. I've arrived ahead of the race weekend so that I can see what it takes for the team to bring the circus into town. It means that when I approach the motor home to meet the project manager, the work in progress under his watch is at its most intense. Outside, build technicians on a hydraulic work platform are applying trims to the facade. I wait until it's safe to pass before negotiating entrance steps draped in dust sheets. As Genrich and I settle at a table to talk, one of the few fittings in place within what will be the ground floor dining area, we do so to the squeal of power drills and beeps of forklift trucks in operation. "The motor home is made up of thirty-two modules," explains Genrich in his German accent. "They arrive on twenty-one trucks and I have a team of eighteen people who construct it in four days."

With his corkscrew curly hair, round glasses, and throaty voice, my host is as distinctive as the creation taking shape around us. A master carpenter by trade, Genrich arrived with a reputation for the highest standards of craftsmanship. Gesturing away from the table, he shows me where two modules meet. Floor tiles neatly camouflage the horizontal join beneath our feet, while the vertical seam is designed to look like a groove in a single pillar. It's a clever construction, with each module hardwired with fittings such as counters, windows, and doors. When Genrich drops in that the finished structure weighs in at 200 metric tons, I ask about the foundations.

"We use wooden blocks," he says casually, which is not what I expected to hear. Genrich looks up pictures of a recent build on his phone to show me. Once we get beyond the shots of the initial leveling exercise—which looks worryingly like concurrent games of Jenga—and into the sequence in which the steel strut substructure is lowered into place, it all appears very solid and efficient. From here, Genrich's pictures tell a story of rapid construction as modules are plucked by crane from the fleet of trucks that transported them and then maneuvered into position. The montage captures his workforce in action, crawling all over a construction that's been engineered with the same level of precision and ingenuity as the cars themselves. As we scroll to the end of the pictures, I am aware that the electrician has emerged from under the stairs. He's dressed and hovering for a word.

With the build some way from completion, and trackside personnel already beginning to arrive at the circuit, the head of the Mercedes F1 motor home crew has a race of his own on his hands.

Formula 1 is a global sport in every sense. It appeals to a billion-strong television audience, and in 2024—with the return of the Chinese Grand Prix—it will stage a record twenty-four races around the world. Such a punishing schedule requires forward planning on a military scale by all the teams. It isn't just a question of making sure the cars arrive at each circuit on time, which is a challenge in its own right. With the weekend workforce in the mix, hospitality and office space requirements, as well as the resources required to build, furnish, and equip a modern F1 garage, the air, sea, and road transport logistics placed on teams like Mercedes F1 is immense. Planning begins up to eighteen months in advance, with the team seeking to make savings in terms of time, cost, and—critically—carbon emissions.

Without a doubt, F1 comes with rising environmental responsibilities. There is much talk of the push for net zero by 2030, but frankly the sport will have to go much further than current goals to maintain global appeal. It isn't the twenty cars on the track that contribute most to the footprint. At the cutting edge of engineering, they're already streets ahead of road vehicles in terms of fuel-to-power efficiencies. It's the impact of staging each race— from the movement of freight and personnel to the crowds that flock to watch. The solution requires a collective effort, while individual teams like Mercedes F1 pursue their own initiatives to optimize their logistical operations. Over the course of the previous year, the team's investment in sustainable aviation fuel reduced their overall air travel emissions by 21 percent. In addition, a recent conversion of their European fleet of trucks and generators to biofuel use will see emissions drop this season by 67 percent.

Like the motor home in the paddock, Mercedes F1's efforts to lead the way in the drive for sustainability are a work in progress. The commitment and the vision exist for them to achieve their own race-team-controlled net zero by 2030, but ultimately F1 as a whole will have to undergo a fundamental reimagination to be truly sustainable. For now, it isn't just the team's freight trucks responsible for delivering the motor home to the paddock that are powered by biofuels but also their race support vehicles. Having left Tobias Genrich to complete the build, I make my way up switchback flights of metal steps to the walkway behind the pit lane. Parked side by side, with enough space in between to cut to and from the garage entrances, these gleaming custom-built trailers look like the *Transformers* of the race haulage world.

Mercedes F1 sport three distinctive models with names that wouldn't appear out of place alongside Megatron, Wheeljack, and Sideswipe. On sweeping into the circuit earlier in the week, Race Liner, Sky Rise, and Race Base all arrived looking like articulated trucks, only to unfold, elevate, fuse, or fan out in different ways. Race Base is perhaps the most impressive. It comprises two trucks parked side by side, leaving the width of a third in between. A laser guidance system is used to position the vehicles, ensuring they are level, parallel, and planted. Six huge pods are then lowered across the parallel pair, with sliding doors and a spiral staircase fitted at one end. Powered up and plumbed, the finished structure provides a huge ground floor tire hangar flanked by workshops, with office space upstairs for a workforce of thirty. This is the engineers' HQ, along with private rooms for the two drivers.

One day earlier, on Tuesday morning, the bays outside the pit lane garage stood empty. Now, the three giant spaces are already home to the technicians and mechanics here to furnish the garage and build the cars. It provides them with a professional environment, from workshops to locker walls and parts storage, treatment rooms for the team's doctor and physiotherapist, and even an air-filtered lab for testing oil, fuel, and transmission fluids. Throughout the European leg of the season, Mercedes F1 deploy nineteen trucks to equip and service the garage and transport the two cars. Between the first and last of these races, there can be no scope for screwups. Should anything fail to show up, by accident, oversight, or at the hands of customs officials, the consequences could be catastrophic for the fortunes of the team. It's a huge undertaking, recognized as being one of the most demanding roles with the greatest responsibility, and that falls to one man.

I find Karl Fanson inside Race Liner. The truck is custom-built to carry freight from one track to the next before converting to an air-conditioned office and workshop during a race weekend. I climb in through a smoked-glass side door. Fanson is at his desk, hunched over a laptop with his back to me. He's a big, towering guy with a personality to match. When he turns to greet me, I see that he's holding what looks like a little Harry Potter wand between his thumb and forefinger.

"Broken compressor." Fanson swishes the tip of the truck part through the air. "They don't often go wrong, but it's on me to get it up and running again." The task is a small one but unless it's fixed then the choreographed flow of freighted equipment through the race calendar will quickly fall apart. As Head of Race Team Logistics, it falls to Karl Fanson to keep the Mercedes F1 show on the road.

"Matt Deane, the Chief Mechanic, is in charge of everything related to the car," he says, to sum up his role. "I look after everything outside of that." In terms of what that entails, Fanson proceeds to run through a dizzying list. He oversees the trucks and their drivers ("the truckies"), the garage interior, and the technicians responsible for the build. Then there are the tires, the pit stop equipment, and the engineering stations, while he also ensures that all the air lines, power generators, and electrical cables are in place and primed to deliver for every race weekend. Managing all the freight transport by road, which connects the European leg of the calendar, to the air and sea freight demands for the long-haul races, Fanson carries a huge load on his broad shoulders. As he breezes through what sounds like steps to maneuver a battalion, which is effectively what's involved in delivering everything here to Spa from the last race in Hungary one week earlier, I quickly appreciate that he really is a general in this season-long campaign.

"One year our garage failed to show up in Brazil on time," he says, when I ask about a worst moment. "It was supposed to have arrived on a plane from Mexico City on Monday, but we were left waiting until midweek."

"That sounds more like a close call," I suggest, when Fanson tells me that the freight hadn't gone missing, which would've triggered the emergency dispatch of a backup garage from the factory, but was simply delayed in transit after the plane had made an unscheduled refueling stop en route. Like Tobias Genrich, his counterpart in charge of the motor home, Fanson can be proactive in the face of the unexpected, but ultimately places a great deal of trust in the logistical process.

In order for the Head of Race Team Logistics to all but guarantee that everything will be in the right place at the right time, that process takes shape long before each season starts. Fanson jokes that it begins with drawing lines on a map of the world, but even on a conceptual level it seems sensible. While he has extensive experience charting a course through previous seasons, since taking on the role in 2016, the race calendar tends to change from year to year. With costs and emissions in mind, Fanson sets out a plan that's both as efficient and economical as possible. The key is in having six duplicate sets of everything the team require to race at a grand prix weekend. Apart from the cars, that extends to all the garage components: from the walling system that defines the internal space to the central engineers' station, the pit lane gantry, VIP seating, tool cabinets and trolleys, power, communications, and lighting rigs. The savings come with transport choices and by striking early. With Europe covered by trucks, Fanson calls upon a combination of sea freight where possible, as well as air and road. This way, he can station resources at strategic points around the world and also stay one jump ahead of a challenging transition where time is at a premium.

"At the start of the year, we sent one set to Bahrain, one to Saudi, one to Australia, one to Azerbaijan, and one to Miami," he says. "That last one stays in the Americas, for example. So after Miami it goes to Canada, and then back down to Austin and across to Vegas. It means the cost of building extra set is quickly offset."

With fourteen garage technicians to manage, as well as nineteen truck drivers for the European leg, while also working with international couriers, Karl Fanson strikes me as the team member with the longest to-do list. With so much pressure on him to deliver, and so many moving parts, how does he stay confident that the choreography behind his grand plan is holding together?

"We have a WhatsApp group," says Fanson, and he goes on to use the current phase of the calendar as an example, which sees his fleet of biofueled trucks collectively cover 386,000 kilometers across Europe. "We have someone tracking each vehicle by GPS, and they send out an update every five minutes." It sounds like a lot, but as Mercedes F1 can't function without a garage and supporting equipment it's the price that has to be paid for Fanson's peace of mind. "I can basically just look at each update and discard it, but if there's a problem I know about it right away."

Despite his ability to effectively monitor the fleet in real time, Fanson considers the European road leg to be the most challenging. This largely comes down to red tape after the UK left the European Union (EU) in 2020, and this must be considerable in view of the borders and goods that are involved.

"It's all about carnets," he says, referring to the documentation required by EU customs for the temporary admission of goods.

Everything on the truck has to be itemized and accounted for on return, and this can prove taxing for an F1 team with a dynamic logistical schedule. On a recent visit to 10 Downing Street, in fact, Toto Wolff and other leading team members lobbied government for help in streamlining the process. "We can send out the complete car with the chassis, engine, and gearbox," he offers as an example, "but after the race it'll be stripped. Potentially, it could return on several trucks, and so we have to cover off the paperwork."

The travel has two sides for the 46-year-old Fanson, who first joined the team under Honda in 2006 as a generator technician and truck driver. Professionally, he's in the driving seat for one long point-to-point endurance exercise that supports the F1 season. From a personal perspective, and by his own admission, he just loves to be on the road. As a trackside "lifer," Fanson recognizes that spending so much time away from home means that Mercedes F1 have become more than just a race team to him.

"My other half and two beagles are always happy to see me," he says, "but when we're away as a team we work and socialize with each other. It's my auxiliary family!"

"Could you adjust to a full-time role in the factory?" I ask out of curiosity, and in response an expression midway between amusement and anxiety crosses Fanson's face.

"I don't think it would be just me who needed to do the adjusting," he says eventually, which must be the case for others like him who seem most at home in the garage.

In this neck of the woods, the weather doesn't know what to do. Since Wednesday, storm clouds have churned restlessly over the Ardennes. When rain falls it comes down hard, as it did in 2021 to curtail the entire race after two laps behind a safety car. This year, brilliant July sunshine keeps breaking through as if to make up for a mistake in the seasonal master plan. It's chilly and then roasting hot, squally but often quite still. For Mercedes F1 and all the race teams, such atmospheric unpredictability is all but guaranteed at this track. It's long enough for drivers to encounter wet and dry conditions on the same lap. With such an entertaining wild card in play, it's no surprise to find the grandstands are full early on Friday morning, while fans emerge from the forests surrounding the circuit like hidden people braving daylight for the first time.

In the paddock, I find not a forklift truck or packing crate in sight. Instead, race team members, media crews, and VIPs fill a thoroughfare flanked by finished builds. Many hurry along to minimize their exposure to the rain, and I join that rank on my way to the Mercedes F1 motor home.

Inside, it feels like Tobias Genrich's electrician has wired a sense of energy into the interior. On the ground floor, team personnel are enjoying breakfast freshly prepared by a brigade of chefs in the kitchen behind the serving bar. People from all departments sit across from each other at bench tables; engineers and marketeers, technicians and personal trainers. There is no hierarchy here. Surrounding them, in a space sculpted by soft lights and indoor plants, wall-mounted screens toggle through slick photographs from last week's race in Budapest: George Russell exchanging fist bumps with two mechanics; Lewis Hamilton climbing into his cockpit. Despite the numbers, the space doesn't feel cramped or claustrophobic. Essentially, it's home for a race team family.

When I'm greeted by Senior Media Manager Adam McDaid, who has offered to take me on a tour, I remark that the place is about as far removed as can be from the popular concept of a motor home. "The team can be quite squeezed at some circuits outside Europe," he says. "When we can bring this with us, it just makes all the difference."

For every race, Mercedes F1 travel with at least 100 personnel. That's a sizable number of people, many of whom require a desk or meeting space, plug and USB points, as well as food and drink throughout the weekend—not just for the team but also partners and guests. In this light, as we head up one of two flights of stairs to the next level, the motor home doesn't seem like an extravagance but an extension of the Brackley campus. The next floor serves to host guests. It's an attractive space with comfortable seating and rooms around the perimeter, including Toto Wolff's private office. The door is ajar. It's early, as well as nice and quiet. Now, I think, would be a great time to check in with the team boss. I glance inside. The desk is as yet unoccupied.

The third floor, under the sky, is known as the sun terrace. As we step onto the wood decking, it's abundantly clear that this is very much a VIP space. With a glass cube structure housing the bar and dining area, and tasteful outdoor furniture to accommodate invited guests, it could be the roof garden of a London club. I look out over the paddock, noting the view of the track at the top end where it exits out of Turn 1. Without a doubt, for those who will spend time here, this is the dream ticket.

Back on ground level, I join McDaid in the office space he shares with the communications team. It seats twelve at three desks, which is tight but well-engineered. All bags are stowed in cupboards, and when one of Lewis Hamilton's bodyguards swings open the door I find myself momentarily hemmed against one. The driver is accompanied by a security detail wherever he goes. Projecting themselves with polite intent rather than a show of muscle, they're skilled at keeping a low profile while scoping their surroundings for potential threats. Whenever I register their presence, I'm struck by the fact that they have usually seen me first. Just now, the visiting bodyguard is focused on not dropping any of the gifts in his arms, from good luck charms to drawings, cards, and teddy bears. They've been presented to the driver by fans as he made his way into the paddock. Handing in the haul for safekeeping, the guy confirms he's checked everything for trackers and thrown away the liquids.

"That's pretty dark," says McDaid as he finds a box for the items.

Hamilton's bodyguard shrugs as if to suggest that he can never be less than constantly vigilant.

The Belgian Grand Prix is one of six in this season's calendar that will also host a Sprint race. It's a recent addition, in a bid to ramp up the racing action. The Sprint takes over the Saturday timetable. It starts with a qualifying session (known as the Shootout) followed by a cut-down race in the form of a 100-kilometer dash to take the checkered flag. With eight points on the table for P1, down to one point for P8, the outcome contributes to the World Drivers' Championship and could potentially mix up the standings. As a result of the extra event in the schedule, however, only one practice session is available to the field, which kicks off proceedings on the Friday, followed by qualifying for Sunday's race. For every garage along the pit lane, that means limited time to nail the setup and be race-ready as a team. "It's not an easy task to get the car in a workable window with such little running," laments Shov after wet weather compromises FP1, "and certainly not with a car that can be as tricky as the W14."

It's both uncomfortable and revealing to observe the eight-times winners of the World Constructors' Championship continue to struggle for consistent performance. The previous week's race in Hungary had been a case in point. A dazzling qualifying pole by Lewis Hamilton had shown what the car could unleash, only for him to struggle in race trim to cross the line in P4. By contrast, George Russell had lined up on the grid in P18 after a compromised hot lap and then fought his way to an impressive P6 finish. Despite the mixed fortunes, the team's efforts have increased the gap to Aston Martin and then Ferrari in the constructors' fight for second place. They've had to scrap for every point, which is easily overlooked in view of the frank reality that Red Bull are alone in truly harnessing the ground-effect potential from these cars. The frustration in attempting to settle the W14 has seemingly caused gravity to weigh a little heavier on every team member in pursuit of their goals. Nevertheless, Mercedes F1 have thrown themselves headlong into this season's battle and made gains by pushing constantly. It's just becoming a grind for position rather than a tilt for victory. Midway into the race calendar, it's clear that for all the updates and refinements the car will not miraculously find another gear to trouble Max Verstappen at the front of the field.

In line with the relentless demands of this sport, Mercedes F1 can only look ahead to this weekend with fight and focus. While that afternoon's qualifying session for Sunday's main race sees Hamilton and Russell on P4 and P8 respectively, any sense of disappointment is squeezed out by the determination to maximize the opportunities presented by the grid order. Despite their best efforts, however, this year's Belgian Grand Prix weekend will continue to be largely pedestrian for Mercedes F1 in both the Sprint race and the grand prix itself, with Hamilton finishing P4 and Russell in P6. At the same time, Hamilton will take an extra point into the two-week summer break after the strategists make a sharp call for him to pit for softs right at the end of Sunday's race. With the podium out of reach, the fresh tires allow him to claim the fastest lap. It might not seem like much, but it sends out a clear message to the rest of the field about where the Mercedes F1 mindset lies.

Performance, it seems, is fueled by purpose. From chasing a single point to learning lessons to prime next year's car, an F1 team must maintain direction. It cannot just give up on a season, because in doing so the impetus is lost. A case in point is pit stop practice; the relentless drills conducted through a race weekend in a bid to perfect technique. Midway through the weekend, intent on catching up with Karl Fanson, I walk through a largely empty garage on George Russell's side to find the car is out in the pit lane. Standing beside the front wing, displaying all the discipline of a military drill sergeant without the shouting, Chief Mechanic Matt Deane instructs his soldiers to run through another wheel change. Despite the rain, which is falling hard, a huge crowd of guests and press photographers look on from behind the tape barrier as Russell's #63 car is manually pushed into the box. While the pit crew pounce upon the wheels and then spring back from what seems like an act of noisy magic to replace them, I focus on one individual at the back. To those who follow television coverage of the sport, Karl Fanson's giant frame makes him a familiar figure during Mercedes F1 pit stops. Even in a fire suit and full-face helmet, he's literally head and shoulders above his teammates. For the Head of Race Team Logistics plays another role during race weekends that is quite literally pivotal. As Rear Jack Operator, Fanson must lift and then drop the tail of the racing car with the aid of a hydraulic trolley so his teammates can go to work.

"It's a knack," Fanson says in a break between drills, responding to my observation that it looks like quite a skill. "It's about positioning yourself so that when you push on the jack you get it over the tipping point."

Having watched him step in behind the car as it arrives in the pit box, slip the scoop under the car's jacking point, and then bear down on the handle—all in one fluid sequence—he makes it look easy. For a big guy, Fanson swivels and drops down on one leg with balletic grace. I'm also well aware that during a race, the car isn't pushed in benignly by two mechanics as it is now. Even with the pit lane limiter activated (restricted to 60 kph at this circuit), Fanson must step in behind Lewis Hamilton and George Russell as they brake hard to stop in the box. It's an act that doesn't just require practice but trust. Fanson jokes that the Front Jack Operator is the real hero, while also reminding me that the crew are working with some of the best drivers in the world.

"They're rarely far out," he says, when I ask if they always hit the precise floor markings, "but it's easier if they stop long as I can lean in to scoop the car. If they stop short, I have to reposition myself. There's a lot to go wrong in not a lot of time," he adds, before returning to his position to rehearse another four stops.

Despite towering over his colleagues, Fanson sells himself short somewhat on his contribution to the Mercedes F1 pit stop. On being called home for personal reasons during the Japanese Grand Prix one year, the team were forced to replace him on the rear jack with not one but two mechanics. Fanson reasons modestly that the jack itself has been custom-built for him, but I'm in no doubt that he owns that position.

This comes into hard focus at the end of the drill when Fanson looks across at me and tips the jack handle in my direction. I glance behind me, figuring he's gesturing at another team member, but when I turn back and tap at my chest he nods solemnly. Even the rest of the pit crew are watching and waiting.

As if I've just been press-ganged, I step out into the rain and take the handle from Fanson. Telling myself not to mess this up, I focus firstly on positioning the scoop under the jacking point. I know for a fact that the car weighs a minimum of 798 kilograms—just over three-quarters of a metric ton—because the FIA mandates it. Despite the hydraulic assistance it's going to take some heft for me to get the back end off the ground.

Leaning over the arm of the jack, I take a breath and then push with all my might. There's none of Fanson's elegance in my movement. In fact, I'm sure I share the face of a guy trying to twist the jammed lid off a pickle jar, but somehow I feel like the jack is working with me. A moment passes before I register that the car is indeed rising upward. Then the stopper under the arm of the jack connects with the ground, which means I have done my job.

What I hadn't banked on, which kills any sense of elation, is that the elevated rear of George Russell's W14 is now balanced in such a way that it begins to wobble from side to side. All I can think is that about £8 million worth of engineering and aerodynamics is in my novice hands, and I gingerly set it back down to the ground. Such a stress-inducing maneuver has taken me way too long to qualify for a place on the pit crew, but I've gained a keen appreciation of the physical and psychological demands.

"There you go," says Fanson, taking the jack handle from my grasp like he's just disarmed me. "I told you it was a knack."

Five minutes later, having left the pit lane and returned to the paddock through the back of the garage, I wonder how long it'll take me to stop shaking. Leaving Fanson and the rest of the pit crew to return the car to its bay, I'd thanked him for the opportunity and sought a moment to myself. Instead of finding space to calm my nerves, however, I discover a scrum of racing fans at the foot of the spiral staircase to the engineering office. The difference here is that nobody is looking at me.

Apart from one individual, I realize, as one of Lewis Hamilton's bodyguards nods at me from where he's standing just a few feet away. The #44 driver is currently with his race team in a briefing, which explains the scene.

Unlike other drivers, the seven-times world champion possesses a magnetic pull that just draws people into his orbit. Hamilton handles it very well, especially when it comes to younger fans, and yet such is his superstar status that his presence in public can swiftly create a frenzy. No doubt it offers him little solace, but the popular view that he was robbed of the 2021 World Drivers' Championship has seen race fans around the world get behind him. Even though most people here are clearly just holding out for selfies, the sheer level of interest and excitement his presence creates makes security a sensible precaution.

In many ways, Lewis Hamilton's security detail offers a sideways insight into the life of the Mercedes F1 driver. From a logistics perspective, it's one thing being in charge of moving palatial motor homes and garage equipment around the world, but quite another to guarantee the safe passage of a racing legend. I really want to ask what training and experience is required, but just then Hamilton emerges from the engineering office on the upper deck of the race truck. Immediately, his bodyguard is in position at the foot of the spiral staircase ready to transport him away.

The Bahrain Grand Prix, 2023. The W14's maiden race on the desert circuit. One week earlier, the same Gulf-state track hosted three days of testing in which every team evaluated their new challengers ahead of the season.

George Russell on track during the night race.

George Russell climbing into the W14.

Lewis Hamilton during a pit stop.

The pit crew readied for action.

Toto Wolff at the helm of the engineers' station, a central island that divides the garage into two bays.

The Miami Grand Prix, 2023. George Russell getting into the "zone" on the grid.

George Russell and Lewis Hamilton warming up their tires on track.

The Mercedes Pit Crew featuring Tom Cruise.

Guests enjoy the trackside Miami Club.

Sarah Morgan, Head of Hospitality and Events, hosts Brian May at Silverstone.

"Top Guns" Lewis and Tom.

George takes P4 and Lewis takes P6 after a battling race.

Tennis legend Roger Federer swings by the pits.

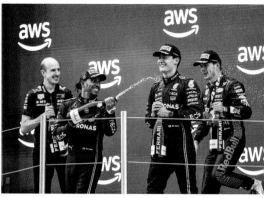

The Spanish Grand Prix, 2023. George Russell wheel-to-wheel with Ferrari's Carlos Sainz.

Mercedes F1 secure a double podium. Lewis Hamilton finishes P2; George Russell finishes P3.

"We did our job," says Chief Mechanic Matt Deane (left), who is in charge of Mercedes F1's 26-strong crew of mechanics.

The mechanics after the race with Lewis Hamilton. They swap their black shirts and overalls for luminous team T-shirts, a safety precaution as the pit lane fills with forklifts and freight containers after the checkered flag.

Lewis Hamilton, Toto Wolff, and Michael Sansoni enjoy the weekend after a tough start to the season.

F1 has strict limitations on preseason testing and race weekend practice on the track and in the wind tunnel. For this reason, the virtual world provides critical tools for gathering data. Mercedes F1 reserve driver Mick Schumacher plays an important role working with race engineers in the simulator.

Matt Whyman is just one of a handful of outsiders who has been permitted to view Mercedes F1's latest driver-in-loop simulator in operation. As a measure of the technology hidden away here, Mercedes F1 recently hosted a knowledge-sharing delegation from NASA.

During the 2023 Silverstone Grand Prix weekend, with data gathered from FP1 and FP2 at the Silverstone Circuit, Schumacher completed well over 100 laps of the virtual track, in a bid to fine-tune performance. Schumacher drove twice the distance that Lewis Hamilton and George Russell would complete in the race itself.

The Mercedes F1 motor home.

Tobias Genrich heads up the motor home crew. Across nine European races, he oversees the transportation, construction, and disassembly of the team's trackside HQ. The finished structure weighs 200 metric tons, is made up of thirty-two modules, and arrives on twenty-one trucks. Eighteen people construct it in four days.

Race Liner. The truck is custom-built to carry freight for the team from one track to the next before converting to an air-conditioned office and workshop during each race weekend.

As Head of Race Team Logistics, Karl Fanson oversees the trucks, their drivers, and the garage interior. Like many Mercedes F1 staff, he also plays another role during each grand prix weekend. As Rear Jack Operator, Fanson must lift and then drop the tail of the racing car with the aid of a hydraulic trolley so his teammates can go to work.

James Allison (above left) returned to the front line as Mercedes F1's Technical Director in 2023, assuming responsibility for the performance of the W14 while overseeing the concept, design, and direction of the W15.

Allison works with Chief Operating Officer Rob Thomas (top right) and the thousands of colleagues in the Mercedes F1 factories at Brackley and Brixworth to bring the team back into contention on the track.

The Singapore Grand Prix, 2023. Lewis Hamilton takes P3 after a dramatic race.

The pit crew react to George Russell's crash on the final lap while chasing McLaren's Lando Norris for P2.

The scooter is often the fastest transport around the paddock.

Team Leader of Trackside Electronic Systems Evan Short and his colleagues face "the racks" in the pit garage, where they monitor every mission-critical electronic component of the car. Wearing a cooling vest ahead of qualifying in stifling humidity, George Russell looks on with interest.

The Japanese Grand Prix, 2023. George Russell in the garage (top) and on the grid with Lando Norris ahead of the Drivers' Parade (above).

Lewis Hamilton on track.

Senior Race Strategy Engineer Joey McMillan: "The strategist's job is to take whatever car you are given when the lights go out and then get the best place you can for it."

The team's Race Support Room (RSR) in Brackley. At this state-of-the-art control center with up to thirty colleagues, the team have access to the same real-time information and telemetry as the trackside crew.

CHAPTER SIX

PREPARE FOR TAKEOFF

Mercedes-AMG PETRONAS Formula One Team HQ
Brackley, Northamptonshire
August 3, 2023

"The only time I stop thinking about work is when I'm up in the air."

James Allison is keenly aware that his role within the team can be all-consuming. The 55-year-old son of a Royal Air Force officer has recently returned to the front line as Mercedes F1's Technical Director, assuming responsibility for the performance of the W14 while overseeing the concept, design, and direction of next season's challenger. The expectations facing him are immense, which is why Allison has come to rely upon his passion for piloting light aircraft as a means of rising above it all. "I try to stop thinking about it when I'm at home, but it's difficult and annoying," he says with his characteristic knack of remaining cheerful in the face of adversity. "It's also a tax I pay for having the most interesting and thrilling of jobs."

Allison relishes his position, and the battle to bring Mercedes F1 back into contention for the championship. He has form after all. Starting out in the sport in the early nineties as an aerodynamic designer, Allison put in two stints with the Benetton team, notably winning trophies with a young Michael Schumacher. He then rose to serve as Technical Director at Renault and then Ferrari, where he enjoyed success with Fernando Alonso before being reunited with Schumacher.

It's also not the first time he's occupied this role at Mercedes F1. Allison arrived in 2017 to continue the run of success enjoyed by the team in the Constructors' Championship in cars that also powered Lewis Hamilton to four of his seven drivers' crowns. In 2021, however, he elected to take a step away from the vanguard. With Mike Elliott promoted from Technology Director to take over as Technical Director, Allison became the team's Chief Technical Officer. In this role, he could focus on long-term engineering development strategies and effectively enjoy partial retirement from a stellar career that had contributed to eleven constructors' titles.

Now Allison is back, after trading places with Elliott in May in the belief that it would allow the pair to play to their individual strengths. He returned to a car that Toto Wolff had described as a "nasty piece of work" in terms of its handling characteristics on the track. Nevertheless, Allison brings with him a revitalized sense of purpose and energy. The W14 is without a doubt a frustrating entity, and yet he knows how to bring out the best from the team in drawing performance from the car. A schedule of updates follows the launch and runs deep into the season, all of which demands factory manpower. At the same time, from the moment he stepped back into the breach, Allison immediately spearheaded the campaign to create a successor for the 2024 season: the W15.

"I'm always busy," he says about what is an annual drive to manage both projects simultaneously. "It's just the nature of what keeps me busy changes through the year. Early on, developing the current car takes up most time but then the new one starts to become pressing. Eventually those demands cross over, and the only effect that the W14 has on the W15 is to rob me of people. Add them together and I barely have a moment to myself from January to December."

Like the rest of the team, James Allison is about to be forced to relinquish his tools for F1's mandatory summer shutdown. It isn't just the Technical Director who could benefit from an enforced fortnight away from the front line. In discussing the colossal operation to finesse one car through the current season while creating a new one for the next, Allison is at great pains to stress that he is akin to being a colonel in charge of a battalion that does the "heft" of the work. The unsung heroes, he stresses, are the personnel at the factories here at Brackley and at Brixworth.

In a sport that has come to venerate the Technical Director as the "mastermind" behind the car, Allison is very clear that it is in fact a collective effort led by a handful of senior team leaders. The key, he maintains, is in how the troops are structured behind them.

"The team is set up so that it is capable of fighting a current championship without ignoring the championship that's coming along," he explains, in addressing how work commenced on the blueprint for the W15 before the W14 had even seen a racetrack. "We have a small concept group charged with broad brush design studies of interesting things that we can't change once a car is launched. It could be chassis, suspension, or cooling system layouts, or the exact position of the driver, engine, and gearbox in the car."

Tasked with addressing fundamental questions, the team's concept group features individuals representing the design office, aerodynamics, and vehicle performance areas. "The design people will be mostly concerned with the physical shape, size, and weight of things, while their advance guard counterparts in the other areas will be looking at the impact that might have on downforce or tire grip. The group will also bring in others with the expertise to explore these future things, all of whom work under the gentle direction of folk like me."

For a modest band of engineers with the luxury of dreaming big, the concept group doesn't entirely start from scratch. A new challenger takes to the track each season, after all. To what extent does the performance of the current car influence the next?

"We're guided by it," says Allison, who sets out what he believes to be a fundamental issue with the present machinery in a way that can only heighten respect for the efforts of Lewis Hamilton and George Russell to keep it in contention. "The W14 is telling us that it's persistently giving the drivers a lack of confidence at the rear. They turn into a corner with the gentlest of touches and the car breaks away from them at the back. It feels like a betrayal of what they're doing with the wheel, especially at speed when the consequences of losing control are very serious, and so we're keen to dial it out."

Next Allison moves on to the subject of downforce, and how it is created, which is central to performance in the sport. "We had been relatively conservative in how near to the ground we were prepared to go," he says of the W14 and which has informed what he hopes to be a bolder aerodynamic package for 2024. "The closer you can get the more the car sucks, and I don't mean that figuratively."

Allison is not shy of admitting that the team have struggled since the new regulations came into force in 2022. He acknowledges that the W14 "isn't a much-loved car," citing reliability as perhaps the only significant feature that the team intend to bring to its successor. Beyond that, the concept group have been gathering pace in their efforts to create a change in fortunes for Mercedes F1. What starts out as blue-sky drawings, informed by "rule of thumb engineering judgment" and "virtual calculated results," evolves through a process of rigorous consultation, simulation, and assessment to detailed 2D drawings and 3D modeling covering every component of the car.

"Since Easter, we've had a broad direction of travel. Now we know where the main masses are going to be placed in the car," he says, referring to the big-ticket items that the concept group first considered, like the chassis, engine, and gearbox. "The drawings start to be released around now, which marks the start of a horrific curve," Allison continues, describing the rate at which production at the factory drives the rest of the year. "It steadily steepens with the number of releases until it's almost vertical. In that time, a dizzying number of things are pouring into the supply chain every day, all of which need to be cataloged, tested, and tracked."

In terms of coordination alone, it takes hundreds of people working with 10,000 bespoke components and parts—and over a million discrete items from screws to washers and wires—to create a potential championship contender. Throughout this phase, every member of the factory's procurement and production departments must play to their strengths to realize the vision of this immense technical project.

"I will just know which bits of the car are being birthed easily and which are more breech," observes Allison, adding that the constant quest for improvements in performance will invariably gnaw at the schedule. "The longer you can think, tinker, and develop in the wind tunnel, and also change and weigh up different ideas, then generally speaking the quicker you're going to be. It's just you're required to have the car on the grid for the first race of the next season. F1 won't delay it for you. So you can play chicken with delivery as much as you dare, but you can dare too much." Allison confesses to learning from bitter experience at a previous team ahead of the 2011 season. "We got it horribly wrong," he confesses. "A decision taken in the summer had a bearing on the whole timetable, which meant the car wasn't ready on time. The only reason I am still in a job today is because the Arab Spring happened and the first race was canceled."

For someone who is quick to play down his role in the team, Allison is considered by Toto Wolff to be his "technical twin." He keeps his reading glasses slotted into the neck of his shirt and wears his heart on his sleeve when it comes to the fight to lift Mercedes F1 above the clouds once more. Allison knows the team face an enormous challenge and has come to value the experience as much as the reward. "It's not every year you win a championship," he says, "but I'm lucky enough to say that's been the case for 40 percent of my career in the sport, and those years are fantastic."

Rob Thomas is a man with a plan. "It's massive," says the Mercedes F1 Chief Operating Officer and the individual whose vast scope of responsibilities includes the factory push to bring the new car into existence. "The core of it is making sure that everything we design gets to the circuit as actual hardware."

Reassuringly, for a team faced with a complex and uncompromising undertaking, the 54-year-old Thomas, who started his career working on oil rigs, comes across as naturally organized. He's assured and collected in his thoughts as he discusses the practicalities of aligning thousands of personnel around the same objective: the manufacture, testing, assembly, and delivery of two Formula 1 cars in time for the start of each new season.

"It contains about 30,000 lines of data," he says of the "mother of all planners" set up earlier in the year. "We establish the key milestones and then break it down into specific areas of the car like the chassis or transmission. The plan provides release dates for everything and goes into huge detail. So you can go from the front wing into the flap and then down into the individual elements."

With such a complex project driven by an aggressive schedule that requires the factory to operate day and night, how does Thomas accommodate the inevitable bumps in the road? "We're in a business that is trying to find performance," he answers, "and yet there's no contingency in the plan. It's just designed to give aerodynamics as much time as possible to find that performance, and then provide engineering with enough time to design it." The upshot, he admits, is that the manufacturing arm is squeezed and the pressure intense. What matters, Thomas maintains, is communication between departments so there are no surprises, and a shared desire to produce a winning car. "It's a tough time, and an intense time," he acknowledges, "but it's a controlled time."

Thomas can point to another reason why he remains so calm in the eye of the storm. Arriving in his post fourteen years earlier, fresh from HPP in Brixworth—where the hybrid power units are produced—the COO found the plan had room for improvement.

"It wasn't really respected," he reflects. "It just relied on the experience of people to worry about things at the right moment. *The build* is what we call the work that takes place over the winter. At the time it was this crazy period in which everybody worked themselves into the ground and we somehow ended up with a car at the end of it. But it was always partially complete, with bits still coming through. So we worked toward a process of encouraging everyone to buy into the plan and maintain the discipline to be agile but still hit the dates.

"Slowly but surely we got better," says Thomas. "People weren't destroying themselves. They still worked very hard but in a joined-up way. It became a nice culture to work in, rather than one that left you dribbling in the corner after having worked seven days a week for four months. As a result, the car that left the factory was complete and we had much better tests," he concludes, referring to a period that would lead into Mercedes F1's long run of championship success.

Like Allison, Thomas is a passionate cheerleader for the workforce at Brackley and Brixworth, not least because their efforts are invariably eclipsed by the sport's visible front end. Having pressed hard throughout the first half of the season to deliver a stream of upgrades to the W14, the factory team are steadily turning their efforts toward the W15. After what has been a difficult few years, how is morale maintained in what has to be a relentless push regardless of results?

Thomas acknowledges that it was tough for those who had enjoyed the golden era. "In 2022, 60 percent of the team had never lost," he says, referring to the season when Mercedes F1's reign as Constructors' Champions came to an end. "At first there was a period of denial followed by a dawning realization that we weren't going to bounce back immediately. So we've just aimed to be open and transparent."

Thomas cites regular briefings and the sometimes disarmingly frank nightly reports to the factory throughout each race weekend penned trackside by either Shov or James Allison. "Rather than just saying, 'We got it wrong and let's hope for better luck next time,' they offer their view of what's happened and set out what we're going to do about it. That's enough, I think, for people to get behind the plan."

Thomas pauses to consider what internal communications strategy has emerged from this tough time and is likely to endure as both a bonding agent and motivating force regardless of the team's fortunes. "That's leadership."

CHAPTER SEVEN

ON THE RACKS

The Singapore Grand Prix
Marina Bay Street Circuit, Marina Bay
September 15–17, 2023

I have arrived in the future. At least that is my first impression of Singapore's Marina Bay Street Circuit. Home to this weekend's grand prix, it's a night race set against a cityscape of bold and breathtaking architecture. High-rise buildings take cues from the tropical vegetation that climbs, spirals, and fans from parks and planters, and also from the straits the city overlooks in the form of giant glass structures shaped like shells and cresting waves. The track itself, carving through urban thoroughfares and avenues usually crawling with traffic, has been transformed into a high-speed raceway defined by catch fencing and powerful floodlighting. Viewed from above, which is easily done in a city on so many levels, it looks like a sanitized spin on *Blade Runner* overlaid with the best of *Tron*.

In such a highly developed setting for this race weekend, it's fitting that I'm here to meet Mercedes F1's Trackside Electronics Leader. Evan Short proudly describes himself as the team nerd. In effect, he's responsible for the car's central nervous system. This immediately comes to mind when Short shows me a schematic diagram of the vehicle. Even with the bodywork and mechanical parts stripped away, the proliferation of sensors, controls, and gizmos still defines the shape of the W14. Then there are the wiring looms. These aren't housed in heat shrink sleeves, which can be prone to wear and tear caused by movement and vibrations. Instead, the wires are embedded in solid carbon fiber wafers that are in turn shaped to occupy the minimum amount of space. With copper veins, vessels, and arteries branching from nose to rear wing, this is the car's vascular network. It feeds everything from the driver controls to the hydraulic power and the raft of data monitoring that a contemporary F1 team demands. It's a huge undertaking, but Short is on it all with self-deprecating good humor and brio. A tall restless Canadian with a boyish smile and laurel crown of hair, Short wouldn't look out of place wearing a white lab coat rather than the team's engineering shirt. He's an engagingly clever individual, who once sent a Lego man into space in his spare time from a field outside Oxford. "Electronics is in everything," he says ahead of FP2. "At least a little bit."

I meet Short as he hurries from a driver briefing in the engineers' office. It's on the second floor of the team's hospitality suite, where electronics are definitely in play as the air conditioning keeps the space pleasantly cool. As soon as we head down into the paddock, after Short invites me to cross with him to the garage, it feels like we've stepped into a furnace. In this tropical quarter, the heat and humidity are intense. Even after dark, the temperature only drops a few notches from the oppressive 32 degrees centigrade that dominated the day. The upcoming practice hour is the only one of the three to take place after dark. It makes it the one truly representative session in terms of temperature and track conditions, and so the learning to be had here will be vital. After mixed fortunes at the Dutch Grand Prix—with a P6 for Hamilton and P17 for Russell after suffering a puncture—and finishing as the third-fastest team at Monza, behind Red Bull and Ferrari,

Mercedes F1 are seeking to move forward here. Both drivers have been largely positive in their feedback following FP1, at a high-downforce circuit with short straights that should suit the W14. Even so, there is still a great deal of setup work to be done.

Entering the long corridor into the garage, we pass the recessed wall of headsets that also houses Niki Lauda's red cap. Short taps the peak twice for luck, almost without thinking, as if he does it so often it's becoming automatic. "Part of my job is to check everything," he says, seemingly at peace with his superstitious leanings. "But still . . ."

A little red ring pull is fitted on one side of each car just behind the air intake. Short visits one side of the garage after the other and gives them a testing tweak. "It's the kill switch," he says. "In case we need to shut down the engine and the system in a hurry."

Without fail, Short carries out the same routine inspection before the cars head out for the track. The ring pull is a deceptively simple precaution, despite being one that could save lives. It's also in contrast to the technological complexity of the next stop on our tour when Short scuttles into a screened-off work-space at the rear corner of the garage. Here, the Trackside Electronics Leader introduces me to his ordinary world, which he calls "the racks," and it's the place he clearly feels most at home throughout a race weekend. I find myself looking at an eight-strong workbench in front of a wall of data screens and communication panels. The number of digital graphs, tracers, and readouts is overwhelming to my eye. It's also an indication of the intensive monitoring operation that Short and his group oversee for every mission-critical component of the car. Just now, only one seat is occupied. Within minutes, however, as FP2 approaches, this back room will be full.

"So there are two sides to trackside electronics," says Short, when I ask where he begins. "During a test event or a race weekend, we're directly tuning the cars from gear shifts to race starts. But then we're also gathering data, and that's vital for the engineers and the folks back in the factory to improve performance."

In total, Short works with a group of forty engineers. With such complex systems at play, even this famously hands-on electronics wizard must delegate roles and responsibilities. "We have the systems engineers," he says. "They calibrate and monitor the sensors related to the physical operation of the car. Then there are the electronics technicians, or the sparkies, who look after the wiring and installation. Finally, we have the control systems engineers, who manage the driver interface such as the steering wheel. That role is split between Chris [Nelson] here," he says, introducing me to his colleague at the workbench, "and Mad Dog back at the Race Support Room in the factory."

Short seems to recognize that might need some explanation, for it sounds like one of those nicknames somebody tried to get off the ground themselves. "His real name is Marcelo Martinelli," he tells me. "He's known as the calmest guy in the team, and so he earned it."

"Do you have a nickname?"

"Not that I know of," says Short, having first looked at Nelson, who immediately returns to his work. "Which worries me."

With the timer started on the sixty minutes available to all teams for this second practice session, the track quickly fills with traffic. As Hamilton and Russell leave the garage in turn, preparing to run a preplanned program to help set up their cars, I sit beside Short and watch every tracer tile on the screens pulse into activity. The software responsible is a commercially available, customizable platform that presents the real-time data he needs from the cars on the track. Each tile, representing a critical component on the car, describes a geometric waveform. Some oscillate in smooth arcs. Others switch up and down. Short draws my attention to one that produces a strange haze for a nanosecond every lap.

"We discovered there's a bridge at the track that wasn't demagnetized at construction, which it should have been," he explains, and goes on to tell me how an exploratory walk with a compass caused the needle to spin. "It means we lose data every time the car approaches it, but we have a work-around for it now."

Evan Short is a man who finds peace of mind in knowing that the cars are constantly talking to him. Throughout the hour that follows, over 1,500 onboard sensors transmit data to the racks—and also the Race Support Room in Brackley—hundreds of times per second. With the suite of monitoring tools available to them, Short and his team of electronics engineers can divine real-time patterns that reflect performance or foretell problems. Ultimately, they can make a valuable contribution to the team's fortunes on the track.

"I'm aware that it looks like I'm staring into the Matrix," he says, revealing an easy sense of humor under pressure. A few minutes later, in a space that is oppressively hot, Short presses a button on his communications panel to address his fellow electronics engineers. "Shall we take a moment to appreciate that we don't live in Singapore? How is it back at the factory?"

"Freezing," reports "Mad Dog" Martinelli through our headphones from his station more than 10,000 kilometers away.

"Oh, fuck off," laughs Short, and lifts his attention to the rack's upper screens.

Observing him hawkishly scan every tracer, including a panel of tiles with a traffic-light color scheme to indicate the health of critical car components, Short strikes me as an engineer who thrives on the edge. Like a broker on the trading floor, focused on a stock price ticker, he's braced to recognize the slightest curiosity in data behavior and react decisively. At any moment, a tracer might stray from its pattern, or a green tile could turn yellow or even red. Whatever the changing status, Short is on it decisively and quick to interpret what it means for the car. Indeed, toward the end of the session Short and Nelson discuss an anomaly with one of the readouts. It concerns a shift between two gears on George Russell's W14, and though the pair monitor it intensely Short tells me it's just cause for investigation after the session has finished. We're at the vanguard of technology here, and the Mercedes F1 Trackside Electronics Leader has seen it come a long way in a career that started with Ferrari back in 1999.

"My first job was as a radio spy," he says breezily, once the second session is complete, and takes me back to when the young electrical engineering graduate found himself tasked with working out how to eavesdrop on race communications between a rival team's driver and his engineer. Crucially, an instruction to pit the car could prove invaluable to a competitor; allowing them to make strategic calls and steal an advantage. "The communication channel wasn't open like it is today," Short explains, and anyone who has followed a race broadcast on TV or radio will be familiar with the choice communications from all teams aired by the FIA. "Teams like McLaren would encrypt their radio. As they were Ferrari's main competitor, my job was to find a way to intercept it."

"And that was allowed?" I ask.

Short offers the smile of a man who knows he got away with a coup. "Arguably it was *morally* forbidden," he concedes. "In those days, analogue encryption relied on automatically shuffling the communication through a sequence of radio frequencies," Short continues. "One of McLaren's sponsors was an encryption company, and I knew they only used a limited combination of sequences. So I built something that followed each combination. McLaren would use the same one for an entire race weekend. It meant once I found it I could chase the communication."

While the information allowed Ferrari to seemingly second guess their rival's pit stop strategy, Short agrees that he gained most satisfaction from the success of the technical challenge.

"We did it for about two years before McLaren worked it out," he says. "We were reacting to things on track that we couldn't possibly know any other way. They had an engineer called Tyler. He suspected we were listening and sarcastically started saying good morning over the radio to my boss, an engineer who used to work with Senna at McLaren called Giorgio Ascanelli. My job was to transcribe everything for him, and so I would dutifully write down: *Tyler says hello*. When it became obvious what was going on, Ascanelli got on the radio one day, waited for the greeting and then replied: 'Good morning Tyler!'"

While the exchange marked an end to Evan Short's hacking escapade, it coincided with a proliferation in the number of teams setting up masts at the side of the track and connecting their drivers to the garage by radio. As Short goes on to explain, this also allowed them to take tentative steps into what is now represented by the banks of screens in front of us.

"There was no live telemetry when I started," he says. "When we did learn to get some transmission of data from the car, it was only once a lap. So for the next ninety seconds, or however long it took for the car to come round again, all the engineers would be poring over the info, and then we'd repeat the process all over again. Around 2003, we developed the means to get a little bit of data coming in from the car all the way around the track. That was transformational. From there, we knew that we could never go back."

Like so many aspects of his work, which saw him leave Ferrari for his current team in 2008, Short tells me that this technological arms race eventually resulted in a paddock summit to discuss a sensible conclusion. "In 2013, all the team nerds sat down and recognized that we were being competitive in setting up masts and receivers when the focus should be on the track. It just seemed more sensible to do it collectively," he says, referring not just to the telemetry harvesting but communications between the driver and the pit wall. "So now Formula 1 Management provide a system that all the teams use. It means we don't have to set up loads of gear around the track, while the governing body can make sure nobody is trying to hide sneaky things they might be doing."

This weekend in Singapore, all the teams are operating on British time. We're eight hours ahead of GMT, but as it's a night race the paddock only fills in the early afternoon and then doesn't empty until way past midnight. It makes sense having traveled here from the UK; minimizing jet lag and maximizing the ability to run on full cylinders. At a briefing, late the next afternoon, Lewis Hamilton's Performance Engineer, Michael Sansoni, makes the point that the team are very experienced at adjusting to different time zones, and also well-supported by the factory. "They provide us with a detailed itinerary," he says. "Some people even set up sleep timetables on a spreadsheet to adjust in the week before and after a race."

As George Russell and Hamilton join the briefing, followed by Shov and Toto Wolff, everyone looks strikingly fresh. Despite such a punishing, season-long travel schedule, fatigue has no place in a sport decided by such fine margins. Race-critical demands are placed on everyone in the team, from the drivers to engineers like Evan Short, who cannot afford to miss an electronic heartbeat.

Throughout FP3, and in approaching qualifying, an air of quiet confidence begins to bind the team. "We are consistently going quicker over the three sessions," says Russell, who completed the final practice hour in P2, just one hundredth of a second behind Ferrari's Carlos Sainz. Hamilton had been more circumspect in the last debrief, having finished in P6 as lap times tumbled in the closing minutes, but overall he echoes his teammate's view that the performance direction is encouraging. This high-downforce street circuit speaks to the normally recalcitrant W14, and though the field is tight, Verstappen is also struggling for speed and grip. In Shov's view, Red Bull have been forced to lift the ride height of their car's floor to accommodate a bumpy track. Potentially, he thinks, they've paid a price in loss of downforce. As the Mercedes F1 cars are set up for race pace over single-lap pace, a potential vacancy has just opened up at the front of the field.

"There is a possibility here," says Wolff when the briefing concludes, and yet cautions his troops to be thorough in their preparation. As people filter out, the team boss leads by example by asking the tire guys to go over their strategy with him one more time.

Now that night has fallen, the paddock and the walkways surrounding the track are illuminated by giant lanterns. The track itself is lit up like daylight, while the temperature also seems to be defying the fact that the sun set hours ago. In their enclosed space at the back of the garage, Evan Short and his squad of electronics engineers settle in before the racks and roll up their shirt sleeves in more ways than one.

"While we wait for quali to start," he says into his headset microphone, "who would like a drink from the fridge?" As the orders flow in, Short looks at me wearily. "I'm running out of arms," he cautions.

"You?" Controls Engineer Chris Nelson looks across at him. "Never!"

As Short heads out to the garage's kitchen area behind the partition walls, I wouldn't put it past him to come back wearing some kind of Doc Octopus rig with techno-tentacles clutching cans of Coke and water. Short just strikes me as someone who is constantly innovating in his mind. Each practice session has seen him run "experimental stuff" on the car, and when he returns with a clutch of drinks cans in the crook of one arm there is talk about bringing a component "out of quarantine."

"Sometimes we need to take an item off the car for investigation," he explains. "It might not be at fault but a symptom of something else, and this is how we find out. Rather than leaving it on a surface in the garage, however, where it's at risk of being picked up in a hurry and put back on the car again, we tag it and then completely remove it from the live environment."

As he speaks, to the sound of the engines firing up in this cavernous garage, the tiles of data across his screens tweak into life. "I've pushed the pit limiter to 59.6 kph," Nelson informs him, which sounds horribly close to the 60 kph speed restriction to which all cars must adhere on entering the pit lane.

"You're a wild man," replies Short, craning his neck to monitor the upper display panel once again as Russell and then Hamilton head out onto the track.

For the next eighteen minutes, which define the first of the three elimination sessions, Evan Short barely has time to blink. He's nervous but acts on that constructively by priming himself to jump at the first hint of an issue. When the system flags a problem with Hamilton's umbilical cord, the physical cable that provides an encrypted communication link between the driver in the car back in the garage to the engineers, Short rushes to plug in a replacement. Out on the track, it's only when Lance Stroll walks away from the wreckage of his car, having activated a red flag after slamming his Aston Martin into the wall on the final turn, that

130

the man beside me turns the dial down on his vigilance. Both Mercedes F1 cars go through to the second knockout round, but it's been messy with traffic impeding push laps for both drivers. In between sessions, I find George Russell standing directly behind me with his race suit peeled to the waist, an ice vest strapped to his chest, and his gaze locked on the telemetry tiles. To the trained eye, there is data here that doesn't just help Short and his team to feel connected to the car but also the driver behind the wheel.

The second qualifying session starts late, due to the barrier repairs required after Stroll's dramatic accident. In the fifteen minutes that follow, cheers erupt from the grandstands when both Red Bulls fail to make the top ten. With a strong showing from Russell, who finishes in P2, those guests in the VIP gallery behind the Mercedes F1 car bays find themselves witnessing a team who know how to seize the opportunity opening up to them. Moving into the final ten-minute session, the electronics engineers in front of the racks seem to pull themselves even closer to the screens. On their first hot laps, Hamilton slots into P5, just one-tenth of a second off his teammate in P4. Short stares at the telemetry in silence. On his main screen, he's summoned a panel of tiles that shows the health of key car components. Every tile is green, but the Trackside Electronics Leader is primed for any change.

When one tile does turn red, just as the cars hurtle through their final laps, it's me who takes a breath. Short's only response is to register it with a glance. "Pressurized fuel cell," he says to help me out, and judging by his tone it isn't as panic-inducing as a puncture or engine failure. "It's not unexpected."

As the cars whip over the line, George Russell's P2 is less than one-tenth of a second off pole. It's both frustrating and impressive for a car that's proved so challenging this season, and while

Hamilton takes P5 it falls to Sporting Director Ron Meadows on the pit wall to put it in perspective. "Reminder of the long runs," he says over the radio, referencing the pace both cars produced in practice with high fuel loads.

This day belongs to Ferrari, with only Russell preventing a front-row lockout by the team from Maranello in Italy. Pole-sitter Carlos Sainz and Charles Leclerc in P3 have been looking strong on a single lap all weekend. In race trim, however, Mercedes F1 will line up tomorrow with every chance of finishing with a driver on the podium.

Heat governs this city. It dictates how the population lives and works. Setting out for the twenty-minute walk from the team's hotel to the paddock the next afternoon, I find barely anyone out in what feels like an open-air sauna. With a street race taking place this weekend, many of the pristine avenues have been closed and screened off to accommodate the circuit. On foot, the only quick access is via the network of underground shopping arcades. It's only when I ride the escalator down into this giant subterranean world that I come to appreciate why it's so busy: air conditioning. The stores, restaurants, cafes, juice and coffee bars are buzzing, as if the temperature up top has preserved the kind of mall life last seen in the nineties.

Feeling out of sync on British time in Southeast Asia, and now disorientated by the labyrinth of identical walkways, it only takes a few turns for me to realize I am lost. I decide to retrace my steps, and imagine that Mercedes F1 mechanic Ben Pettifer must wonder why I seem so pleased to see him. "It can be confusing," he says generously as I fall in with him. "But you get used to it."

"How about the jet lag?" I ask.

"We're so busy in the garage over a race weekend that I don't have time to feel tired," he says. "We have a job that's got to be done. It's only when I'm home, with time off, that it catches up with me."

I am mindful of Pettifer's take on passing through the swipe gate into the paddock. Wherever F1 is in the world, there is an energy within this racing enclave that's infectious. Every team present is in hot pursuit of performance, after all, and this demands commitment and attention at the highest level. Yesterday evening, in the debrief following his P2 qualifying finish, I watched George Russell take his seat looking like the physical attrition from such a punishing session on the track had no bearing on his focus. A fresh shirt did little to hide the fact that he was cooked, and yet once the round of applause on his entrance subsided, the Mercedes F1 driver had been keen to get down to business.

"A really great job, everyone," he said. "A well-maximized session. I just feel confidence in the car."

"What defines that confidence?" asked Shov, speaking for the engineers keen to translate that human feeling into the language of mechanical and aerodynamic systems. Russell explained that it came from having begun the weekend on softer suspension than usual, and then optimizing it from there. "We used to start low and stiff," he said. "This is a better starting point for me."

The 25-year-old speaks with clarity of purpose. There is no self-doubt here. Just a recognition that everyone present is working toward the same pressing objective. In this view, there's no space for anything other than absolute honesty. Later in the debrief, Russell pointed out that a recommended time he'd been given to complete an out lap had turned out to be a little tight.

"I know you're good at doing two things at once," said Shov, "but we try to avoid talking to you on a lap."

"This is the highest level of sport," Russell replied bluntly. "It's fine."

When I catch up with Evan Short, as he prepares to play his

role in another pit stop practice ahead of the afternoon's race, I ask how he feels about such plain speaking. Lewis Hamilton can also be direct in briefs and debriefs. He'll often challenge his engineers about setup and development progress in ways that make me glad I'm not on the receiving end. It's expressed with respect, but with the intensity dial turned to eleven. I sense it's a way for both drivers to test their engineers to be sure that they're giving 100 percent. I just wonder how it feels to be put on the spot in this way.

Short offers me a wry smile. "I have made very slow progress toward realizing that being the correct voice in a discussion is not as important as communicating. It's far more important to focus on what will make us faster than to come out thinking, *Well, I showed them!*"

On the subject of speed, the Mercedes F1 team's pit stops are coming under increasing press and public scrutiny. This is largely down to the fact that Ferrari, Red Bull, and McLaren continue to steal an advantage of up to half a second on the Silver Arrows in sending their cars back out onto the track. While the cost cap prevents new wheel guns coming into service until next season, Matt Deane and his pit crew can only commit to consistency in the shortest time possible with the tools at their disposal. It makes these dress rehearsals even more critical, with all eyes on Short to put a figure on each drill. *Two point four seconds*, he'll call out each time the guns fall silent . . . *Two point two.*

The Trackside Electronics Leader stands before a trolley-mounted electronic instrument that could double as a bombproof briefcase. The screen displays another suite of figures that go way beyond recording the overall pit stop time. In between drills, Short explains how it can determine the time for each gun as well as the torque and position. "It also holds the car if something hasn't gone well; for example, if a wheel hasn't been tightened sufficiently. But it is a system and systems can fail," he adds. "That's why Matt [Deane] has a controller with an override switch and a trigger guard in case he drops it."

The next time the car is rolled into the box, I watch Deane flip back the guard like a sharpshooter cocking the hammer of a gun. Short's system works perfectly, however, and the data it provides is central to helping the pit crew finesse the sequence. His role is one of brain over brawn, as I am reminded by Rear Jack Operator Karl Fanson after the final run-through.

"Evan's actually got a full head of hair," he says, addressing not just me but the man who knows he's about to become the punchline to a joke. "It's just it can't cover his massive egg head. The surface area is too big!"

Every time a Mercedes F1 car takes to the track, the onboard sensors can beam back five to six gigabytes of data. With the umbilical cord plugged into the vehicle in the garage, which serves as a hard link as well as an encrypted communication channel between the driver and engineers, Short can extract up to seven times that volume. It's a hugely specialized field, and beneath the banter from his colleague lies a deep-seated respect for the work his group undertakes. In order to stay at the bleeding edge of technological innovation, Short also considers his role to be one that must constantly evolve.

"Over the next few years we will see an increasing reliance on AI and machine learning," he tells me. "In my job we look for patterns, or worrying trends, and at present these are done by coding we prepare manually. Eventually, when we're looking for something like a hydraulic leak, for example, we can teach a system what the leak looks like and leave it to watch out for one."

"Could the time arrive when you don't need a driver?" I ask.

Short responds as if this is something he's already considered at length. As much as I'm sure he'd love to develop a self-driving

Formula 1 car, he recognizes that's not what motor racing is about. "There was a period where we were allowed to directly reprogram the cars on track, but it didn't last very long," he says. "I think the FIA and the fans began to feel that the engineers were driving the cars. As it is, I get to deal with systems and electronics, and also human beings—athletes at their absolute peak—and that's exciting."

In the final minutes before the race, in the heart of a city after dark, a sense of expectation presides over the paddock and the grandstands. In the Mercedes F1 garage, VIP guests take to their seats in the rear gallery. As the mechanics return from the grid where the drivers await the formation lap, Toto Wolff settles into his high stool at the head of the engineers' central island. Like a captain on the bridge of a ship, he looks composed, calm, and confident in the crew surrounding him.

On the racks, hidden behind the screens from the roving F1 TV camera operator, Evan Short is struggling to stay cool. He's laid an ice pack on his lap, which stayed solid for about two minutes. It's as hot as a commercial kitchen here, but it's also easy to assume the sweat on his brow isn't entirely related to the tropical temperature. I know he's on top of the data in front of him. Even for a man of his intelligence, however, it demands a great deal of organic processing power. As I watch the cars undertake the formation lap via the TV feed, a host of varying waveforms begin their cycles in the telemetry tiles surrounding it. Beside me, Short scans the tracers like an orchestra conductor following sheet music. While it falls to him to detect that one odd or missing note that could undermine the entire performance, everything is currently playing to expectation.

"Give me something to worry about," he asks his group nonetheless.

"Climate change." The reply comes out of nowhere, and quite

possibly from back in the Race Support Room at Brackley. "Join the conversation."

Evan Short nods as if the suggestion is a fair one, if perhaps not what he was expecting as the cars return to the grid.

Watching a race unfold from the garage is a unique experience in many ways. It's an opportunity to see the engineers and pit crew at work in real time, but you're also strangely disassociated from the action on the track. The F1 broadcast feed is exactly what is broadcast into homes around the world, but in here it's stripped of running commentary. Instead, through my headphones, I listen to the voices of a team steering both cars from the sidelines. Engineers are relaying data long before lights out, and when that happens Short checks in with Chris and Mad Dog to be sure the launch has gone to plan. As the cars surge around the first corner, Hamilton is forced to cut the next turn to avoid contact with both his teammate and Lando Norris in the McLaren. He's on the radio straightaway, anxious not to cede places unnecessarily, and triggering an intense discussion between Wolff and Sporting Director Ron Meadows, on the pit wall. "Leaving the track and gaining an advantage," Meadows clarifies insistently, as if knowing that a five-second penalty is about to drop.

When another voice cuts in to inform them that the FIA is awaiting a response, Bono instructs Hamilton to return the positions. The driver obliges at the first opportunity, but not before being assured that it's the only option available.

From there, over the course of the race, my ears fill with a steady stream of status updates and strategy calls, as well as communications that climb the chain of command to the drivers. It can make following the overall narrative of the race quite challenging. At the same time, I am entirely up to speed on the Mercedes F1 story. With Max Verstappen struggling for grip as predicted, the Silver Arrows are in the running for a win alongside the two Ferraris and the McLaren of Norris. "It's been a while since we've gone this far in a race with so many cars this tight," says Short with just seventeen laps left.

As if in response, just two laps later Esteban Ocon's Alpine malfunctions abruptly. The loss of power forces him to pull off the track, triggering a virtual safety car period.* At once, the strategists ask Russell and Hamilton to give up second and fourth place respectively and come in for fresh tires. Why? Because when compared to the fading grip of those cars that stay out, the team's tacticians believe they can catch up and then shoot for a one-two finish. It's a gamble that leaves the duo chasing Sainz, Norris and Leclerc, but sets the scene for a thrilling endgame. "I suspect this will be tense," says Senior Race Strategy Engineer Joey McMillan from his command post back in the factory. "Regardless of how it ends, it was the right call."

Within minutes, as the tire advantage kicks in, Russell makes a bold move on the Ferrari of Leclerc. "Come on, George!" yells Adam McDaid, who is watching from behind me while providing race updates on the team's WhatsApp group chat for key personnel.

Since exiting the pits, Hamilton has closed the five-second gap on his teammate. He can't afford to get caught behind Leclerc, and a victorious roar erupts across the garage on lap fifty-four as he also passes the Ferrari to move into fourth place. The Mercedes F1 drivers now have eight laps left to reel in Norris and Sainz at the head of the field. Judging by the closing interval times in every sector, there is a growing possibility that Russell and Hamilton will bring their cars home first and second.

Beside me, Short toggles through the telemetry menu. Jabbing

---

* A slower speed limit enforced electronically—without a physical safety car on the track—while marshals clear a hazard.

at the keyboard, he summons the traffic-light tiles that signify the health status of the cars' critical components. Several are on amber. One or two are on red.

Short activates the communications channel to talk to his group. "These are the warnings we definitely shouldn't ignore, right?"

"Apart from now," replies Chris Nelson.

Underneath the TV feed on his screen, Short has activated four smaller windows. They provide a dual view from each cockpit, with one camera positioned just behind the driver's helmet and another facing him from in front of the steering wheel. Russell is now so close to the back of Norris that he's effectively driving blind, relying on the position of the McLaren and muscle memory to stay on the racing line. Nose to tail, and traveling at 300 kph in places, it's incredibly brave and reflects a high level of trust between rival drivers. All he can do now is steal a moment to pounce on Norris, who is relying on the DRS* advantage from Sainz less than one second ahead, and this gives his Mercedes F1 teammate time to join the train. A true apex predator, Hamilton is just as committed as Russell, though with just two laps left— and Sainz reporting that his tires are gone—the pair are running out of track.

On the racks with Short and his engineers, all eyes are on the F1 broadcast feed as Russell vainly sets up one opportunity after another to get around Norris. There's no air inside this suffocatingly hot space, it seems, but then nobody dares to breathe anyway. I can't say if the communications channels have fallen quiet or whether I've tuned out of everything but the action on the track. On the final lap, I only register the exasperated cries from the pit

---

* DRS (Drag Reduction System) is a mechanism that reduces aerodynamic drag by opening a flap on the rear wing to increase straight-line speed.

wall to the factory when Russell attempts a slightly wider entry than Norris into Turn 10 in a bid for better exit speed. While the McLaren is already close enough to brush the wall, Russell clips it with catastrophic effect. In a shower of sparks, as the other cars wheel left, his car barrels on into the impact absorption barrier. For one awful split second, I wrongly interpret his howls to be one of pain and not anguish. While the polyethylene foam blocks serve their purpose, it does nothing to soften the emotional impact of the crash. It might not be fit for broadcast in its entirety, but we hear every word over the radio channel.

"No. *No!*" On the feed with the reverse view into the cockpit, I can see the whites of Russell's eyes behind his visor as he strains to catch sight of Hamilton, Norris, and Sainz disappearing toward the last few turns of the race. *"You fucking rookie!"* he cries in self-admonishment, which is how he sees himself in that moment despite this being his fifth season in Formula 1. The supreme confidence I had witnessed in the debrief after qualifying has evaporated. It's required by all drivers at this summit of motorsport, and yet one wrong move can be humbling. Later, in front of the cameras in the media pen, Russell will be close to tears.

By now, Hamilton has crossed the line in third. Ahead, it's Sainz who claims a well-earned victory. In the closing stint, the Ferrari driver had deliberately kept Norris close with clever DRS deployment to cover the threat from Russell before his accident. Any celebration in the garage for Hamilton's podium finish is muted by the shock of what's just happened to his teammate. By now the stricken Mercedes F1 driver is out of his car. I only know this having turned to exchange words of congratulations and commiseration with Short, because when I look back at the cockpit's reverse-facing camera it shows an empty seat. As for the tracer lines for Russell's W14, many have maxed out as if recording an earthquake and then seemingly frozen in time. It's jarring to see the car so still in the front-facing feed, in fact, with two wheels buried in the barrier and overheated brakes smoking heavily.

Then the first flames catch, a malevolent lick around the bodywork, and the Trackside Electronics Leader is up on his feet immediately. "Fire!" Short says anxiously into his mouthpiece, clearly aware of the value of the sensors and components on the line here, and then rushes from the racks to sound the alarm in the most conventional way possible. *"Fire!"*

CHAPTER EIGHT

REMOTE CONTROL

The Japanese Grand Prix
Suzuka International Racing Course, Suzuka
September 22–24, 2023

The pit wall is a challenging place for quiet concentration. It takes the form of a covered stand across the pit lane from the garage. With the track on the other side of the parapet in front of them, it couldn't be more exposed to noise and distraction from all sides. On each pit wall, perched on high stools under a canopy, a clutch of team players face a bank of monitors and an intercom panel while trying hard not to get their backs wet if it rains.

Conventionally, alongside senior race engineers and many team principals, this is the command post from which the strategist calls the shots. As the individual who must effectively peer into the future of the race and divine a path for the optimal outcome, it's a role that demands both deep-thinking and an ability to respond fast to unpredictable events. For this reason alone, Joey McMillan prefers to set himself apart from his pit wall colleagues. As the Japanese Grand Prix weekend gets under way, at a snaking figure-of-eight circuit that stands out from an otherwise industrial hinterland near the city of Nagoya, he also won't be found tucked away in a space at the back of the garage. There's always an option for him to work there alongside the engine

142

technicians and trackside electronics crew. It's just this Mercedes F1 Senior Race Strategy Engineer favors even more peace and quiet in which to make informed decisions about the race.

Which is why McMillan is working remotely in the most extreme sense, seated more than 9,500 kilometers away at the factory in Brackley.

He may not be able to smell burnt rubber in the air, but the 34-year-old race tactician has all the tools he requires to fulfill his role. At his triple-screen workstation, McMillan can choose from a suite of data maps, charts, and diagrams, many of which evolve dynamically throughout each session. If he looks up from his post, on the back row of a tiered auditorium that accommodates some thirty operatives, he can view a live video feed of the race on one of the large screens that fill the front wall. Along with the data on the monitors before him, McMillan is able to consult the leaderboard and weather radar, check the time at the track, the countdown to the next session, or live cams from the garage to the pit lane or even from the Mercedes F1 driver cockpits. It's all very space-age, and indeed the engineers and technicians that currently populate Mercedes F1's Race Support Room (known within the team as the RSR) are set to oversee an event that is taking place a world away.

Despite being on continents separated by a nine-hour time difference, Joey McMillan and his trackside colleagues have access to the same real-time information, with the factory and the garage connected by an enhanced communications link. In Formula 1, milliseconds don't just matter when it comes to lap times. Any "mission-critical" personnel—those involved with the racing action—cannot afford to work with lag, and McMillan is a case in point. So when he confers with a teammate on the pit wall, ahead of the upcoming qualifying hour, it's as clear and sharp as if the pair were sitting shoulder to shoulder.

"Joey, if you remember what happened in Mexico 2019," his colleague suggests as they discuss precedents for a proposed run plan, at which the strategist rolls his eyes.

"Mexico 2019?" McMillan laughs. "I don't even remember the race last week!"

As he signs out of the conversation to snatch a break before the session gets under way, I sense this is a man with little time for the past. Responsible for tactics in a race, his focus lies with the present and—critically—the future. In shaping a course of action on the track for his team and two drivers, Joey McMillan really is one of Formula 1's fortune tellers. The mists he peers into take the form of numbers from data streams that eddy and swirl, but they also form patterns very few can see. And the decisions he makes—even from afar—can win or lose a race.

"The strategist's job is to take whatever car you are given when the lights go out and then get the best place you can for it," he says.

In the few minutes of downtime available to him, McMillan has planted himself outside a fire exit with a vape between his thumb and forefinger. In Japan, it's approaching midafternoon. Here on the fringe of a market town in west Northamptonshire, where McMillan began work at two o'clock this morning, he stands in a pool of exterior lighting with dawn still a long way off. It's disorientating, but then preparation is central to strategy. "We spend a long time exploring scenarios before each race," he says. "We build a baseline plan, with alternatives, but it has to be a flexible plan. We don't have to decide until the race starts which way we're going to go."

Before the battle begins, a strategist like McMillan—who works alongside several key figures in his department—can only count on a handful of certainties. In effect, he'll know the track layout and the number of laps that make up the race. He'll also have detailed information to hand on the performance of the W14 throughout the season to date and from the practice sessions at Suzuka this weekend. From there, the forthcoming qualifying session will give him the order in which all the cars will line up on the grid, as well as a picture of how the team's rivals are performing. Then there are the tire choices. With the same limited number available to each team throughout the weekend, McMillan has been canny.

"Degradation is an issue at this track," he says, which means the more durable hard tires should allow a team to run longer. "And we've saved two sets for the race."

Beyond these tactical race basics, almost everything else is subject to change. From the weather conditions to track temperatures or racing incidents, a branching path of variables can swiftly open up. As McMillan sets out how he navigates this labyrinth, it becomes clear that there's a fine line between forward planning and thinking too far ahead.

"For now," he says, "we're just asking ourselves when does a one-stop look good and when does a two-stop look good? If everything goes as we predict, which it won't, then our baseline plan takes us to the finish. But what if we are quicker? What if other teams are quicker? What if the tires do this or that? Before the race, it means we need to know what will trigger the switch from a one- to a two-stop."

"And beyond that?" I ask.

Drawing upon the device in his hand, Joey McMillan responds with a long, meditative exhalation of vapor into the air.

In the moments before the pit lane opens and qualifying begins, the RSR shares the same atmosphere of studied calm and contemplation as a university library. Most stations are now occupied by personnel in team shirts and headsets. The F1 broadcast feed occupies the biggest screen on the wall, currently cutting between establishing shots of the circuit and team garage interiors, but McMillan and his colleagues pay it little attention. "It's on a ten-second lag," he says, referring to the broadcasting delay built in to comply with regulatory requirements. "There's nothing for me to see that would be useful."

Time is of the essence in McMillan's role. In order to look ahead with clarity, and make informed decisions, he has to be anchored in the here and now. To this end, as the first cars exit the pit lane, he summons a circuit map into the viewer on his screen. It features a GPS overlay that displays the live position of every car on track—each denoted by a tag in team colors featuring the first three letters of that driver's surname—as well as the time between them to a tenth of a second. McMillan then admits that he prefers "the circle map," and switches to what looks like a clock face with the tags revolving around the dial perimeter and a full lap ticking over at twelve o'clock. The circuit turns serve as unevenly spaced markers around the dial, which explains why we soon see the tags slow down as the cars on track approach each corner and then speed up on exit.

"It's just cleaner," says McMillan as I begin to appreciate the simplicity. Suzuka's iconic figure-of-eight design might be striking, but when it comes to making strategy calls the layout is a distraction. Along with the timing screen, which he locks alongside the circle map, McMillan summons data tiles from a bespoke software suite in much the same way as his colleague on the racks. While Evan Short is focused on the internal workings of the car, McMillan's selection concerns the outcome in terms of its position in the field—either present or predicted.

"The aim is to get out on the right bit of track," he says of this first of three knockout rounds. "We make the calls about getting the drivers into clean air and predicting what everyone else is going to do."

When McMillan talks about his work in the third person, primarily he's referring to Rosie Wait. As Head of Race Strategy, the widely respected 35-year-old engineer leads a team of ten in devising tactics, developing software tools, and undertaking competitor analysis that seeks to give the two Mercedes F1 cars a competitive edge. Then there's Leonardo Donisete Da Silva, who shares the same job title as McMillan and serves as his trackside counterpart. Also in his early thirties, the Brazilian-born Senior Race Strategy Engineer performs an identical function. It's just while one works in the calm detachment of the RSR, like a chef drafting a menu in a closed dining room, the other sits on the pit wall and performs in the heat of the kitchen. The pair are in constant communication throughout this race weekend, either in video-conference when it comes to strategy planning or in its execution via headsets during a session. They make an odd couple, by McMillan's own admission, but also one he firmly believes to be stronger than the sum of its parts.

"A few years ago there was a time when Leo and I suddenly found ourselves to be the most senior people," he says, referring to a period when Wait was on maternity leave and the former Mercedes F1 strategy maestro—and current Williams team boss—James Vowles (known as JV) had moved away from the pit wall. "I think JV always wanted to pitch Leo and me against each other, so that he could choose the best, but we weren't going to play that game," he says. "You could argue about who is the better strategist between Leo and me. We've all got different strengths, after all. It's just we found we liked working together, and we support each other."

McMillan smiles when pressed about his weakness. "Once I get an idea in my head, I often think I'm right," he says with endearing candor. "Leo is very good at making the counterpoint."

"And how do you support him?"

"He can be more risk averse," says McMillan without hesitation,

147

as if this is a conversation they have had many times between themselves. "But that comes from being on the pit wall," he adds. "There's less pressure here."

With their working relationship in mind, I am struck by just how much dialogue McMillan and Da Silva share over the Mercedes F1 strategy channel. As more rival cars start their Q1 session, the race team's intercom network starts to fill with updates from engineers and technicians about the likes of sensor statuses, tire and brake temperatures. Meanwhile, the chatter between the two tacticians could easily be one individual talking to himself.

"We should wait a few minutes to maximize space," says Da Silva, as the two Silver Arrows remain on standby in the garage. Track grip is also a consideration here, which is likely to improve as cars circulate and lay down rubber onto the surface; the later the lap, the faster the time. Which all feeds into the test of nerves currently keeping the cars on hold.

"Just go if everyone else goes," adds McMillan, mindful that leaving it too late could mean Hamilton and Russell find their efforts to get into Q2 compromised by traffic. As with any aspect of strategic thinking in this sport, nothing is ever determined by a single factor.

On the big screen tiles at the front of the RSR, among the various webcam feeds the team has set up for itself, I find the view of the pit wall. Leo Da Silva sits alongside Shov, the team's Sporting Director Ron Meadows, and Chief Engineer Trackside, Simon Cole. While Meadows is on this race front line principally to communicate with the FIA over any issues concerning sporting and technical compliance, Cole is responsible for overall vehicle reliability. Viewed from behind via a camera mounted above the pit garage, all four sit with heads bowed, focused intently on the telemetry screens in front of them.

"Let's go!" Da Silva issues the command over the airways. In response, one after the other, the two Mercedes F1 cars launch into the pit lane.

Over the course of the next sixty minutes, the two race strategists negotiate a path for Lewis Hamilton and George Russell to secure P7 and P8 respectively on the grid for tomorrow's race. Across all three knockout rounds, McMillan and Da Silva reach decisions based on everything from track space to surface evolution and tire wear, while keeping a close eye on competitor lap times throughout. They're precise and assertive in their calls (*We need to be eighth car out. Eighth doesn't get any traffic*) and reactive when required (*We don't think we're going to be safe so we're going to run again on new tires*). When Logan Sargeant rakes his Williams across the gravel and into the barrier on the final turn—walking away unharmed but triggering a red flag just ten minutes into Q1—McMillan and Da Silva calmly review the most advantageous time to exit the pits once the session resumes. The Brazilian is keen to get out early, given the limited time left. McMillan is not so sure. For a few minutes, as the stricken Williams is cleared from the track and notice is given that the session is set to resume, they circle around their options.

"Why wait?" asks Toto Wolff, who is also operating remotely this weekend from his home in Monaco as he recovers from knee surgery. Like Shov on the pit wall, the boss also has access to the tactics channel. While the two strategists are generally left to talk between themselves, with Shov also in the mix, Wolff has a keen ear and will sometimes ask questions seeking clarity.

"The problem . . ." begins McMillan, who has been concerned that a car on an early push lap may well encounter rivals on their out laps, only to pause in astonishment as Sergio Pérez appears set to illustrate his misgivings. On the big screen, we watch the Red Bull trundle to the top of the pit lane and then stop to wait for the green light. "The problem is that Pérez is *fucked!*"

As the session resumes, McMillan's confident foretelling appears to play out. It comes down to a difference in tactical thinking between the teams, because in due course Pérez does hit traffic. Instead of securing an early pass into Q2, the Mexican driver finds his lap time compromised and has to work that little bit harder in the time left to get the job done.

Ultimately, Q3 ends with a dominant display from Max Verstappen after his uncharacteristic struggle with setup on the Singapore street circuit. This weekend could even see the Dutch driver tie up the World Constructors' Championship for Red Bull. It's an uncomfortable reality for Mercedes F1 as much as an incentive to keep pushing if the team are to return to the very front of the grid. With this in mind, and the qualifying results allowing the strategy plan to evolve, the team set targets for Sunday's race that are ambitious but also achievable. "Red Bull are clearly very quick," concedes Shov in his postqualifying report to the factory. "McLaren also could be out of reach, but Ferrari could well be close enough that we can start to give them problems. The other thing that could definitely cause them a problem is that we have two hard tires and they do not."

Half an hour after the late afternoon session has ended in Suzuka, Joey McMillan offers to talk through what will happen overnight. Even as he says this, we look at one another just to anchor where we are in time.

"Overnight in Japan?" I say to clarify.

McMillan takes a moment to think. "That's right," he replies, though it didn't come easily and I feel his temporary confusion. Locked away through the early hours in the RSR, with no windows to the outside world and with live pictures, communications, and data pouring in from the other side of the world, it's easy to become snagged between two time zones. "Tonight, *Japan* time, we'll run approximately one million sims of the race on a computer cluster. We'll base it on the proposed tire choice, with variables thrown into each race, and that will spit out an average outcome."

Now it's my turn to pause for a second, because frankly I'm stuck on the huge, seven-figure number he's just thrown in.

"It would be impossible for a human to visualize all the ways a race can play out," McMillan tells me, explaining that the variables are random, such as overtakes or a tweak to a rival team's strategy. "We also run the sim during the race and take each last lap as data. So with every lap it becomes more accurate."

Their target for the weekend, McMillan reveals, is Ferrari. After victory for Carlos Sainz at last week's Singapore Grand Prix, compounded by George Russell's last-lap crash, the battle for second place in the Constructors' Championship is tightening considerably. For Mercedes F1, the runner-up prize has acquired a rising sense of importance. It means their fight is with Ferrari.

"They won't be looking to take risks," says McMillan about the team who have qualified well, with Leclerc in P4 and Sainz in P6. "The safest option is the strategy with a 90 percent chance of delivering that result in the race. It's the right thing to do mathematically, but it takes away the chance of sneaking extra points. That's why there are times when you deliberately have to do the *dumb* thing," he says, playfully describing a strategy call with a low probability of success but minimal downsides. "It's just you need a team that has confidence in you, and in that 10 percent chance of scoring more points."

When it comes to making unconventional calls, Joey McMillan has form. He's part of a strategy group that famously executed a tactical move late in the 2021 Spanish Grand Prix that initially baffled rivals but enabled Hamilton to claim the win from Verstappen. It saw the Mercedes F1 driver sacrifice track position behind the leading Red Bull, to pit for a second time in the race. Despite some misgivings from the driver himself, Hamilton's improved pace on fresh rubber forced Verstappen to defend, ultimately causing the Red Bull driver's tires to degrade at a faster rate. In the closing laps, as calculated by McMillan and his colleagues, Hamilton delivered the pass that would claim a memorable victory.

If this was McMillan's definition of a foolish move—and it seemed that way to many when Hamilton gave up a close chase to peel off into the pits—it made heroes of those who called the shots. In this view, that outside chance he clearly often favors is more of a fiendishly informed gamble. For now, as I leave the Mercedes F1 strategist to prime the sim to spin through a seven-figure variation of the same race, the spare set of hard tires the team have so carefully saved will remain in his back pocket. What it gives him is that all-important flexibility. Depending on how the race evolves tomorrow, Joey McMillan can play it safe or do the "dumb" thing—whatever it takes to optimize the outcome for the team.

Each weekend, the strategy group is supported in the RSR by a small band of university students on industrial placements. These aren't indifferent youths who have yet to find their calling in life. In Mercedes F1 polo tops or engineers' shirts, the young men and women at their workstations have been carefully selected from a huge and diverse pool of applicants. Every single one has worked hard to be here, on a program that can span a season, and they make a valuable contribution to the team's fortunes on the track. They're unquestionably smart, proactive, and dedicated to their work throughout each session. The only nod to their student background is the fact that they've named their dedicated channel on the intercom panel "Potato," which can only earn a smile when viewed alongside the likes of "Tactics," "Toto," and "Lewis." Above all, the group are hugely proud of the opportunity to gain knowledge and experience in this environment.

On my return to the RSR, now emptying out after qualifying, this is evident in their shy request for me to take a group photo for them in front of the big screen. "What you learn at university puts you in a great place to understand the theory of what's going on here," says Kat Tse, a postgraduate engineering student from Cambridge University who has earned a place here before returning to study for her master's degree. In talking about her experience, it's evident she feels as challenged by the opportunity as she does valued by the team. "What it doesn't prepare you for is the process of having three people talking at the same time over different channels, or a race going wrong and we only have a minute to figure out why it's happened."

Despite finding themselves in what could feel like a fathomless deep end, Tse and her fellow students are closely supervised and supported by McMillan and his colleagues in the RSR. They're often given specific responsibilities, like identifying brake degradation rates or fractional differences in correlation between the cars on the track and the race simulator. This weekend, Tse has been tasked with investigating why Lewis Hamilton is losing two-tenths of a second at Turn 14 (the exit of the famously high-speed Spoon Curve at Suzuka) compared to George Russell. It's something Hamilton had specifically asked about during a session debrief, where any query raised is doggedly probed by the team. In this case, Tse's enquiry involved studying reams of tracer charts with forensic precision. "We found that George was constantly taking the entirety of the turn wider than his teammate. We told Lewis what we'd spotted. The next time he went out," she says proudly, "he took that same line."

Like every permanent member of the team, and as an engineer with a bright future ahead of her, Kat Tse is determined to contribute her tenth of a second to performance. Judging by her beaming smile when she shares the outcome of her work for this grand prix, it's clear she's delighted to have delivered not just one tenth but two.

"Morning all! Just back from the nightclub."

Ron Meadows, the team's long-serving Sporting Director, is the first voice on the conference call. The quip from the 59-year-old is met by laughter from others logged into the session. It's 1:15 a.m. here in Brackley, while those participating from the Suzuka circuit are looking forward to lunch. Unusually this weekend, Meadows isn't operating from the pit wall but the RSR. While McMillan sits before his laptop, alone in a meeting room, Meadows is either at home, on the road into the factory, or at his desk somewhere in the building. Frankly, it makes no difference. Such is the communications technology enabling key race team members to make a remote contribution to the Japanese Grand Prix, he could be on Mars.

"So this is the first of two race plan presentations," McMillan tells me, having muted his microphone. On the screen from Japan, Bradley Lord has just signed into the meeting. With Wolff absent from the circuit, Lord is standing in as the eyes and ears for the Team Principal. "This presentation is for the directors," he continues, as Shov also joins the call from trackside, "which is a useful way to stress-test the plan before we present it to the drivers."

Over the next thirty minutes, McMillan and Da Silva take these central players through every aspect of the strategy. Having run a million races since qualifying, the sim has helped to refine the plan. In theory, it's produced the most likely outcome of the race. In reality, any number of events could force the pair to chart a different course. As a result, they present a solid framework that can be modified at a moment's notice. "We're targeting a two-stop race," says Da Silva, having shared one of several slides that visualize the data under discussion, "but a one-stop is not ruled out."

As the presentation progresses, the strategists cover off everything from the latest track temperature forecasts to the likely wind behavior in a race that is traditionally unkind to tires. This reinforces their belief that the extra set of the more durable, hard compound tires could prove to be decisive in their battle with Ferrari, while cautioning that the high rate of wear will still require respect.

In the conference call with the drivers that follows, McMillan and Da Silva bring in an engineer from their group with tire expertise to take Hamilton and Russell through the management required at key turns.

"You didn't leave many corners out," quips Hamilton afterward.

"We can only look ahead," Da Silva reassures him, having asserted that the race will shake out into pace order with nothing behind Mercedes F1 to trouble them and a tire advantage that could take them forward. "It provides an undercut opportunity on Ferrari."

"It'll be hard to finish outside the top eight due to the race gap," concludes Shov, confident that those cars behind the Silver Arrows won't present a threat. "So we can try things."

This weekend, Joey McMillan is never more than a keystroke away from a "race planner." In any other context, it looks like the kind of visual tool on a computer screen that a corporate suit would use to depict economic indications, stock market values, or quarterly revenue streams. Typically, you're looking at multiple strings on a line graph that launch from the same origin point and then climb, drop, and cascade across the screen. It might seem dry at a glance, but as a means of interpreting a Formula 1 race—either as a predictive instrument or a summary after the checkered flag—it provides fascinating insight.

As a lesson in race literacy—with the briefings complete and fuel loads calculated to bring the cars home with the required one-liter sample left in the tank—McMillan loads up a planner in the RSR. This one tells the story of the previous week's F1 round in Singapore. The graph plots the time gap from the leader for each car on the vertical axis against the number of laps on the horizontal axis. Collectively, the ascending progress of each string is interrupted by precipitous drops where the cars have pitted for fresh tires. Most occur within two vertical yellow bands on the graph. These mark the period in which a safety car and then a virtual safety car were deployed (advantageous windows in which the time spent pitting is offset by the speed limitation on track). McMillan draws my attention to the fact that after the first safety car, the strings are tightly bunched behind the leading Ferrari.

"This is Sainz doing his absolute best to keep these cars as close as possible," he explains. "One of the reasons he's driving so slowly is because he knows we want to attack with a two-stop. If we were to do that here," he continues, and draws my attention to the cluster of lines beneath Mercedes and the other front-runners, "we'd come out in all of this hellish traffic."

Next, McMillan advances to the second yellow band, the virtual safety car period triggered after Alpine's Esteban Ocon lost power on the track. While Sainz and Norris in the McLaren remained on the road at a reduced speed, the two Mercedes F1 cars were finally able to deploy the two-stop strategy without paying such a high price in track position. From there, on fresh tires, the catch-up commenced. This is represented by four lines coming close to converging at the end of the horizontal axis, but it deftly outlines what had been a thrilling final phase of the race.

As a dynamic resource, the planner can also present data as it plays out live during a race. Together with predictions from the sim, and the array of supporting data tiles, it allows the strategists to operate decisively. At a glance, McMillan, Da Silva, and their colleagues can determine the performance of any car in relation to the rest of the field and make calls to gain a competitive advantage. In his demonstration, McMillan summons several planners to illustrate points about how to play a smart tactical game. Like the circle map, it doesn't serve to call the shots but render the information he requires to determine the way ahead. To the untrained eye, the telemetry available to him is mesmerizing.

"There are lots of tools," he acknowledges, having filled all three screens. From there, McMillan spins through how he can determine the impact on rivals of pitting either of his cars at any time—critically, in terms of bringing them in early to gain an advantage with fresh tires (the "undercut") or staying out longer to gain track position by exploiting older tires and faster laps after competitors pit (the "overcut").

As much as I'm dazzled by the sophisticated armory at his disposal, I'm fascinated to know what qualities and experience led him to the role. Away from this environment, in civilian clothing, Joey McMillan strikes me as being the kind of affable everyman whose character provides no clue to his calling. All I know from our conversation so far is that he and his wife enjoy a form of ballroom swing dancing called the Lindy Hop, which they teach to a high standard. As I ask more about his background, the lighting in the RSR catches the tragus piercing in his right ear, perhaps the only hint of an unconventional path to this post.

"I'm not an engineer," he begins, counting himself as the only member of the race team without such a qualification. "I don't even know how engines work. I've always loved Formula 1. My dad didn't live with us, but growing up I used to go round to his house to watch it. I shared his enthusiasm for the sport, but really my interest was in mathematics."

Given the demands of his role, it comes as a surprise to learn that McMillan found little connection with the subject at school.

"I didn't really like it," he reveals. "Math at GCSE and A level is very dry. You just repeat what you've learned, which means people who are book-smart tend to do quite well at it. And that wasn't for me. I prefer pure math in the abstract, theoretical and philosophical. I see numbers in patterns," he adds, as if hoping to articulate something that seems quite natural to him. McMillan goes on to detail his awakening at degree level, studying mathematics at Birmingham University, only for his restless gaze to settle as he accounts for why he quit the course before completing the first year.

"My mum got very sick with cancer," he says. "So I moved back home to care for her. I was only nineteen and when her prognosis became terminal I just had to find a way to look after her. We lived in Reading, which has a university, and so in that time I tried to get a place on the mathematics degree there. All the places had gone, and so I went to see the admissions professor. I literally knocked on his door. We had a chat about the subject for five minutes and he invited me to start in the new term." McMillan plays down the conversation, but I imagine it doesn't take long for an expert in mathematics to recognize something special in another.

"I was ready to start again," he continues, "but then Mum moved into the final stage of life. She died in the fourth week of term. I had a funeral to organize. Then I had to deal with her estate, and so I just didn't attend as much as I had hoped." Despite such heart-rending challenges, and missing much of the course, McMillan still sailed through the degree and then into a highly specialized doctorate that effectively combined mathematics with meteorology.

In an alternative timeline, Joey McMillan might well have carved himself an academic life. It's fair to say that a mastery of abstract mathematics has limited practical application. Where it counts, however—in fast-moving fields demanding predictive modeling—such expertise can be invaluable. For those who relied on such a rarefied skill set, this was a young man who could make a difference. Which is how McMillan ended up bailing from yet another course, on receiving an invitation from Mercedes F1 that he couldn't refuse.

Listening to him complete the picture, aware of how calmly and confidently he works, it strikes me that it isn't just his gift for numerical thinking that makes Joey McMillan a successful strategist. It's also his emotional maturity acquired under challenging circumstances. Seven years into the role, McMillan has become key to maximizing a return on the track even when the odds are stacked against the team.

For many Mercedes F1 personnel, the quietest time of the weekend comes just before the start of the race itself. With the cars on the grid, even the assembled mechanics can find themselves looking for bodywork to polish. From the RSR, I watch the live feed on the big screen as the camera closes in on George Russell's Race Engineer, Marcus Dudley. He's standing in front of the #63 car in his headset and aviator glasses. As well as the team communication channels, I have the Sky Sports F1 commentary fed low into my mix. I find it useful, and it seems I'm not alone.

"Hey, Marcus," says a race engineer over one of the channels. "Martin Brundle just said that you're looking very *Top Gun*."

"I'll buy him his pint later."

On the screen, after a slight delay, Dudley can be seen covering a smile as he says this by touching his headset microphone. A moment later, the camera cuts to a lingering shot of Hamilton's former teammate and current Alfa Romeo driver, Valtteri Bottas.

"The coolest man on the grid," observes another voice on the same channel, and indeed the Finnish driver has come to own the mullet he's been sporting this season.

"When fashion comes full circle," jokes Shov, who I can see stationed on the pit wall thanks to one of the many trackside team feeds. Leo Da Silva sits beside him. He looks as focused as his colleague in the room with me, even if the pair also contribute to the casual prerace conversation that ensues about drivers and haircuts.

All day, even though dawn is still hours away here in North-amptonshire, every preparatory meeting and briefing has gone into extensive levels of detail. So what could be seen as trivial chat now is more like a restorative break before a period of intense focus for the race team. Only the drivers stay detached, cut off from all but critical communication in their cockpits.

By the time the covers come off the tires, ahead of the forma-tion lap, everyone both trackside and in the RSR is ready for action. Throughout the weekend I have witnessed the strategy plan evolve to this point. Flexibility remains built-in, but this is the moment when the team must commit to an opening move. While Lewis Hamilton and George Russell start on the medium tires, aiming provisionally for a two-stop race, Da Silva points out from the pit wall that they may be vulnerable to an early chal-lenge by cars that have opted for the faster but less durable compound. "There are three behind George on softs," he observes. Having listened to McMillan and Da Silva continually remind each other that they have a spare set of hard tires for the race, I wonder whether the option to run long against their faster-starting rivals—by switching to a one-stop strategy—has just become more likely.

Across the row, Kat Tse has been tasked by McMillan with lis-tening into rival radio transmissions. On-track dialogue between the drivers and their teams is broadcast on an open channel, but McMillan is specific about who he wants monitored. "Cover Sainz as he's ahead. Also the McLarens and Pérez. I'm not worried about

Verstappen," he adds, given the likelihood that the pole-sitter will soon disappear into the distance.

Seconds after the lights go out on round seventeen of the 2023 season, it quickly becomes apparent that the delayed television feed is all but redundant to everyone in the room. As the cars flock toward the first turn, the action on the screen just can't seem to keep up with the activity across the communications channels that fill my headphones. Before I see it, I know that Hamilton suffers contact with Pérez approaching the first corner, which in turn allows the Aston Martin of Fernando Alonso to capitalize on their misfortune. Like his teammate, Russell also loses a place in the scramble. With the safety car deployed, and the Red Bull forced to pit, the sudden turn in fortune sparks intense debate between the two strategists. "Alonso will soon be struggling on softs," says McMillan, a player now deep in the game, "and we're very much racing him now."

Even though the safety car stays out until lap five, there is no letup in the discussions. With one Red Bull out of the frame, but an Aston Martin in its place, Hamilton and Russell remain in P6 and P7 respectively. McMillan is confident that on less durable tires Alonso will eventually fall prey to the pair.

It's just nobody anticipates that the two Mercedes F1 drivers will suddenly tussle with each other as racing resumes. First Russell overtakes his teammate in the final chicane, only for Hamilton to regain the place as they shoot into the DRS zone. It's thrilling to see such wheel-to-wheel action, but not ideal for two cars sharing the same livery. Immediately, McMillan and Da Silva debate pitting as a solution. It's just the outcome is not that clear-cut. Bringing in one car will create much-needed space between Hamilton and Russell, and also open up some flexibility in the form of a split strategy. At the same time, it means whoever comes in could miss out on easy meat when rivals on softs start to run out of grip.

Ultimately, the team opt to make the most of their current medium tires and keep both cars out. It's not an easy decision, because with two highly competitive drivers running so close another clash becomes inevitable.

"Who do we want to fight here?" asks Russell angrily over the radio, after feeling he'd been forced wide by Hamilton on a lap sixteen exit of Spoon Curve and lost out on an overtake. "Each other or the others?"

In response, after Russell has been explicitly instructed not to challenge for position, Da Silva calls in Hamilton for his switch to hard tires. Only then, with the possibility that the stewards could be looking at the Spoon Curve incident, does the tactical reasoning become clear. "Had they inverted it would have screwed up the pit stop," McMillan explains, unwilling to forfeit the fraction of a second it would have cost had a stewards' decision required the two drivers to swap places.

As Hamilton embarks on what will become a conventional two-stop race for him, the strategists work with his teammate to roll the dice by pitting just once. Staying out while others pit a second time will give Russell track advantage, but it also means he must manage his tires and also risk being reeled in by those on fresher rubber. With this in mind, Russell duly extends his opening stint for another eight laps, earning himself the hard compound to the finish. Even though the track still isn't proving to be quite as unkind as predicted to any of the tire compounds, the relative degradation still creates what McMillan views as an opportunity that "nobody else will have the balls to do."

This is the long shot that McMillan had championed ahead of the race. For the sure-footed Lindy Hopper as much as the tactician, the single stop is a chance to freestyle surprise points for Russell. The win is all but guaranteed for Verstappen, but while taking a risk with the #63 driver the Mercedes F1 strategists still have their sights fixed on the central race goal. One way or another, they intend to scalp the Ferrari of Carlos Sainz.

As the race evolves, Hamilton is first in line with the knife. "I guess we've been undercut," says the Spanish driver, running in second place on lap thirty-seven when the Mercedes F1 strategy unfolds. Three laps earlier, Hamilton pitted for his final set of hard tires while Ferrari stayed out to focus on keeping ahead of Russell. A smart driver, as demonstrated by his clever control of the Singapore race, it duly dawns on Sainz that they really should have covered off Hamilton by making their second pit stop one lap after him. Instead, running on worn tires, he realizes that when they finally come in the #44 car will steal the advantage. "Yes," replies his Ferrari Race Engineer dolefully, who doesn't need to spell out that the Italian team have left it too late. "Confirmed."

Like any game involving forward thinking, there are consequences attached to every decision. In this case, while Hamilton makes the jump on Sainz, Russell is left with the challenge of making McMillan's gamble work. As the race moves into the final stint, he finds himself defending the track advantage he'd earned on tires that are now significantly degraded compared to his two-stopping rivals. With Alonso seemingly presenting a threat in an Aston Martin that has rediscovered its form from earlier in the season, the tactics group review their commitment to keeping Russell out.

"We're safe to Alonso," insists McMillan, having done the math and figured the odds are in Russell's favor. "But our only way for him to beat Sainz is by staying out, no?"

"Just so you know, I'm in favor of pitting George," says Leo, siding with the fact that returning to a two-stop would give Russell the fresh rubber to guarantee finishing ahead of the Aston Martin. Same aim. Less risk.

"But Alonso is only matching our time," counters McMillan, who is more concerned at the prospect that Russell will give up on a chance of keeping Sainz behind if they pit him. "What have we got to lose?"

On the surface, it sounds like a disagreement and potentially a disadvantage in having two strategists calling the shots instead of one. It's the tone that dispels any sense of conflict, however. For having made his case, McMillan still yields to the fact that Da Silva is trackside and should have the final call. With the options weighed, the Brazilian agrees to keep Russell out. It's a considered decision, but invariably one that opens up another fork in the road within a matter of laps.

This time, it takes the form of his teammate. For Hamilton is behind Russell in sixth position, but among those two-stoppers on fresher tires. On lap forty-nine, with just four remaining, Russell finds his wing mirrors filled with the reflection of the other Mercedes F1 car. At the same time, while Sainz is down, he's clung on to Hamilton's tail and is by no means out. It presents the strategists with an immediate problem to resolve. Should Russell yield to his teammate, despite feeling as if he lost out on their earlier encounter, or be allowed to defend his position and potentially risk the Ferrari stealing a march on them both? Out of nowhere, it seems, the team are faced with a dilemma loaded with multiple consequences. The discussion lasts for a lap, and the tension rises by the second.

"Swap position."

Toto Wolff might be convalescing at his Monaco residence, but the instruction from the Team Principal over the tactics channel confirms he's entirely engaged in the race. As ever, since lights out, Wolff has played an active role in discussions with McMillan and Da Silva, seeking clarity of thinking behind strategic options. In this case, with Sainz inside the DRS zone behind Hamilton, the switch had become an inevitable call. With the strategists on board, it's executed with immediate effect.

Within the closing laps, Sainz delivers the move on Russell that Wolff feared he would make on both cars. It's disappointing but at least not a double blow. While media attention focuses on the Verstappen win, sealing the 2023 Constructors' Championship for Red Bull, the Mercedes F1 strategists are left to digest a P5 and a P7 finish for Hamilton and Russell respectively.

"I did not expect so much opposition to stopping George," says Da Silva over the tactics channel.

"From me?" asks McMillan, but the exchange is lost amid procedural chatter across all the channels as the cars come into parc fermé.

For Mercedes F1, it's not a race that sees champagne corks popping in the garage or the RSR. Nevertheless, the team achieved their objective of taking at least one position from Ferrari. Points are the priority, and yet when Wolff addresses the race team ahead of the driver debrief, he's clearly mindful of the manner in which they arrived at this outcome. "Racing each other like we did—in the beginning pushing the other guy wide—sets the tone for the rest of the race," he says, unhappy that his drivers had potentially cost the team points. "I didn't like it."

As the RSR powers down, from data tiles on the big screen to personnel in need of a stretch, Joey McMillan and Leo Da Silva are in agreement that the on-track relationship between the two Mercedes F1 drivers is beyond their control. Both are quite at peace with Wolff's call. He simply voiced the decision they'd just reached themselves, says McMillan. Within the hour, during the debrief, it's striking how readily both Hamilton and Russell step up to take responsibility for the cause of the boss's displeasure. They seem genuinely respectful of one another, and united in wanting to crack the car that continues to challenge them.

"I'm not going to apologize for racing, but with the struggles I had it was more aggressive than normal," admits Hamilton. "George has always been fair throughout."

"I'm totally on board with all of this," says Russell, who returns the compliment about his teammate. "The one-stop wasn't optimal in terms of race pace, but I'm glad we did it. We just need to make this car faster."

"I know you're working toward something better for next year," adds Lewis, addressing the wider team, and now it seems the pair are speaking for each other, "but it has to be drastically different. It can't be the sister car to this one. Or the evil twin to last year's," he says, finishing on a note that draws both grim amusement and agreement from the team.

With the debrief concluded, I join McMillan as he collects his vape pen and makes his way through the building toward a side exit. He seems satisfied with how the strategy played out as well as the fact that the drivers have headed off any wider complications. What bothers him, I sense, is the postrace remark from his colleague at the track in Suzuka.

"It was only ever going to be fifty-fifty," he says of Russell's chances of beating Sainz, as if he needs to justify it out loud. In the same breath, McMillan recognizes that the one-stop strategy denied Russell the opportunity on fresh tires late in the race to take a point for the fastest lap. As an F1 tactician, when faced with the outcome of a call, there must be times when hindsight is hard to handle. It's a weird science, after all; one that doesn't just call upon detailed analysis, precision planning, and execution but also sometimes subjective decisions, an appetite for risk, and ultimately the desire to win.

"There will always be nuances like this," he acknowledges, and returns to the fact that every decision the strategists make is shaped by the circumstances at the time. It's another reason,

McMillan tells me, why he favors the circle map and the visual approximation of a lap. "We've always got sixty seconds to talk about things. That's loads of time for us."

Just before the race, having operated on Japan Standard Time all weekend, a perky McMillan admitted that he is one of those people on the team who deploys a strategy spreadsheet for sleep. Effectively a bedtime bar chart, it incrementally brings him into the right time zone over the course of the previous seven days. As we step out into a service area to find the sun behind the tree line, I am genuinely unsure if it's dawn or dusk.

McMillan draws deeply on his vape pen. As he does so, his mobile phone chimes. It's a message from Da Silva, trackside in Suzuka. It could be that the nicotine hits home at the same time, for as McMillan turns the screen to face me after reading it himself, a weight seems to lift from his shoulders.

Maybe you were right about staying out.

"Leo and I do butt heads," says McMillan, "but the beauty of our relationship is that we're always honest. We'll review what happened, and probably come to the conclusion that it was down the middle."

CHAPTER NINE

THE NARRATIVE DRIVE

The United States Grand Prix
Circuit of the Americas, Austin
October 20–22, 2023

This weekend's F1 rodeo takes place in Texas. It's only 9 a.m. on Saturday but already the sun rides wild across a big, open sky above the Circuit of the Americas (COTA). The brightness is more intense than the heat. Given that we're in cowboy country, amid rolling terrain and farmland to the southeast of the city of Austin, a Stetson makes perfect sense. It's not lost on several drivers in the paddock, notably the former Mercedes F1 driver Valtteri Bottas, who somehow makes it work along with a neckerchief and aviators.

Worn without the same carefree panache, but simply for practical purposes, many race fans have also gone with the state's signature wide-brimmed headwear. Ahead of today's Sprint race, preceded by the qualifying Shootout, the grandstands and grass banks are packed. Most popular of all is the vantage point overlooking Turn 1, a boldly steep climb from the start line 200 meters back, with a blind crest and a drop left into a stunning sequence of high-speed curves. It's the kind of layout that kids build from Scalextric using cushions to stack up the track, and here that same ambition has given rise to a compelling spectacle. It's also a challenge for drivers as they hit the thirty-meter incline at a speed close to 300 kph and experience significant compression into their seats. The work of renowned circuit designer Hermann Tilke sometimes invites criticism for playing it too safe. Since Formula 1 arrived for its inaugural race in 2012, however, the heavy braking zones and wide run-off areas around this anticlockwise track have produced gripping racing.

COTA isn't just rated by fans but also by the drivers. Starting tomorrow's big race from the third grid slot, having missed out on pole by just 0.14 seconds, Lewis Hamilton is hoping to make up lost ground following his first-corner DNF at the previous race in Qatar. With George Russell lining up in fifth place, and a final update for the season that has at last brought some stability to the car's rear end, the mood in the Mercedes F1 camp feels different this weekend. The team are realistic about their immediate fortunes, with Red Bull's dominance resulting in Max Verstappen claiming his third drivers' title in the desert just a fortnight earlier. Now the race is on for second place in the constructors' fight. It's a step down on the podium from the prize chased by every team, but for Mercedes F1 it's also a long way up from that dark time in the garage at the opening race in Bahrain. With Ferrari behind them in third place, and gaining ground with their resurgent form, it's shaping up to be the story that closes the season.

Which explains why Mercedes F1 photographer Sebastian Kawka finds himself jostling for position among a greater media presence than usual awaiting Hamilton's arrival. When the seven-times world champion does appear, sporting a casual top and jeans by team partner Tommy Hilfiger, the Mercedes F1 photographer is quick to capture the moment with a volley of shots. He knows that the driver waits for nobody just as he sometimes forgoes team apparel for his paddock entry in favor of high fashion.

Sebastian Kawka is one of several photographers and "content creators" tasked with the visual documentation of the organization's activities, not just during race weekends but also throughout the year. Alongside his colleagues who deal with the written and spoken word, Kawka's role is to work with the visual element of the narrative maelstrom that swirls around Formula 1 both on and off the track. The spotlight is intense, as is the surrounding chatter. It can transform the paddock into a hotbed rife with drama and politics from which often baseless rumors quickly solidify into seemingly immutable facts. In a sport that demands focus and not distraction, and with teams backed by huge investments in terms of money, time, and energy, clarity is critical. In Formula 1, even reputation can have an impact on performance.

With the shots he's been tasked to capture safely embedded in the memory card of his digital camera, Kawka hurries to his back-room desk behind the hospitality suite. Later, the most compelling images will be shared across the team's social media platforms as well as with relevant partner sponsors and in response to media enquiries. It's just one small element in a wide and often frenetic range of activities undertaken by the trackside communications team as the Mercedes F1 story unfolds over the race weekend.

The challenge, I discover, is in defining their relationship with that narrative.

When I ask if they're leading, chasing, shaping, or curating it—for consumption both internally within the organization and by its partners as well as by the wider world—I'm met with mildly pained expressions as if it's not that easy to pin down. Ultimately, it falls to Bradley Lord, Mercedes F1's long-standing Chief Communications Officer, to bring it all together by recognizing first and foremost that the story is governed by what happens on the track. "It's like we're on a boat," he begins. "We don't have control of the flow, but we can steer a course. We want to avoid the rocks but also make it exciting for our passengers."

With a trim beard and solid handshake, Lord carries the charm and authority of a regimental officer liked by both the troops and top brass. He's good company; articulate and quick-witted. Lord points out that those on board for the ride represent everyone from hardcore race fans to casual viewers, all of whom must be addressed in appropriate language and tone. He also suggests that the first interpretation of the story falls to the race commentators, in broadcast media and then in print. This requires the communications team to have a keen ear for nuance and detail and an ability to place a hand on the tiller before the vessel veers into danger. With potential for the wrong word to spill across to social media and then both warp and amplify, Lord aims to address the source before it spreads. "We might need to react to something that's been said," he continues, "correct a mistake or just change the perception."

Lord cites the 2021 title climax in Abu Dhabi as a case in point, when Max Verstappen snatched the World Drivers' Championship from Lewis Hamilton and the boat effectively entered white water rapids. "We stayed very quiet for a very long time," he says of the aftermath, in which Lord sought to maintain a calm presence in the face of a crisis. "It was still evolving, and we were putting in protest documents and waiting for adjudications. We also needed to reach a settled and considered view of the situation." Ultimately, after the FIA agreed to a commission looking into improving the rules, and recognizing the unlikely prospect of a successful appeal, Mercedes F1 opted to pursue victory on the track and not in court. *We have always been guided by our love of this sport,* read the official team statement a day after the race, *and we believe that every competition should be won on merit . . . Max, we congratulate you and your entire team. We look forward to taking the fight to you on the track next season.* In a carefully constructed communiqué, Lord had put Formula 1 first. Ever since, perhaps drawn by the team's dignified response to a perceived injustice, Mercedes F1 have enjoyed an enduring groundswell of support from fans around the world. "The ability to find the right message, the right nuance, and the right words is powerful," he says.

On other occasions, when it seems as if the boat is set to be swept away, Lord and his communications team know when to get on the horn. A case from this season, I suggest, is the high-speed tangle between Lewis Hamilton and George Russell during qualifying in Barcelona. The clash of wheels on the home straight forced Hamilton onto the grass and immediately triggered pundits into proclaiming that it marked the start of a war for supremacy between the two drivers.

In reality, there was no inter-cockpit conflict. The team had simply been guilty of what Shov described at the time as "inelegant coordination" when it came to informing each driver of the available space on track. The incident looked bad, but also occurred as Bradley Lord served as Sky Sports F1's on-call team representative for the session. As a result, when the commentators came to him for insight, Lord was able to present the facts on air in the immediate aftermath—even if it didn't paint the race team in the best light—and defuse what could have become the talking point of the weekend.

"The story of division is way more compelling than the story of harmony. So if anyone can stand up a story of potential division, it will happen," says Lord, who joined Mercedes F1 in 2011 having worked as an interface between media and motorsport throughout his earlier career. Fluent in both French and German, he's an eloquent communicator who has learned his craft from decades of experience. Lord downplays it as a niche field. Either way, he has an instinctive appreciation of the value of reputation in motorsport. "We can't make the car faster in what we do in communications, but we can reduce distraction for the team," he continues. "That's a net gain, because it means minds are focused on the job and not on annoying headlines or whatever it may be."

As well as working with the media, the Mercedes F1 communications team recognize how fans can also shape the narrative. They also play a pivotal role in the story. With several hours to go before the Sprint Shootout, I join Rosa Herrero Venegas, Senior Public Relations Manager, on a roaming assignment around the paddock periphery. She carries a folded umbrella with her, despite the clear sky and searing heat, as she has done for years at every race weekend around the world come rain or shine. Along with her tumbling dark hair pinned back by sunglasses, the umbrella makes Herrero Venegas easily recognizable from a distance, and its primary use will become clear later in the race weekend.

For now, our first port of call is a row of garages behind the side entrance to the paddock. This weekend, it's home to the teams contending in a new race series for young female drivers. F1 Academy is in its debut season. Here at COTA, in an important step, this final fixture will appear on the timetable as part of the United States Grand Prix. Managing Director Susie Wolff has grand designs for the series as both a springboard and showcase for new talent and ultimately as a catalyst for raising female participation in motor racing. Wolff might be familiar to *Drive to Survive* fans as the wife of the Mercedes F1 Team Principal, but she is in fact a former professional racing driver of note with just the right credentials for her current role. After rising through the ranks in Formula Renault, Formula 3, and DTM, Wolff served as an F1 reserve for Williams. She drove in both test and practice sessions during the 2014 and 2015 seasons, and in doing so became the first woman to take part in an F1 race weekend in twenty-two years. With just a handful of female drivers preceding her in the history of the sport, Susie Wolff is on a mission to open up the road ahead for more women in motorsport.

This morning, as a show of support, George Russell has arranged to drop in to meet the current crop of racers. From next season, all ten F1 teams will be backing a driver and featuring their livery on the car. The lineup and pairings are yet to be announced, but as the 2024 F1 Academy season is set to become an official support race during a selection of grand prix weekends, it's an exciting time for Wolff and her young hopefuls.

Herrero Venegas and I arrive just as the Mercedes F1 driver sweeps in with the F1 Academy boss. Finding himself surrounded by drivers keen to engage with him, Russell represents exactly where they aspire to be in the coming years.

Amid the media scrum for pictures, Russell, in his white team T-shirt and dark glasses, is both encouraging and entertaining in the drivers' company. The photographers swarm around the gathering, seeking out the best shot, which is when Herrero Venegas steps forward and quietly turns Russell around by ninety degrees. I look at her quizzically as she returns, aware that the photographers have all now rotated accordingly to keep his face in the frame. "He was in front of a banner for a brand that conflicts with one of our sponsors," explains Herrero Venegas. "I do it all the time," she adds, which explains why Russell didn't question the steering.

From then on, I watch his short tour of the garage through a different lens. Frankly, there are banners everywhere, and I leave with a keen appreciation of such an eye for detail. Team partners are important to Mercedes F1. Understandably, they want to see returns on every level of their investment. It means that if a driver goes on a side quest to the central storyline of the weekend, as Russell has just done here, then it falls to the communications people to be sure that it still contributes to the overall team narrative.

As Russell completes his tour, leaving the F1 Academy drivers with the prospect of meeting Lewis Hamilton later in the day, I look around to find that my communications companion is already on her way to the next assignment. I hurry to catch up, aware that Herrero Venegas—born to a Chilean mother and Spanish father, raised in Germany and British-based—is constantly on the move throughout a race weekend. In a team that measures time in milliseconds, she's not far off such exacting standards.

"Where are we heading now?" I ask.

"The track," she says simply, handing me another lanyard to accompany my paddock pass.

The new card around my neck won't open doors, but it does permit me to follow Herrero Venegas through a gap in the debris fencing closely guarded by security. I step out onto the edge of the home straight in front of the grandstand. There, we join one of several small groups of fans clutching crash helmets. All of them look electrified by excitement and absolutely terrified. At this moment, some half-dozen high-performance road cars are tooling around the track. The drivers decelerate after the final turn, maintaining a parade formation in their growling chargers before each peeling off to stop in front of a group. The Mercedes-AMG GT that pulls in beside us features the regular F1 safety car maestro, Bernd Mayländer, behind the wheel. He peers through the passenger side window and smiles at the assembled gathering.

"I think I'm going to be sick," one girl says to her partner, and though the pair can't stop grinning it looks like he might beat her to it.

This is the Pirelli Hot Laps program. It's an opportunity for a select few to ride in a supercar with a professional driver behind the wheel, and for car manufacturers involved in F1 to showcase their road vehicles. With Mercedes-AMG providing a car for the

175

weekend's prerace program, alongside McLaren and Aston Martin, Rosa Herrero Venegas is present to ensure Mayländer's passengers-in-waiting enjoy this supercharged experience courtesy of the team.

Notably, these individuals aren't associated with sponsors. The Mercedes F1 contingent are simply racing enthusiasts whom Herrero Venegas has picked out from an earlier roam around the public areas of the circuit. They might have been wearing a team cap or T-shirt, or even just a bright smile or a look of wide-eyed wonder. For in her mission to engage with Mercedes F1 fans of all ages and backgrounds, this is someone who enjoys nothing more than inviting ordinary people to become part of the team's story. With her help, even proposals of marriage have taken place in front of the pit garage. As Mayländer takes off for a lap of the track that his passenger won't forget, Herrero Venegas looks on well aware of what an experience like this can mean.

In 2019, shortly before the Spanish Grand Prix, a terminally ill five-year-old boy called Harry Shaw sent a video message to Lewis Hamilton wishing him good luck. The sweet, seventeen-second clip came to the driver's attention, and he couldn't help but feel moved by Harry's plight. On winning the race, an emotional Hamilton stood on the podium and dedicated the victory to the boy. "The team had sent him a few bits like a signed cap and T-shirt," Herrero Venegas says, "but I thought we could do better."

With Hamilton's support, and time sadly not on the little boy's side, she and several team members rushed back from the circuit to the UK to put a plan into place. The next day, having been transferred from hospital to the family home in Surrey for his final days, Harry was carried outside in his father's arms to find Hamilton's car on the drive. To complete the surprise, Harry was even presented with the trophy his hero had won that weekend.

Even now, as Herrero Venegas tells me about the logistics, time and energy that the team put into making it happen, her eyes shine with emotion. Moments like this, and the many other charitable acts that she pursues for the team, quite clearly mean a great deal to her. She comes into her own as someone with a gift for welcoming people in from the outside and making them feel at home. As Mayländer's Mercedes-AMG GT reappears from the hot lap, the young woman riding shotgun climbs out looking both stunned and elated. Smiling, Herrero Venegas is on hand to return her gently to reality.

In terms of support, I wonder what the team means to someone who spends so much time on the road each season. "Everyone looks out for each other, which is a nice feeling. If you need anything people will always help." Overseeing the next passenger switch, Herrero Venegas tells me how Ferrari are always warm and courteous to her after she handed out ice creams to the Mercedes F1 crew one race weekend and then shared the rest with their Italian rivals. "We're a family away from home," she says simply.

"And how about your real family?"

"We're very close and I miss them a lot," she replies at once, and right there I understand why it's so important for her to reach out to those who believe in the team and then help them to feel valued. In watching this side of her communications work, I have come to consider Rosa Herrero Venegas to be Mercedes F1's ambassador for kindness, which is a race story in its own right.

Later that afternoon, with a stubbornly intense sun over the circuit, Adam McDaid gathers in the cool of the garage wings to watch the Sprint race. Standing in front of a screen showing the F1 broadcast feed, he dons a headset to monitor race team communications. With his phone in hand, he prepares to go to work.

As Senior Media Manager, much of McDaid's race weekend is spent as the conduit between the team and journalists, television and film crews. It's by no means a straightforward role. From sup-plying facts and comments for media stories to stripping back rumors, running press conferences and overseeing briefings and interviews, McDaid is one of those team members who never stays still in the paddock for more than a minute. He's also searingly passionate about Mercedes F1, prone to expressing it in the heat of the action like a soccer fan in the North Stand, and deeply knowledgeable about the sport. During sessions on the track, this combination of fire and insight makes him ideally placed to pro-vide race updates, clarity, and comment on several key WhatsApp groups. It's a combination of internal communications, with one large group dedicated to a broad range of stakeholders in the team, including representatives from key departments, and external messaging to media players should it be required in the moment.

Given the solitary hour of practice we have very little tire degrad-ation information, he begins, addressing the internal group via the keypad on his phone. *The Sprint will be useful for adding that knowl-edge ahead of tomorrow's race.*

Like mechanical greyhounds braced in their traps, the cars are lined up in grid position. Hamilton sits in P3, his confidence emboldened by a floor upgrade that could also serve as a test bed for next year's car. Russell is back in P11, having taken a three-place grid penalty for unintentionally blocking Charles Leclerc on a push lap in the Sprint Shootout. Despite the setback, on lights out both cars are in contention with their immediate rivals, with Hamilton claiming second and Russell into eighth by the time the pack come full circle in this nineteen-lap race.

"C'mon, George," urges McDaid in between updates. Having climbed four places, Russell prepares to attack Oscar Piastri. On his tail coming out of the long back straight on lap three, he sweeps around the outside of the McLaren to claim P7. It's a bold move, but McDaid spots that the Mercedes F1 car is just outside track limits even before the stewards place the overtake under investigation. "You could say Piastri forced him wide but I doubt they'll see it like that," he tells me. Sure enough, as Hamilton breaks from the rest of the pack to chase Verstappen, the stewards hand his teammate a five-second penalty.

"Harsh," mutters a technician at a workbench under the monitor, and McDaid doesn't disagree. "It's one thing in a full-distance race," he complains. "In a Sprint, five seconds can make a huge difference."

The Sprint race might be in its infancy, with opinion divided about the format, but if the aim is to deliver a quick hit of racing action it's certainly over in no time. *P2 for Lewis and an F1 Sprint podium,* writes McDaid, having provided concise, informative updates from the team's perspective for an audience ranging from trackside personnel hosting commercial partners to driver management and brand representatives associated with Mercedes F1. It's quite a responsibility, as are the clarifications and corrections he often has to put out to race commentators, pundits, and journalists during a session to keep the story honest.

"It's not about being controlling," he says afterward, when I ask about the line he takes both internally and externally. "It can't be PR nonsense because people see through that." As we talk, I come to appreciate Bradley Lord's assertion that the action on the track is central to the narrative drive. The communications team can only work with the material as it plays out lap after lap and just serve to bridge the gaps. "If we didn't, people would fill them with their own takes and biases or whatever, based on 15 percent of the story. We're here to provide the other 85 percent." At the same time, McDaid concedes that the truth is often not as entertaining as stories aimed at grabbing headlines. "People watch sport for incidents and drama," he agrees. "Our job isn't to minimize interest. We want people to root for our team because hopefully we're successful but also because we stand for things that chime with them."

In his early thirties, with a dark beard and head of hair that looks like he's been out in the frost, McDaid lives and breathes Formula 1, with a side interest in cricket should it happen to be on a laptop screen in the garage. As well as responding to the turn of events on the track, McDaid also seeks to set up stories that reflect what he calls "pride values." "We'll always be thinking about opportunities to put our people forward to tell them," he says, citing a piece with Head of Race Strategy Rosie Wait, after tire wear concerns at the Qatar Grand Prix saw last-minute rule changes to mandatory stint lengths. It could have played havoc with the race plan had Wait not pulled an all-nighter to rewrite the computer code behind the simulations that ultimately helped the team to shape their strategy. "Rosie showed absolute determination," says McDaid, "and we wanted to share that with the wider world."

Like Bradley Lord, his group boss and mentor, McDaid must be prepared to react as well as act in steering the story of the team. No two race weekends are the same, and he's well aware that the inherent danger of motorsport can give rise to an unthinkable narrative.

"When Romain Grosjean crashed in Bahrain 2020, it wasn't immediately clear what car had gone into the barrier," says McDaid, his voice softening as he recalls his experience of witnessing one of the most horrifying, fiery accidents in Formula 1 history from the garage at Williams where he worked at the time. "There had been a moment as the car went off where it looked like one of ours. Until it became clear who it was and that he'd survived, I feared I was about to deal with one of the worst moments of my career."

It's a sobering account, and one that serves to regularly remind

McDaid that on the narrative front line, representing a Formula 1 team, he must be prepared for all eventualities. Messaging of any kind brings a sense of responsibility, even when communicating updates on a session that proved encouraging for Mercedes F1. "There are ex–racing drivers in that group and people new to the sport," he says on signing out of the session following the Sprint race. "I need to convey information that's useful rather than hit them with everything that's going on."

When McDaid leaves the garage, the brightness of the day is beginning to dim at last. So too is the activity on the walkway now that events on the track have drawn to a close. Making his way back to his desk, to consult with Shov on the nightly report to the factory that occurs through every race weekend, McDaid seems to be on nodding and smiling terms with almost everyone. It reflects the range of contacts he has in his role as well as the five years he spent at Williams before joining Mercedes F1. In that time, he worked with George Russell in his first years in Formula 1. In some ways, the pair are peers in this upper echelon of motorsport. They certainly have a healthy working relationship. As is evident the next morning on the freeway out of Austin for the circuit.

Just a few kilometers beyond the city limits, the SUV I'm traveling in alongside members of the communications team overtakes the car carrying the Mercedes F1 star. "Hey, George!" yells McDaid, winding down the side window to salute him glee-fully with his middle finger. Russell might be concealed behind a smoked-out window in the back seat, but the fact that his trainer, Aleix Casanovas, can be seen grinning from the front passenger seat speaks volumes. The pair travel everywhere together, after all. In response, after our SUV slots in front of the car amid much laughter, Russell's man behind the wheel takes the next oppor-tunity to signal and then calmly pulls ahead of us. "He's in no mood to yield to anyone," says McDaid approvingly on what is Russell's 100th race weekend as a Formula 1 driver. "Good man."

The team bring some confidence into this race day. With the floor upgrade delivering to expectation, both cars have performed strongly over the weekend. Nobody is expecting a sea change in performance, but after the challenges this season has presented, people seem to be genuinely enjoying themselves.

From the desk space hidden behind the hospitality suite, where McDaid and his communications colleagues are based, the sound of a birthday celebration for a team member spills over the partition wall. As slices of cake appear on napkins, delivered by personnel keen to make sure everyone shares in the moment, it begins to feel like this race might mark another significant occasion for Mercedes F1. If Hamilton can capitalize on his P3 starting position, with a car that for once feels like it's coming to him, it could earn the team precious points in their fight with Ferrari for second place in the Constructors' Championship.

This morning, in the buildup to the race, the social media wing of the Mercedes F1 communications operation has uploaded several posts to the team's platforms. One is a dynamic montage of Lewis Hamilton and George Russell meeting the F1 Academy teams. Another captures a moment in the pit lane as Susie Wolff hitches a ride on Toto's electric scooter and jokes about his driving ability. The content is contrasting in nature, typical of posts through the season that range from slick coverage of the cars and drivers to short, daft challenges that frequently rope in team personnel. Across the board, each offering is carefully produced and purposely pitched at audiences from X to Instagram, Facebook, YouTube, and TikTok. Boasting millions of followers on multiple platforms, Mercedes F1's social media presence is not to be taken as lightly as some of the posts. It's also treated with the utmost seriousness by the man on the ground orchestrating both tone and voice.

I've arranged to meet Daniel Paddock, Mercedes F1's Creative Social Lead, at the top of the fire escape behind the engineers' room. At every race weekend, with platforms to populate with content that involves working closely with the team's photographers, videographers, and content creators, he's constantly glued to a phone or laptop screen.

This rare break for Paddock, who has taken himself and a coffee to a cool spot out of the sun, seemed an appropriate time to explore his work. It's also a chance for me to visit another building in the team's allocation from the circuit that houses the engineers, team boss, and drivers.

"What's wrong with these steps?" On his way out to the garage, Evan Short has just skipped down the flight from the briefing room as if every step burned his feet. He stops at the bottom and invites me to guess. "It's been driving the engineers *crazy.*"

I consider the metal staircase. Nothing registers at first, but then I don't immediately see things as forensically as these people. With this in mind, I pay closer attention to detail, namely the screws designed to lock each footplate to the frame. Judging by their skewed appearance and battered heads, I realize they have been hammered in. "Why?" decries the Trackside Electronics Leader, pressing his palm to his forehead. "Who would do that?"

On my way up, I find I can't stop looking at the workmanship. I'm so focused on the janky screws that it takes me a moment to realize people are waiting for me at the top so they can come down. It's Prince Harry and a small entourage, along with two NASA astronauts in agency jumpsuits. These guys are from the Artemis space mission to return humans to the Moon, their calling signposted by patches emblazoned across their breast pockets. I hurry to clear the steps, exchanging nods and polite smiles with them all.

A minute later, when I find Paddock on the fire escape and

share my encounter with some of Mercedes F1's guests for the day, he doesn't remark on the wild pairing of royalty and rocket men. He just wants to know whether a team photographer was following them. A forward-thinking, almost restless member of the team's social media group, with a bold mustache growing thicker through the season, Paddock doesn't like to miss a moment. As I settle beside him on the top step, he seems visibly relieved to know the tour that their notable guests are enjoying will produce material to feed his different channels. "We map out a plan before every race weekend," he says, explaining how he manages a steady stream of content tailored to different platforms. "But then you can't brief for everything."

A scroll through any of the Mercedes F1 accounts doesn't just reveal a broad scope of material. The level of engagement from users is significant, with posts of all stripes drawing a sustained chorus of responses. Having helped grow the team's largest platforms, Instagram and TikTok, by upward of 10 million each since he came into the role in 2017, Paddock has a nuanced understanding of how to connect with the audience. The result is one that arguably doesn't immediately seem on-brand for a pedigree team such as the Silver Arrows.

On the Friday ahead of the opening race of the season in Bahrain, Paddock posted a video skit to TikTok. It opens with a shot from the pit lane of the mechanics working on the #44 car, with a caption stating that Toto Wolff had asked them to take the platform more seriously. Accompanied by the kind of tinkling chiptune soundtrack you'd expect from a vintage arcade machine, the camera then pulls back and upward to reveal the overlay of a giant cat looming over the garage. Throughout the three days at the circuit, despite its trivial nature, the upload proved inexorably popular. To date, it has been viewed more than 22 million times. "That was our worst weekend of the year," says Paddock ruefully, referencing the realization across the team that the W14 car was off the pace, "with the highest engaged piece of content we'd ever made."

Such a commanding reach reflects the fact that social media plays a central role in Mercedes F1's approach to communications. It's drawn a new, younger audience to the team. The lighthearted, quick-fire content is underpinned by the serious business of bringing fans together behind their efforts on the track, but is it all about a race for likes and followers? Paddock believes it's far more than just a numbers game.

"We want to be the most engaging team," he says, "which means the team that has the best story. Ultimately, it's an extension of what these guys are doing," he adds, gesturing toward the engineers' room where the drivers are currently in a briefing. "How they perform sets the agenda in terms of what the message needs to be. We just go about it in our own way. We're trying to explain not just what happens, but how the team *feels*."

Paddock sees a pointed correlation between the downturn in the team's fortunes over the last two seasons and the upswing in humor present across the platform. "We had to reset expectation," he says. "We never sat down and decided we needed to be funny. We just found out very quickly what worked at that time. It's like a test session with the car. You find out straightaway whether it's good or bad. It's the same with a post when you look at the response, and in this case it was positive. Obviously we weren't happy with our performance on track, but with no results to offer, people recognized why we were leaning into it."

Paddock speaks candidly and with conviction. While deadly serious in his efforts to tell the Mercedes F1 story in a contemporary medium, he possesses a hyperactive sense of humor that regularly reduces team members to fits of laughter. He can be relentless with his quick-fire wit, rarely letting up, which makes him instinctively attuned to mining short attention spans on social media for maximum appeal. He's comfortable striking a balance across the channels between being entertaining and informative, knowing when to shift the tone appropriately, and recognizes the disconnection that would occur between fans and the team if he failed to acknowledge reality. The playful side of Paddock's work is not an invitation to laugh *at* the team but *with* them, offering some light relief from the huge operation going on behind the scenes to return to title contention on the track. Ultimately, it has a unifying effect.

In many ways, the work of the social media team brings character to the Mercedes F1 story. This weekend, Paddock has printed and framed an AI rendering of Toto Wolff in the style of a 1990s college yearbook photograph. Paddock plans to plant it on Wolff's desk and quietly film his response. "If the team boss is OK for me to do that then he must be a pretty chilled-out guy," he reasons. "It shows a very different type of Toto than perhaps you see on the television every race weekend when things haven't been going well. In the same way, when the moment is right we put him out there in a leadership role."

As Paddock's time-out from his phone screen expires, I'm left with the impression of a man who saw an opportunity to speak to fans at a challenging time and give them every reason to get behind the team. Everyone is working flat out toward a new chapter when a positive performance leads the narrative once again, and yet no doubt those cat, boss, and driver memes will continue to play a role in propelling the story.

The next time I see the social media team in action, from the pit garage later that afternoon, the race is under way. There, his colleague Tom Dodd is providing coverage of the action to the Mercedes F1 X account. Adam McDaid is also present, his WhatsApp group in hand, as Lewis Hamilton puts on a barnstorming show. From the outset he's in podium contention, even after Verstappen has worked his way to the front from sixth on the grid. Clearly in tune with the car this weekend, Hamilton fights hard to topple Leclerc, who started in pole, which leaves him to fight with Lando Norris in the McLaren for second place.

"Let's go, Lewis . . ."

McDaid barely blinks as he watches the action on the monitor. Like Dodd, he breaks only to punch in an update to the group. He has a seasoned eye for the race story as it takes shape, condensing key moments into dispatches that foreground the team's fortunes on the track. Like any form of sports commentary, it's harder than it looks, but McDaid makes it seem effortless.

"Oh, *big* send!" he yells when Hamilton makes his move on Turn 1, only for Norris to draw level as they drop into Turn 2. "Don't fucking hit him," he growls at the McLaren driver, visibly relieved when Hamilton claims track position and with it second place.

Throughout the race, with George Russell holding station in fifth, both Mercedes F1 drivers endure a challenging ride. From on-foot experience, I know that the track surface is far from optimal as a result of long-term subsidence issues. The layout might be fast-flowing but it's undulating, with scars in the tarmac where cars have bottomed out. As Hamilton pulls away from the McLaren in the final phase of the race, and even works to close the gap on the seemingly untouchable Verstappen, I note his yellow helmet rocking and bobbing excessively in the cockpit. That sparks frequently fly in the wake of the W14, as the car "bottoms out" on the track, makes it clear just how low the team are running the car this weekend. While the setup aims to increase ground effect, the payoff must be an uncomfortable experience in the race seat. It can only add to Hamilton's relief when he crosses the line just 2.25 seconds behind the Red Bull in a car that seems to have come alive at last. It also gives Mercedes F1 something to celebrate, as is evidenced by an outpouring of team members from the garage to parc fermé in front of the podium.

Rosa Herrero Venegas hangs back from the crush barrier between the paddock personnel and the cars as they pull in. It's a scrum, but above all the Texan sun is beating down on this exposed strip of pit lane. We're going to be here for the next twenty minutes as the top three driver interviews take place, followed by the trophy ceremony and champagne celebrations, which is why Herrero Venegas has unfurled her umbrella. That's not the reason why she carries it, however, even if it can be useful in both rain and shine. Its true purpose only becomes clear after Max Verstappen, Lewis Hamilton, and third-place finisher Lando Norris have climbed down from the podium. When the drivers next appear, popping out into the crowded paddock from the back of the FIA building, Hamilton is met by Herrero Venegas. His bodyguard is also on hand. Both are here to protect him in different ways.

The media pen is effectively a corral for F1 drivers. After the race they gather within this space defined by crush barriers, with broadcast crews jostling for position on the outside, and circulate from one radio or television interview to the next. Every driver must make themselves available, steered by team representatives to be sure that journalists don't stray in terms of times and subject matter. Ultimately, these chaperones serve as benign reminders that facts matter. George Russell, as P7 finisher, is already accounting for his race. This weekend he's accompanied by Mercedes F1 Communications Manager Charlotte Davies. As Russell answers questions in front of the camera, she stands just out of frame while recording it all on a pink iPhone that she holds aloft as her sword of truth.

In the same way, Herrero Venegas will have Lewis Hamilton's back under the camera lights. It's just first he has to reach the pen.

"Lewis . . . *Lewis!*"

The enthusiasm for the Mercedes F1 driver is intense. As soon as one fan calls his name it draws others. Within seconds there's a swarm, with photographers and camera crews in the mix, and finally Herrero Venegas deploys her umbrella for the purpose she intended. In one smooth move, as the minder keeps things moving, she wields the folded device like a guard rail between Hamilton and anyone who looks like they might get too close. At the same time, she and the driver swap a few words.

A moment later, with Hamilton inside the pen and answering questions from the media, she reveals that the quick exchange was the only chance she had to brief him. On this occasion, Herrero Venegas needed him to know the reason for a slower than expected pit stop. The timing had been picked up by the commentators, potentially refueling criticism of the team who must see through the season with the problematic pawls. As a result, Herrero Venegas has anticipated that he'll be questioned about it. "Lewis actually stopped long in the box," she says, which explains the delay, and indeed the driver is quick to accept responsibility when asked. It snuffs out what could have become a distracting narrative and frees up Hamilton to talk about the race on his own terms.

In this light, Herrero Venegas's trusty umbrella plays an important role in delivering the team's story. Without it, she would have struggled to snatch a few seconds to brief him. By her own admission, the umbrella only serves as a psychological barrier. It's by no means as physically effective as Hamilton's security detail, which makes it all the more impressive to learn that for years Herrero Venegas was in sole charge of his safe passage around the paddock.

"I used to run about and recce places," she says, reflecting on the time from the middle of the last decade when Hamilton's fame began to escalate toward the realm of global superstardom. "I'd look for alternative routes if I needed them, or ask the circuit if they could help me." As interest in the driver grew, so Herrero Venegas found her role became more physically challenging. She can reel off the times she's been accidentally hit in the face by cameras like a boxer recounting blows in the ring. "For so many people, when they see Lewis it's a one-time chance to get the shot or the autograph. They just lose their minds."

The tipping point for Herrero Venegas, when it arrived in 2018, took the form of a video shot on a phone by a Mercedes F1 mechanic from a balcony above the pit lane at the Monaco Grand Prix. She shows me the clip, as if no words can illustrate what she was facing, and she's right. The crowds surging uncontrollably around Hamilton and Herrero Venegas might be friendly fans and media, but frankly they look like a zombie horde and the pair in the middle seem lost. Shortly afterward, with the recruitment of a security presence, Herrero Venegas regained that precious space to equip Hamilton with the information he needed to account for his side of the race. "Lewis and I have learned how to deal with it together," she says of this one aspect of her job that has transformed beyond recognition. "I just try to stay out of the picture."

Within an hour, shortly after Hamilton has finished with the press conference for printed media, all such smiles, along with the team's good news story from the United States Grand Prix, will be entirely eclipsed.

Apparently we will be disqualified.

So reads the shocking news on the communications team's WhatsApp group.

Toto just telling Lewis.

Across the paddock, in the wake of a successful race weekend for the sport, the teams are packing up. In a week from now, Formula 1 will be racing in Mexico City, and so travel time is of the essence. With floodlights keeping the dusk at bay, the pit lane is congested with industrial-sized flight cases and forklift trucks. Mechanics in high-visibility "pack down" T-shirts are busy stripping the cars while the last of the guests drift along the paddock walkway for the exit gates. As news breaks in the form of an FIA decree that Lewis Hamilton has been stripped of his second-place finish, the Mercedes F1 communications team go into overdrive.

In the workspace behind the team's hospitality area, Bradley Lord and Adam McDaid sit opposite one another. With fingertips flying over their laptop keyboards, they barely blink in a bid to keep the ship from listing. "It's the plank," explains McDaid in a momentary break from the press release he's redrafting in the wake of the Hamilton ruling. "We were under."

In F1, downforce underpins performance. Dropping a car's ride height can strengthen the suction to improve grip and speed in corners, but there are limits to how low teams are allowed to go. In this view, the FIA requires a ten-millimeter-thick laminated composite plank to be fitted under each car from front to back. Some wear is acceptable. Indeed, those dramatic sparks are caused by integral metal inserts in the plank connecting with the ground. Ultimately, however, these inserts must measure a minimum of nine millimeters after the race.

A spot check on Hamilton's car, as well as Charles Leclerc's Ferrari, found both had exceeded the permitted tolerance.

"There had been some concern after qualifying that it was wearing more than expected," McDaid explains, before outlining how the engineers had lowered the ride height on Hamilton's car as far as they dared in the hunt for performance. The resulting plank wear wasn't just down to the bumpy track, however. There was also the fact that in a Sprint weekend only minimal changes are permitted to the car after Friday's qualifying session. Unable to lift the ride height, forfeiting some downforce but preserving the plank, Hamilton's team just had to hope that it would endure through Saturday and Sunday. Across the teams, such a restriction has been widely considered to be an unfortunate consequence of the new race format. This weekend, in an infringement measured by a single millimeter, two drivers paid the price. "We took a gamble and lost," McDaid says simply.

As the hospitality suite powers down, it takes with it some of the spark that had lit up the team all weekend. Inevitably, people are deflated. With both Mercedes F1 and Ferrari penalized, the fight for second place in the Constructors' Championship moves on from Texas without much change in the points. Still, there are positives to take away on the car development front. Things are moving in the right direction, even if they arguably went a fraction too far today. With George Russell promoted to P5 and a disarmingly upbeat Lewis Hamilton putting his head around the back-room door to wish everyone a good week, both drivers leave the circuit feeling motivated. In the immediate aftermath of the United States Grand Prix, however, and manifest in quotes gathered from the major characters by Lord and McDaid, there can be no excuses. *Others got it right where we got it wrong,* says Toto Wolff in the official statement that will be released later that evening by the team, *and there's no wiggle room in the rules. We need to take it on the chin, do the learning, and come back stronger next weekend.*

Despite the team's disappointment, the dismantling work continues at pace. As Bradley Lord heads out into the night to address questions from a waiting journalist, and remaining personnel clear their desks, one of the team's logistics guys arrives to start stacking chairs. He works the room methodically, leaving McDaid until last. Finally, with the team Wi-Fi set to go offline and every chair but one ready to roll, he braves asking.

McDaid is on the last paragraph of the release that will acknowledge the late turn of events. Like an F1 driver on the final corner of the race, there's no stopping him now. He's in a zone of his own making, seemingly oblivious to the fact that his workspace is on the way to becoming an empty shell. Without dragging his eyes from the screen, McDaid stands to let the guy take the chair. Only then does he seem to register what he's about to lose here and sits down again smartly.

"Give me one minute," he pleads, and with that he returns his focus to getting a revised story of Mercedes F1's race weekend over the line. It's one that had been packed with promise but now carries a twist in the tail.

CHAPTER TEN

MAN MACHINE

The Brazilian Grand Prix
Autódromo José Carlos Pace, São Paulo
November 3–5, 2023

Outside Toto Wolff's trackside office, at a circuit where he had taken the checkered flag for the team one year earlier, George Russell spreads his hands wide. "I need a cuddle," he pleads, not entirely seriously but under the circumstances it wouldn't hurt.

We're at the back end of the race weekend here in São Paulo. The Brazilian Grand Prix closes what has been a punishing tripleheader across the Americas that left the high drama of Austin, Texas for the rarefied air of Mexico City and then finishes here at an iconic track on the outskirts of another sprawling metropolis, São Paulo. It's been three weeks without a break and comes at the tail end of a long season. When teams talk about resilience in the sport, this is where it can count.

In the Mercedes F1 camp, after a weekend in South America that has fallen well short of expectation, Russell's jokey appeal seems to sum up the mood. Having come so far, not just from home but also in terms of performance progress in the last few races—notably a P2 finish for Hamilton in Mexico with an intact plank—everyone could do with a reassuring embrace. In any venture, it's only natural for a setback to trigger an emotional reaction. Even if it's just a sense of heaving disappointment across the team, it can have an impact.

So, how does a Formula 1 driver deal with what is effectively a healthy response without it playing out in their performance? In the cockpit, there can be no room for anything but supreme confidence and self-belief. Any kind of psychological or emotional blip could have a direct bearing on a driver's focus and ultimately their fortunes in the race, which simply cannot be allowed to happen. George Russell and Lewis Hamilton are often likened to machines, but clearly they're human like everyone else. Despite being alone behind the wheel, there's a good reason why both drivers are connected to an external support network dedicated to keeping them on track in every sense.

The Autódromo José Carlos Pace—a circuit commonly known as Interlagos after the local neighborhood—lies on a hillside to the southwest of São Paulo, some distance from the pockets of skyscrapers that vaguely define the commercial and financial center. From the first day of the race weekend, teams travel to the circuit in a series of small convoys. They also wear casual clothes and ride with a security officer in each vehicle. Over the years, some F1 personnel have been victims of armed roadside robberies. Wearing team gear, following familiar routes, they have made easy targets in this sprawling megalopolis with a socioeconomic spread to match. While many in the paddock feel such precaution is unnecessary, it's still a sobering reminder of the poverty issues in some quarters of this region. Given our privileged reason for being here, it's uncomfortable to parade out of the city in this way. That changes, however, as we pass through several favelas close to the circuit. Ramshackle streets are peppered with potholes and lined with shacks fronted by plastic chairs, but they're also heavily decorated with checkered flags and motorsport murals—notably cheery portraits of Brazil's racing god among mortals, the late Ayrton Senna, and the country's adopted F1 son, Lewis Hamilton. For we're in a city and country that is wildly passionate about every aspect of motorsport. When the lights go out, it's a great leveler. All that matters is the race.

Formula 1 first came to Interlagos in 1973. Over time, it's become a mainstay for good reason. The comparatively short 4.3-kilometer track is built into a hillside. It features gradient changes at almost every turn, a twisting middle section, overtaking opportunities aplenty and a long, swooping climb into the home straight that can spit drivers into wheel-to-wheel racing. In a humid, subtropical region that sees rain sweep in with little warning to mix things up, it's a venue that can deliver motor racing that is both thrilling and unpredictable.

Mercedes F1 have history here. In 2012, Michael Schumacher made an emotional farewell to the sport from the cockpit of his Silver Arrow. Six years later, at what is a prized race weekend in the calendar for every team, Lewis Hamilton and Valtteri Bottas secured the team's fifth consecutive constructors' title. While Hamilton has enjoyed three victories at Interlagos, as well as famously claiming his first World Drivers' Championship here in 2008, it's also a special place for George Russell, having taken his first F1 win in his maiden season with the team in 2022. As a result, in view of their strengthening form over recent races and despite the challenges of the last two seasons, Mercedes F1 inevitably bring a sense of expectation with them.

Arriving at the circuit ahead of the business of the weekend, fresh from his podium finish at the previous race, Lewis Hamilton is in a buoyant mood.

"You're still here!" The Mercedes F1 driver expresses mock surprise on running into Ryan Lewis, the team's Head of Client

Services. "You could be the new Bernie," he jokes, referencing the infamous former F1 rights owner and confounding nonagenarian Bernie Ecclestone. The poor guy he's just greeted is decades away from that age, but his relationship with the driver predates their time with the team, which makes it all the more amusing for them both. Hamilton claps him fondly on the shoulder on his way out. "You know I love you, really."

"I used to look after Lewis when he was racing karts," the Mercedes F1 man tells his colleagues afterward by way of explanation. "It was just him on track and me in the stands with a hot dog."

Like his teammate, George Russell is in relaxed form. Nursing his car to a P6 finish in Mexico had been frustrating for him, largely because of overheating brakes, but given the initial pace of the car that all seems to be behind him now. He's happy to pause briefly so fans can take selfies with him outside the swipe gates, even if he is tight for time. This weekend sees the final Sprint race of the year. With only one hour of practice before parc fermé, the engineers and drivers will be presented with pressing challenges. With this in mind Shov is prompt in opening the first briefing. As the conference call gets under way, hosted from a cramped room behind the garage, the Trackside Engineering Director begins by greeting everyone around the tables and also those logged in from the factories back in Brackley and Brixworth. Before he can proceed further, the #63 driver jumps in from over the airwaves. "I'll be thirty seconds," says Russell, having logged on via his phone; he's hardly late but is well aware that every second counts. "I just got held up in the paddock."

Achieving a solid base setup is key before it's baked in for the weekend. Having been caught out at COTA in Austin with plank wear during the last Sprint weekend, the team must nail the ride height for both cars. Tire degradation is also high on the agenda, faced as they are with old, abrasive tarmac that will require some running to understand. Then there is the question of optimizing the rear wing level. This plays an important role in generating the downforce that helps to press the car to the track. In effect, it's about finding the balance between grip (high downforce) and straight-line speed (low downforce). The nature of the circuit is a determining factor at Interlagos, where the first and third sectors are relatively fast but the middle sector snakes and turns. Here, the planted nature of a high-downforce setup might favor drivers on a single qualifying lap. It's just that any low-downforce rivals might make the most of the straights and come back at them in a race. Setting the wing is a mechanical, aerodynamic, and strategic alchemy of sorts. All of which means everyone on both sides of the garage must work through a formidable task list on limited time.

An army of engineers is responsible for the setup of an F1 car. Mechanical, aerodynamic, and electronics experts must work as one to optimize the vehicle for the track. When it comes to the human component in the Mercedes F1 #63 cockpit, however, there is just one individual whose role is to ensure the driver fires on all cylinders. Aleix Casanovas is qualified in a different way to the men and women attending the briefing. He doesn't concern himself with optimizing the car but its driver. In doing so, George Russell arguably spends more time with Casanovas than he does with his partner, Carmen Montero Mundt.

"Carmen comes to more races now," Casanovas says of the 26-year-old former investment banker, "which helps me because she understands him as an athlete. It also gives him someone else to talk to," he adds, before outlining the importance of communication as a tool to prepare Russell for the demands placed upon him as a driver.

Officially, the Catalan-born Casanovas is a performance coach. Not every driver on the grid works with one, but those who do consider them to be an essential part of the toolkit. For Casanovas, it's a broad role that goes way beyond talking a good game and delivering Russell to the track in peak physical condition. As he grabs breakfast in the hospitality suite while the driver is in the briefing, he comes across as a human engineer operating on a precision level. Casanovas doesn't speak in terms of heave and roll, traction and torque. Instead, this intensely passionate individual is fluent in the language of strength and conditioning, diet and psychology. Having worked with the driver for seven years, Casanovas has developed an intuitive understanding of what makes George Russell tick.

"I recognize how complex we are," he says, "and how little we know about ourselves." In this view, Casanovas takes a holistic approach to his work. "So many things impact upon performance, but much of it is connected. Take the gut and the central nervous system. We know that we have to eat well to work out or perform and that makes us feel better. It has a cascading effect. So if we can be healthy in one aspect of our lives, it has an impact elsewhere."

On a practical level, Aleix Casanovas is never far from his client. He moved to Monaco soon after Russell relocated to the principality and from there manages everything from his nutritional requirements to his mindset and workout routine. When it comes to physical fitness, an F1 driver must be able to endure the intense demands of high-speed racing in order to execute a precision drive and maintain concentration and focus. In particular, Casanovas aims to prepare Russell to withstand a cycle of gravitational forces every lap from rapid acceleration, deceleration and cornering. "The neck is probably the biggest factor," he says. "Not just in terms of strength but durability, because it has to sustain the load for a long period of time."

During a race season, the pair frequently travel together while a weekend at the circuit sees Casanovas at his side right up until the moment that Russell pulls out of the garage. From monitoring his fluid intake and body temperature to keeping him cool in hot or humid conditions—and even "micro training" exercises shortly before Russell gets behind the wheel to raise his heartbeat and prime response times—this is a performance coach who takes nothing for granted in preparing his driver to go racing.

Asked if there is any piece of the performance puzzle that is more significant than the others, Casanovas is unequivocal. "Sleep," he says. "It's king during race weekends, because in Formula 1 there is no consistency." For a sport that is always on the move through different time zones, paying no heed to our natural body clocks, Casanovas is well aware of the detrimental effect this can have on everything from mood and focus to energy levels. For a driver operating in margins measured in milliseconds, this could win or lose a race. That's why at every opportunity he seeks to minimize the disruption on Russell by making the transition from one circuit to the next as smooth as possible. "Humans can tolerate only one hour of change to their sleep routine per night. Any more than that can be a struggle," he explains. In smoothing each transition, Casanovas deploys a battery of aids from blue-light-blocking glasses (aiming to reduce eye strain and sleep disruption from exposure to artificial lighting) to switching Russell to his next-destination time zone from the moment he finishes a race. For the big jumps, Russell is permitted to sleep in. "It can be a huge challenge when we go to places like Australia or Japan," says Casanovas. "In those situations, I'd rather George slept for ten minutes extra than do a bit of mobility in the gym."

For a performance coach with so much influence over his driver's life, Casanovas knows how to let Russell breathe. Despite the intimacy of their working relationship, the Catalan's great skill is to create both physical and emotional space for him to maintain his independence. When pressed to explain his approach, Casanovas returns to his belief that communication is key. At the same time, he acknowledges that as a teenage driver in the early stages of his racing career Russell had to recognize the benefits of opening up about his thoughts and feelings.

"George is a complex but extremely smart individual," he says. "He understands that we need to overcome the stigma that men don't share emotions. But honestly in the first two years he wasn't willing to share many things. I needed to build his trust and that meant being patient. Now, we know each other really well."

In developing that aspect of the relationship, Casanovas calls upon the "sideline dad" for comparison. "You get the bad examples," he laughs. "The parents who yell and scream at their kids that they suck. Some tolerate it and end up being really good athletes, but generally it's not good for them. I feel you need to be supportive. You need to be there for that person and let them speak when they feel the time is right."

As he says this, I'm mindful of the heartbreaking last-lap ending to Russell's Singapore race this season. The driver had emerged physically unscathed from catching the barrier in his bid to overtake the McLaren of Lando Norris, and yet the emotional impact on him was evident.

"You can be the best sports psychologist in the world," says Casanovas, "but when that happens you just have to be there. In the beginning, you have to show them you care and that you're there with them. And listen a lot," he adds. "It's not a time to ask questions straight after a race because the answer is just something you want to hear."

No matter what has happened on the track, Aleix Casanovas has learned to wait before putting a performance into perspective with his driver. "The Monday is my listening time. On Tuesday, I can start asking some questions based on what he's said. Then, on Wednesday, I can address anything that I feel can be improved."

As an approach, it clearly works for George Russell. It allows the driver to come through what Casanovas describes as an emotional "hangover" after the adrenalized rush from the race and begin to process his own thoughts. In effect, he stops Russell from retreating inside his own mind. As for dealing with the crushing disappointment of Singapore, with just a week before the next race in Japan, Casanovas turned to a trusted means of creating an environment for talking.

"We went running for forty-five minutes in Tokyo," he says. "We all know the benefits of exercise when you're down, and often that's when you get the best conversations."

Casanovas can talk at length about the detailed physical and psychological process involved in getting his driver race-fit. While his knowledge is underpinned by years of academic study, he acknowledges that working as a performance coach in Formula 1 is a specialized area. It's one that relies on experience more than academic papers. "Look at something like cycling," he says. "It's probably one of the most studied fields in sport science. In Formula 1, there are maybe three articles a year, and so I have to create my own program."

Casanovas isn't complaining. After seven years at Russell's side, in a plethora of expert roles rolled into one, he understands what his driver requires to perform at the highest level. Ultimately, that comes down to an intense working relationship built on trust, and the shared faith that the driver has what it takes to become a Formula 1 world champion. "I believe in his abilities," he says with absolute sincerity. "I think he's extremely good."

During our conversation, Casanovas embodies his approach to optimal performance by eating a breakfast of porridge and honey with a sprinkle of sunflower and chia seeds. As Russell's training partner, he's as toned as his client. This is no coach content to stand on the sidelines barking instructions. A former motocross rider of note, before finding his calling in the field of sports performance and now working with the world-leading performance company Hintsa, Casanovas shares Russell's racing passion. In such an intense working relationship, however, in which highs and lows are shared and Casanovas must constantly push his driver, does it ever become too much?

"Even married couples need time out from each other," he says. "George knows it and so do I. For the last three weeks we've been together every day, but after the last race in Abu Dhabi we'll have a break. Then we won't see each other for at least a month and George will take good care of himself. We might send each other pictures from wherever we are, but unless there's a problem to discuss we'll enjoy our time off."

As he finishes his porridge, Aleix Casanovas notes several engineers emerging from the back of the garage. He rises from his seat, for now is not the time to think about a break. A signal that the briefing is over, and the initial car setup established, the performance coach sets out to find his driver and work on ensuring he's equally primed, sharp, and balanced.

Shortly before qualifying, following the Sprint weekend's only free practice session, George Russell arrives in the garage to be weighed. With just one hour to prepare for the hot lap and the long run, every team must place some element of faith in their setup work. In that time, Mercedes F1 have focused on assessing likely tire degradation to crystallize the pit-stop strategy. They've also locked in a less uncompromising ride height than they ran at COTA to avoid a repeat outcome for their efforts. It's not ideal, and yet when Russell steps onto the scales he does so with the confidence of a soldier facing inspection. His height, combined with the race suit and helmet, makes him a compelling presence. Aleix Casanovas stands alongside him, checking the reading for himself as the FIA official registers it on his clipboard.

Once his driver is ensconced in the car, mirrored by Lewis Hamilton on the other side of the garage, Casanovas hands him a drinks bottle with a long straw. He also lowers a bag of dry ice pellets into his lap to keep him cool for the next few minutes.

"Radio check," says Russell over his communication channel.

"Loud and clear."

Marcus Dudley stands with his back to the car. Facing the data screens at his station on the central island, the Senior Race Engineer is responsible for all communication between the team and the #63 driver. As Bono, his seasoned counterpart on the opposite side of the island, prepares Hamilton for the same session, Dudley instructs Russell's mechanics to weigh the vehicle with the driver in position. With the car floating on jacks, they slide a scale underneath each wheel and await the sign-off from the FIA official.

"Fire up . . ." Dudley says next, and as the engine ignites, the garage shakes from floor to ceiling.

From his station, Russell's Race Engineer raises his hand to hold the car in position. Twenty seconds later, with a gap on the track identified, he switches to a thumbs-up and the mechanics take their cue. They snap away the blankets from the tires, and then step aside smartly as if the beast in their care might bite. Let loose, Russell squeals away on the first phase of his mission to circumnavigate the track faster than his competitors. As he prepares to throw the car around corners, piloting a rocket ship on wheels, Marcus Dudley will serve as Russell's lifeline to the outside world.

With the bag of dry ice pellets back in his possession, and the drinks bottle in his other hand, Aleix Casanovas looks out in the wake of Russell's departure at the crowds in the grandstand opposite. Until his driver returns, the performance coach can only watch proceedings with the same intensity as the throng on the other side of the track. Earlier in the day, as the rows began to fill, a joyful atmosphere set in. People are here to have a good time whatever the outcome on track, as is clear from the faces picked out for the broadcast feed. As well as the wide smiles, Brazilian flags flutter in a stiffening breeze. For despite the glaring sunshine and strong humidity, a bank of ink-dark clouds looms over the circuit.

"It would be nice to get a fan," says strategist Leo Da Silva over the airways from the pit wall.

"A screaming fan?" asks Dudley, whose quick wit reflects an ability to think on his feet, only for both drivers to commence their out laps and focus the team's attention.

In the session that unfolds, Mercedes F1 will find themselves frustrated on several levels. Most immediately, after Russell and Hamilton put in strong opening laps in Q1 and then Q2, a combination of track evolution and tire temperatures works against both drivers. It could be setup or car design, or a combination of both, but ultimately it leaves the team—in Technical Director James Allison's assessment—*with tires that gain and lose 0.3sec per lap if you merely look at them funny*. Even if a clever call could have mitigated both factors, there is nothing that can be done for the apocalyptic downpour that calls a halt to Q3. At one point, the hiss of the rain hitting the tarmac competes with the engines as the cars return to the pits. The storm blots out all daylight as it passes overhead, sweeping away the team's hopes that they can build on their resurgent form at COTA and the podium finish for Hamilton in Mexico City to end this triple-header on a high.

After qualifying, with the drivers in a debrief, I find Casanovas under the canopy at the garage exit. He's looking out at the intense rain like some noir detective with a case on his mind. "On the last lap, George asked to pit for new tires when he should have just been going flat out," he says, reflecting on a psychological aspect of Russell's performance just moments before the heavens opened. "We need to work on that, but now is not the

205

time. It might have only lost him a tenth or so, but in a tight field it's significant."

With little respite in fortune come Saturday's Sprint Shootout and Sprint race, it becomes apparent to the drivers that this year's Brazilian Grand Prix weekend does not belong to Mercedes F1 as it had the previous season. With a car that has proved to be a handful all year, it's taken a track that has hosted high points in the careers of both Hamilton and Russell to cruelly call it out. The W14 is overheating the tires on both axles, understeering into corners and snapping out of exits. If any calendar fixture has the potential to break the team's spirit this season, it could happen this weekend at Interlagos.

Sunday mornings at the track always open with a sense of enforced calm. With the cars in parc fermé, the setups can no longer be modified and the focus is on prerace preparation. As a result, engineers pop up who have been otherwise hidden away in briefings and debriefings throughout the weekend. Their work is intense, and so it's unusual to find the likes of Marcus Dudley on a high stool at a table by the window. With a cup of tea in hand— and every suggestion that the pressure of his role has a curiously rejuvenating effect on his appearance—the boyish-looking forty-year-old sits quietly watching the F1 world on the walkway outside get up to speed.

"Today is more about working with the driver," he says, checking the time on his phone ahead of his first meeting with Russell. To any F1 fan, Dudley's deep but softly spoken voice is instantly recognizable from the radio exchanges between the pair whenever the #63 car is on the track. "We'll be looking at issues like what we can do to get the tires in the window, the length of stints, and then discussing how we can be adaptable during the race with the fuel or the brakes."

For the Mercedes F1 Senior Race Engineer, this is a rare break from his preparations to serve as the voice in Russell's earpiece as he powers around the track. In effect, he's last in the chain of command between the team and the driver, and with that comes a weight of responsibility. Unlike many of his colleagues here this weekend, it's also not a role he dreamed of pursuing from an early age. As a university undergraduate, studying for a degree in computer science, this equitable young man found his career path taking an unexpected twist on discovering the existence of Formula Student, a competition encouraging young people to design, build, and race a car on the track. Dudley unleashed a passion that ultimately led him to switch to a degree in mechanical engineering. His parents, however, didn't share his new vision with such clarity and confidence. "They weren't happy," he tells me, smiling as he accounts for his first steps toward a role at the vanguard of Formula 1 racing. "My mum told me I'd end up as a Kwik Fit fitter."

To anyone who listens to the snippets of broadcasted team radio communications between the car and the garage, the role of the Senior Race Engineer can seem like a double-edged sword. As well as communicating essential information to allow their drivers to do their job behind the wheel, the likes of Dudley and Bono are also there for the memorable moments. They're the sidekick to the hero in the cockpit; a voice in the earpiece to share the joy and elation when things go well, from a daring overtake to a podium finish. Without Bono, there would be no emphatic *It's hammer time!* when instructing Hamilton to push. Dudley has only been in partnership with Russell for less than two seasons, and yet already his calm and controlled guidance has become a hallmark of the #63 package.

For all the good times, however, there will be occasions when the Race Engineer must break news that their drivers do not want to hear. Two weeks earlier, at the United States Grand Prix,

Russell had returned to the garage from qualifying in P8 for the Sprint race, only to learn over the radio that the stewards had handed him a three-place penalty for impeding Charles Leclerc in the Ferrari.

"He was on an out lap!" Russell told his Race Engineer with defiance bordering on fury. "He just came barging through!"

"He was on a push lap," said Dudley to correct him, deploying the kind of low voice reserved for telling someone that their beloved dog has passed away.

"So I blocked him?" Russell's question was left to hang in the air. With an eye for economy and efficiency in every communication, Dudley knew his driver had just registered every word. "Oh wow."

In steering the fine line between racing supremacy and catastrophe, barely blinking through lap after lap, drivers are understandably adrenalized. With an imaginary *Do Not Disturb* sign lit up in the cockpit, it means any communication from the Senior Race Engineer has to be as vital to performance as it is clear and concise. Even with a carefully worded missive, however, a driver can still respond combatively.

"Note on comms," George Russell had snapped from the track during FP1 earlier in the weekend. "On one lap you're telling me to manage more, on the next lap to increase pace. When you're driving as hard as you can, you're hot and pushing on the limits, you want clear, concise info and direction!"

Despite the delivery in the heat of the moment, I heard a driver seeking to be constructive. Dudley certainly didn't grimace or flinch at his station. Nor did he come back on the channel to explain or even defend himself. In context, Dudley and his driver enjoy a warm and cordial professional relationship, while Hamilton is on record as saying that Bono is "like a brother" to him. Even so, I wonder how it feels to be on the receiving end of an abrupt response or even a dressing down.

The inaugural Las Vegas Grand Prix, 2023. Home to some of the world's largest hotels and casinos, the Las Vegas Strip was always going to be central to F1's designs for a grand prix spectacular.

George Russell with his performance coach Aleix Casanovas. Not every driver on the grid works with one, but those who do consider them to be an essential part of the toolkit.

Marcus Dudley is Senior Race Engineer to George Russell. Their relationship isn't limited to radio communications between the car and the garage. The pair refine race setups and work together on car development back at the factory.

Senior Media Manager Adam McDaid (left) and George Russell being filmed by the crew from the Netflix series *Drive to Survive*.

Communications Manager Charlotte Davies with George in the media pen.

Lewis Hamilton in conversation with Bradley Lord, Chief Communications Officer, whose role it is to share and explain the on-track narrative with fans and media.

Rosa Herrero Venegas, Senior Public Relations Manager, is adept at briefing the #44 driver in a hurry on his way to the media pen.

Lewis Hamilton and Toto Wolff's close relationship has led to unprecedented success for Mercedes F1.

The late Niki Lauda's red cap hangs in the team garage on race weekends and is often tapped by team members for good luck. Lauda played a key role in luring Hamilton to Mercedes F1.

W15 marked a return to the silver livery paintwork (front nose) of Mercedes F1's storied past.

Before the 2024 season began, Emma Hunter, Senior Reliability Engineer, put the W15 through its paces in testing.

The average pit stops in F1 are 2–2.5 seconds. During the 2023–24 offseason, the Mercedes F1 pit crew undertook an intense training regimen in their bid to chase every millisecond.

The Monaco Grand Prix, 2024. In the tiny principality hemmed into the French Riviera, the race takes place on a tight, narrow street circuit more suited to mopeds than F1 cars.

Andrew Shovlin (center), the team's Trackside Engineering Director, leaving the pit wall from where he manages each track session.

Technical Director James Allison with Sporting Director Ron Meadows. Thanks to a pipeline of car upgrades from the factory in Brackley, the W15 starts to show promise on track by Monaco.

Georgia Parslow, the first full-time female mechanic for Mercedes F1, pushing George Russell's car back into the garage.

Toto Wolff at his office on race weekend.

In his other "office"—the team garage.

Speeding around the Miami Grand Prix, 2023, with Susie Wolff, Managing Director of F1 Academy.

The Austrian Grand Prix, 2024. *"Yabba Dabba Doo!"* —George Russell

Thanks to a fast-improving W15 owing to a regular schedule of upgrades, and after capitalizing on a late tangle between Lando Norris and Max Verstappen, George Russell claims the team's first victory since his maiden F1 win in Brazil back in 2022.

One week later, Mercedes F1's momentum continues at the Silverstone Grand Prix, 2024, with George Russell and Lewis Hamilton locking out the front row of qualifying, and Lando Norris in third for an all-British top three on the grid.

The Silverstone Grand Prix, 2024. A fairy-tale ending.

"Thank you so much, guys. It means a lot to get this one. I love you." —Lewis Hamilton

945 days since his last win, Hamilton storms to victory during his final British Grand Prix with Mercedes F1. After a long period of struggle, the win is earned and enjoyed by every member of the Mercedes F1 team.

"People often think that drivers are shouting and complaining, but this is an elite athlete who has got the car on the edge," begins Dudley. "He's on the absolute limit, and as a race engineer you're asking him to carry more speed or go easier on the throttle or questioning what he wants to do about the aero balance. Sometimes, you just get this emotional response back, and though it's aimed at you in the moment it's not *about* you. So even if they're getting worked up you can't just tell them to calm down," he adds. "As well as a thick skin you need to ask yourself what needs to be done to bring the driver back where you need them."

If composure under fire underpins the Senior Race Engineer's character, the married father of one concedes that it doesn't always translate well from racetrack to home life. "It *infuriates* my wife," he admits. "She can't understand why I don't get mad."

Marcus Dudley's relationship with George Russell isn't limited to radio communications between the garage and the car. As well as helping to refine setups through each race weekend, the pair also work together on car development back at the factory. Like Hamilton, Russell is a critical asset here for one simple reason. "George and Lewis are the only people who have actually raced the car," says Dudley, who liaises with Russell to allocate his time effectively across the departments at Brackley. "We've got lots of very good simulator drivers. They'll do the laps and say whether new parts make the car faster or slower, but it's only when you get the *race* drivers that you can tell if it feels right."

In any track session debrief, Hamilton and Russell describe the experience of handling an F1 car. It then falls to race engineers like Dudley to translate that into practical steps to refine the setup. "You have to understand what he's feeling in the car," he explains. "George can describe things that could otherwise take a little while to find in the data. It could be a tiny thing, like a brake lock, but putting that into words can help to unpick what's happening."

Dudley speaks highly of Russell's precision with language when it comes to explaining his experience of driving the car. In addition to his skill in interpreting that experience to improve mechanical and aerodynamic setup, the Senior Race Engineer needs to be the kind of people person who can get inside the mind of his driver. To this end, Dudley has forged a practical alliance with Russell's performance coach. "Aleix and I have a few chats," he says. "We catch up on how George is feeling just so I can gauge how he is mentally."

In conversation with Dudley—and the same applies when talking to Bono—it takes a while to associate the familiar but disembodied voice from on-track communications with the actual person behind it. Both speak with such a kind of soothing authority, though Dudley admits that he has to be careful not to sound too laid back. "Someone once told me that I'm the most nonchalant person they'd ever met," he says with a quiet smile, "but I have to be careful not to let that go too far and sound as if I've checked out. The fact is I'm very determined," he points out, upon which an intense gaze comes into his expression. "I've always set myself goals, and right now that goal is to win a championship with George."

This afternoon, Mercedes F1 will face a significant challenge in their battle with Ferrari to tuck in behind Red Bull in the World Constructors' Championship. The Sprint race has exposed a lack of long-run pace in the W14 at this circuit, compounded by the indignity of rapid tire degradation, which saw Russell finish in P4 and Hamilton in P7. With parc fermé limiting the engineers to minor tweaks to wing and tire pressures, much comes down to what magic the pair can conjure. As Russell prepares to climb into the cockpit, first unstrapping the ice vest from over his race overalls and handing it to Casanovas, he'll also need a cool head. Starting in P8, having taken a two-place grid drop for a pit lane incursion during qualifying, he'll have to fight hard to exploit his position.

For reserve driver Mick Schumacher, who arrives in the garage ahead of the race, Interlagos can at least bring out the best in a talented driver. "I love this track," he says. "It just flows."

Having completed a lap in running shoes the evening before, I can appreciate Schumacher's view. Even without the forces at play in a Formula 1 car, this anticlockwise track snakes, coils, and unwinds in all the right places. F1 TV coverage considerably flattens every circuit, and this one is a case in point. From the home straight high on the hillside, the first turn is one of three in rapid succession—famously known as "the Senna Esses"—but on rounding the corner the tarmac literally falls away. It's a steep drop into the next two alternating corners, tailor-made for drivers seeking overtaking opportunities. The stands along the straight that follows are as dilapidated as they are historic, having witnessed momentous events in motorsport such as Ayrton Senna taking his first home victory in 1991—so exhausted by the effort that he couldn't lift the trophy—and Lewis Hamilton's dramatic 2008 race to wrestle that year's World Drivers' Championship crown from Ferrari's Felipe Massa. The famously twisty middle section continues to make the most of the circuit's topography. There are elevation changes at every turn, and while the drivers are through it in a heartbeat, the view opens up here of a rolling expanse of favelas bound by clusters of tower blocks and distant skyscrapers. Finally, the long, slingshot climb takes the cars full circle into what will be a punishing total of seventy-one laps.

To excel, the drivers must find rhythm and calm in the teeth of a relentless centrifugal assault. So far this weekend, however, Mercedes F1 have been frustrated in their efforts. Given the evolution in performance that the team enjoyed in the first two races of this Americas triple-header, their experience here in São Paulo feels like another turn of the screw of frustration they've been fighting against all season. Once again, with limited practice sessions available in a Sprint weekend, the W14's operating window has refused to yield an optimal setup. The playing field is level for everyone, of course, even if it feels like an uphill battle for Mercedes F1.

Despite the immediate challenges faced by the team, Mick Schumacher is in bright spirits. He's fresh from the Spanish circuit of Jerez, testing as a driver with Alpine's World Endurance Championship (WEC) team. Later in the month, while remaining in his role with Mercedes F1 for the 2024 season, confirmation will arrive from Alpine that he's secured the seat. For a young driver who has had to dig deep following his release from the Haas F1 team, it's a meaningful opportunity. Away from open-cockpit racing, in the closed confines of a hypercar, it also comes with a seemingly surprise benefit. "The cars have *air con*," Schumacher declares, as if he's only just discovered such a feature exists.

With the countdown to the race under way, a huge carnival has taken shape on the home straight. Drummers, dancers, and stilt walkers parade in front of packed grandstands. It's absolutely wild, with the fans on their feet under a scorching South American sun and not a storm cloud in the sky. The Mercedes F1 team might not have any reason to get into the party spirit, but everyone in the garage, from the drivers to the mechanics, engineers and technicians, appreciates the passion the Brazilian F1 community bring to the event. Indeed, when a mechanical failure cuts short Charles Leclerc's installation lap, flopping him ingloriously into the barrier, the crowd around the circuit share in his despair.

At the same time, Ferrari's premature loss opens up a huge opportunity for Mercedes F1 to solidify their claim to second place in the Constructors' Championship. It also heaps pressure on Russell and Hamilton to outdrive the car in its current form.

As the red lights blink out on the gantry, triggering the start of the race, everyone in the team's garage unites briefly in silence as much as hope. What unfolds, after a first-turn incident sees Alex Albon and Kevin Magnussen crash out and red-flag the race for thirty minutes, brings no respite to the misery that Mercedes F1 have endured this weekend. Following the restart, despite bold moves by Hamilton and Russell to advance from their starting positions (P5 and P8 respectively), both are soon forced into tire conservation mode. Compromised on speed, the drivers fight hard to hang on. As the race plays out across the course of the afternoon, the pair struggle to defend against attacks that drop them painfully out of contention.

From the garage, Aleix Casanovas watches with his arms tightly folded. Late in the race, when Marcus Dudley informs George Russell to retire his car due to the engine overheating, the performance coach shakes his head and disappears to begin preparations to receive his driver. Now is not a time for talking but rehydration and physical recovery. Casanovas has two weeks before the next race in Las Vegas to get Russell back into race trim, and clearly has a great deal of work ahead.

The disappointment is set into faces across the garage. Toto Wolff's silence at his station speaks volumes. A moment after Hamilton nurses his car across the line in P8, he removes his headphones and retreats to the sanctuary of his back-room office. The boss moves briskly, head down as he leaves the rear of the garage and crosses a paddock walkway teeming with media. Another win for Max Verstappen will be the main headline, followed by Lando Norris in the McLaren, and a thrilling photo finish that sees Fernando Alonso in a resurgent Aston Martin claim third place from Sergio Pérez.

The Mercedes F1 story is really just a footnote. That Ferrari faced their own challenges, with Leclerc out before reaching the grid and Carlos Sainz finishing in sixth, means the fight for second in the constructors' race has yet to be wrapped up. It could have been worse for the Silver Arrows, and yet it leaves the team as frustrated as the fans.

It's also felt by the drivers like a gut punch. Postrace, with his duties in the media pen and the debrief complete, George Russell appears in the back room behind the hospitality suite. He's dressed in a fresh team shirt and chinos, but looks tired nonetheless as he approaches Toto Wolff's office door.

"Is he in?" he asks, addressing members of the communications team working at their laptops in the space outside. Wolff has only emerged once to face the media at a press conference, where he summed up the weekend as his worst in Formula 1. With this in mind, Russell is perhaps wise to be cautious.

"You can go in," says Bradley Lord, looking up from his laptop. Keen to lighten the mood, he sounds bright and encouraging. "He's probably on the phone to Susie," he suggests, referring to Wolff's wife, which only causes Russell to hesitate further. "Go on, George! He needs a cuddle."

"What about me?"

It's here that a playful glimmer comes into the eyes of the Mercedes F1 driver as he goes on to appeal for the very same thing.

"*I'll* give you a cuddle." Lord is on his feet, drawing laughter from his colleagues as he spreads his arms and waits for Russell to edge his way around the desk.

The hug, when Lord wraps his arms around him, takes years off the driver. For a brief moment, Russell could be a small boy. Having strived so hard for nothing this weekend, and with so much riding on performance, it's only natural. He's first to break it off, with a brave smile pasted across his face, and the promise that he'll pay it forward as he goes in to see the boss. For all the fun and games of the exchange, it is perhaps a reminder that F1

214

drivers are cut from the same cloth as everyone else. They might be alone in the cockpit, the astronaut sitting in a tin can, but it takes a team on the ground to lift them into orbit. And when things don't go to plan, that solitary individual requires support more than ever before to get the mission back on course. As an elite driver, Russell can count on the likes of his performance coach and Senior Race Engineer to prepare him for the next race so he's in the best possible physical and psychological shape. As a human being, dealing with disappointment, it's only natural that other people will want to comfort him and commiserate.

"That wasn't a cuddle," Lord chuckles to himself as he returns to his seat. "He asked for one but didn't bring it in," he says, before returning to his work with a shrug. "Maybe I'm not much of a consolation."

CHAPTER ELEVEN

HOPES, DREAMS, AND A LITTLE BIT OF CRAZY

The Las Vegas Grand Prix
Las Vegas Strip Circuit, Las Vegas
November 16–18, 2023

"I feel a little like one of the many sad old ladies in our casino-hotel lobby." James Allison sounds uncharacteristically bewildered. "I'm pressing buttons repetitively on a brightly lit screen without the slightest idea of the day of the week, the time of day, or whether the next meal is breakfast, lunch, or dinner."

The usually razor-sharp Mercedes F1 Technical Director is not alone. Like everyone in the paddock, waiting for a red-flagged FP1 to resume, he's found himself somewhat adrift. There are several reasons why upward of 1,000 people that make up the F1 trackside community, as well as marshals, officials, reporters, and broadcasting crews, are currently looking somewhat lost. First, this weekend's Las Vegas Grand Prix schedule only gets started after dark. For most personnel, still adapting to the fact that Nevada's Pacific Standard Time trails the European time zones they left behind by eight hours, it's already been a long day. Under normal circumstances, such seasoned travelers know how to acclimatize to the fact that they're also having to contend with effectively starting a very late work shift. In this case, we're in a city that actively encourages visitors to stay awake for as long as possible in order to keep feeding the fruit machines or throw dice and poker chips across the gambling tables. It's a neon-lit dream come true for some, but for many it can become an unreal nightmare, as Ferrari's Carlos Sainz discovered soon after the opening practice session got under way.

At sundown, the Spaniard had arrived in the paddock looking happy to be here. Like every other driver, he couldn't ignore the air of excitement and anticipation surrounding the event. The city had certainly got behind this race weekend, treating it like another big show. As day turned to night, and the time approached for the curtain to go up and reveal the stage, Las Vegas experienced a transformation. In essence, the traffic that almost permanently blocks the boulevards drained away. Then, with a series of finely choreographed road diversions deployed and debris fencing locked into place, the overhead lighting flared into life and Sin City revealed itself as a crucible for high-speed motor racing.

Home to some of the world's largest hotels and casinos, from the fountain-fronted Bellagio to the Mirage, Cosmopolitan, and Caesars Palace, the Las Vegas Strip was always going to be central to F1's designs for a grand prix spectacular. Setting aside the visual treat, this central boulevard forms the backbone of a street circuit within a working metropolis. It's one of four high-speed straights in a 6.2-kilometer anticlockwise track chained by low- to medium-speed turns. Without a doubt, the circuit designers have done a fine job of showcasing the spirit of the city. All the track lacks now is any racing.

Less than ten minutes into FP1, as fans watched from grandstands and bridges over the circuit, and millions around the world tuned in to witness this much hyped spectacle, Sainz struck a loose water valve cover in his Ferrari and ground to an inglorious halt. The incident led to a red flag that didn't just delay proceedings.

As a safety issue, this unwelcome but wholly avoidable incident threatened to derail the entire weekend. Officials arrived to gather around the hole. There, it dawned on them that the measures taken to secure the valve cover, and dozens more around the track, were no match for an F1 car running so low to the ground. When Esteban Ocon swept over the site in the Alpine, his car's forward floor edge had levered the cover like a beer cap to be collected in full by Sainz. The remedial work, when it began, would take hours; long enough to finally prompt the cancellation of the rest of the session and later a class action lawsuit from fans forced to vacate expensive grandstand seats.

For a city that knows how to put on an extravaganza, with the likes of David Copperfield, Adele, and Barry Manilow performing residencies throughout the month, F1's opening night here is in danger of folding in the most farcical way. It's a shame because this penultimate grand prix of the 2023 season, and the final installment in the American trilogy, has the potential to be the most spectacular of all.

After dark, Las Vegas feels like the playfield under the glass of a giant pinball machine. Everything is lit up, from the track to the billboards and the grand hotel buildings, some of which could serve as large-scale pop bumpers and slingshots.

As for the pinball to complete the picture, the Sphere looms large on the horizon. The latest landmark on the Las Vegas skyline, this 112-meter-high and 157-meter-wide globe-shaped structure houses a boundary-breaking sound and light arena featuring almost 54,000 square meters of dynamic, external LED lighting. One moment it's a seemingly sentient ball, with moving eyes that peer down at us mere mortals; the next it transforms into a spinning crash helmet or shuffles through logos for race teams on the grid. Thanks to the playful designs, the Sphere escapes being dismissed as an eyesore and seems to fit perfectly in this Disneyland for adults. With Turns 6 to 8 orbiting much of the arena perimeter, this modern-day monolith defines part of the track landscape. Complementing the passing cars in terms of sheer dazzle, it could be purpose-built to represent the anchor point between sport and entertainment. As news spreads across the paddock that FP2 will also be delayed, it seems the Las Vegas Grand Prix could offer neither one nor the other.

Despite this early misfire, F1 owner Liberty Media has high hopes and long-term ambitions for the Las Vegas Grand Prix. With the aim of taking the sport to the next level, the commercial rights holder has effectively become the race organizer. It's the first of a three-year contract, with an option to take it to ten, but keeping the Nevada city on board is key. As a sign of its commitment, Liberty has resurfaced roads and invested north of $500 million in the venture. While waiting to find out whether any more of tonight's track timetable will happen at all, we mill around in the willfully low-lit but brand-new pit and paddock complex built on 39 acres of prime real estate.

Such investment is in place for good reason. For F1 has been here before, and the experience doesn't cover the sport in glory. In 1981 and 1982, Las Vegas staged grand prix races in the parking lot at Caesars Palace, which proved to be both slapped together and humiliatingly unsuccessful. Crucially, the hotels and casinos failed to get behind the venture. A motor race just seemed like a distraction from their business of making money. Forty years on, Liberty has been determined to learn from the experience. So as well as going to great lengths to stitch the event into the fabric of the city—by cooking up a circuit that can be switched on and off from the city's road system within a matter of hours—F1 set about selling the sport as an extravaganza worth $1.7 billion to the local economy. Feeling lucky this time, the Las Vegas establishment hasn't just accommodated the 2023 grand prix, it's gone all in. Race banners hang from every building and block. The track's sausage kerbs are detailed with red and black hearts, clubs, spades, and diamonds. Gamblers at the blackjack tables fan hands of F1-themed playing cards while drinkers at the bar enjoy cocktails with names like Slip Stream, the Chicane, and Chequered Flag. From here on, the organizers promised, the future is bright . . . the future is fast. At least it will be once the last water valve cover is locked down.

With the moon through the apex of the night sky, James Allison is just one of many in the Mercedes F1 team who unexpectedly find themselves adrift. Personnel who would normally be mining performance data or priming tires are instead floating around with espresso shots in hand and questioning if a restart will ever happen. Only the commercial and marketing teams continue to work at full throttle. It's a hugely important weekend for them, with partner guests and prospective sponsors hosted in a bespoke three-story speakeasy overlooking the opening turns. While the Mercedes F1 Vegas Club is in high gear with DJs, drinks, and distractions on every floor, the rest of the team are left to kill time in the paddock. This interminable break from the usual relentless pace might be unexpected, but it's also deeply revealing. These people are so driven that they don't know what to do with themselves, which effectively renders them off duty in the workplace.

"I've nowhere else to go," says Ron Meadows, coffee in hand, as he settles at a table outside the team's hospitality suite. "So this is fine."

It's a clear, star-spangled night. In this Mojave Desert city in November that means it's also quite cold. For weeks, the low temperature has been a talking point in terms of its impact on tires and ultimately performance. Engineers from every team expect it means the rubber compound will be more challenging than usual to switch on and provide the stickiness for grip. The cool conditions could even give rise to an unwelcome "graining" effect in which flecks of rubber pull away from the tire to create an uneven surface. With the cars running for just eight minutes, such fears remain largely untested. As Meadows has just demonstrated, the only certainty in a chilly paddock at this moment is that the tables near the patio heaters are highly prized.

Having pounced on one as it became vacant, Meadows checks his phone with the kind of guarded relief of a man who has temporarily cleared his notifications. He might be killing time now, but as the Sporting Director of Mercedes F1 he's been busier than most in the hours since Carlos Sainz stopped on the track in a car that had incurred serious damage. As a result of the collision with the rogue valve cover, which carved through the underside of the chassis, Ferrari have been forced to replace the entire engine. In going one beyond their permitted allocation of four power units for the season, despite arguing that the incident occurred through no fault of their own, the FIA has sanctioned their driver with a ten-place grid penalty.

At first, it reads like an unjust punishment by a ruling body that is also responsible for the condition of the track. In a city home to colossal casinos, where the rules of the game are strictly upheld without compromise, it transpires that the ruling is in line with regulations. It might not seem fair to Ferrari or their fans, but a new engine brings improved performance. Not just here in Las Vegas but also at the final race of the season in Abu Dhabi. In a fight going down to the wire with Mercedes F1 for the runners-up spot in the World Constructors' Championship—and with a difference in the prize share measured in millions between second and third place—that would mean a significant advantage for the Italian race team.

When Meadows presents his case in front of the patio heater, having earlier done so to the FIA stewards in his role representing the team on issues that involve F1 rules, he makes a compelling argument. "I'm not like a soccer manager who puts his hand up for every throw-in," he reasons, having recognized the potential consequences of this unfortunate incident had the FIA not applied the letter of the law.

Born in Liverpool and raised close to the city, the 59-year-old is the team's longest-serving member, having joined BAR in 1999 after an earlier stateside career in the IndyCar series. Meadows began by setting up the team's first factory at the Brackley site, accommodating a workforce of just 250. Nearing a quarter of a century later—and in a racing organization that has grown to almost five times the size—he manages all garage operations while communicating with the stewards from the pit wall during track sessions. Here, Meadows' passion, wisdom, and insight come to the fore. Indeed, for the last twenty years he has also played an important role in helping to shape F1's rulebook. In a sport that is constantly evolving in terms of engineering, technology, and sometimes even the format itself, the regulations surrounding it can be complex.

"The teams are asked to come up with solutions for issues," says Meadows, who represents Mercedes F1 in the Sporting Advisory Committee. "We talk for hours on end, along with the FIA, and between us we come up with a book of rules. In the early 2000s, the book was about 29 pages. Now it's 112. Much of it has been set in stone for ages, but just as you think you've got there something changes," he says with a shrug, and cites the introduction of a Sprint race as a reason why the group have put in long hours lately.

In addition to helping define the sport's rules of engagement, Meadows also represents the team and its drivers should they find themselves in front of the stewards during a race weekend. From an on-track incident to car compliance, he's there to speak for

Mercedes F1 but not always as the default defense lawyer. "I just explain what's happened," he says. "If I think we've got something wrong then I'll admit it. Sometimes we just need to go in and take our medicine."

Meadows cites a tangle between Lewis Hamilton and Alex Albon during the penultimate lap of the 2019 Brazilian Grand Prix that caused the former Red Bull driver to spin out. "Lewis had already been on the radio to say he was at fault, and the move denied Albon the chance for second place," he explains. "So I got on to the stewards and said: "Just give us the five-second penalty now." People asked me why I did that, but it was the right thing to do. I also didn't want Lewis to go on the podium and then receive a penalty thirty minutes later which took that away."

As Meadows talks about his life and times in F1, personnel mill around like guests at a party that has yet to get going. Many are in their twenties and early thirties; free to travel without too many ties. As a team elder, Meadows is able to put this challenging period into context.

"Some people have just known winning and wonder what's gone wrong," he says of those who arrived during Mercedes F1's glorious reign before it came to an end after 2021. "Others have never seen one of our drivers on the top step of the podium. But it's not that anybody here woke up and decided to do a poor job. We just went in the wrong direction. It's also very unusual to immediately bounce back in this sport. We have to keep on doing what we do; follow procedures, get sharper by the day, and have faith in the fact that everyone else is doing their very best as well. That's how we'll find our way." He says this with absolute conviction. "And besides," he says, as word spreads across the paddock that this long night will see a practice session at last, "it's always more enjoyable to come back fighting."

*

At the break of the next racing day, which comes at 5 p.m. when the covers are permitted to come off the cars, the Mercedes F1 garage cranks into life to the sound of Elvis Presley's "Viva Las Vegas." This is followed by "Fast Car" by Tracy Chapman. Within the space of two songs, as mechanics arrive on the garage floor, the tone is set for the Mercedes F1 team to go to work.

This weekend, in a break from the sanctuary of the RSR in Brackley, Senior Race Strategy Engineer Joey McMillan has traded places with Leo Da Silva and is working from the pit wall.

"Do you have a plan?" I ask, aware that he's had just one compressed practice session to formulate a tactical outlook for tomorrow's race.

"Not yet," he says breezily. "Which is how I like it."

We're at an untested track, on new tarmac and in cool conditions: three factors that make it hard to formulate a solid campaign without further running. For now, McMillan's main aim is to navigate his way through the forthcoming FP3 in a way that saves enough soft tires for that all-important qualifying session later tonight. His second challenge, and this applies to every member of the team, is the deepening sense that time has turned upside down.

FP2 had finally taken place as a band of light formed over the mountains to the east of the city. By the time McMillan and his colleagues made it back to their hotel, where the ground-floor casino continued to draw gamblers in huge numbers, he'd been awake for close to twenty-four hours. And yet, despite being beyond exhaustion, he wasn't alone in struggling to sleep. Yes, the team had just pulled an all-nighter while also dealing with jet lag, but this city makes it so hard to find a reference point in reality. Despite committing to precision sleep schedules throughout the season, even the drivers are feeling this one.

"I've just had a nap," admits George Russell on emerging from his room behind the hospitality suite. For someone who had been smashing through the micro sleeps during yesterday's delays, he seems somewhat disorientated. "What time is it?"

Despite this initial difficulty in finding the right gear, Russell is completely up to speed by the time FP3 gets under way at 8:30 that evening. The team's focus remains on how to generate tire temperature in cool conditions as well as setting the ride height to run long straights while coping with several slow corners. The sight and sound of twenty Formula 1 cars punching around the streets of Las Vegas at night is as effective as any caffeine kick. It's all about speed, neon, and sparks as the two Mercedes F1 cars sweep along the Strip in front of the magnificent, lake-like Fountains of Bellagio.

On the garage screens, the overhead shots from the helicopter are dazzling. Watching alongside me, two technicians glance at one another and share appreciative nods. This is backed up by broad smiles later in the session when Russell wakes up the tires and punches home a P1. Just as Hamilton primes his car to follow suit, in the closing minutes of the session, Alex Albon clips the wall in his Williams and leaves a wheel on the track. It's enough to see another session cut short while this time leaving Mercedes F1 with reasons to be cheerful. The fight is still on with Ferrari for second position in the Constructors' Championship, and steadily tipping in favor of the Silver Arrows. With persistence, this difficult, seemingly obstructive car has produced enough solid results to potentially help them win that battle.

This is a team following procedures, as Ron Meadows put it, and seeking to grow steadily sharper. Claiming the runners-up prize would be meaningful. On an individual level, a bonus is traditionally pegged to the team's finishing position. It applies to every individual both trackside and at the factories in Brackley and Brixworth. Everyone wants to take pride in their collective achievements, but the value of the bonus triggered by second rather than third place—as one team member tells me—"will make a difference to my life."

Even when qualifying brings a mixed result one hour after midnight, the team hold on to the positives. After a strong showing in Q1 by Russell and Hamilton, a fast-evolving track in cool temperatures creates an unpredictable outcome across much of the grid. Completing his hot lap just as the rubber laid down on the track improves grip, Hamilton is denied a chance to progress from Q2 and into the top-ten decider by just 0.028 seconds. There, Russell secures a respectable P4 while Verstappen is denied his usual pole by strong hands shown by both Ferraris. With Sainz's ten-place grade penalty applied, shuffling Russell to P3 and Hamilton to P10, this strange nocturnal session would have made fools of anyone moved to place bets on the outcome.

Las Vegas loves risk. From rolling the dice against all odds to making an overtake stick where other drivers would come undone, this is a city that actively encourages gambling no matter what the outcome. Which makes Emma Hunter a seemingly incongruous presence in her race team role as a guardian of reliability. "If a car returns to the garage on the back of a flatbed, or it's on fire, then obviously that's a very bad day," she says, voicing her own worst nightmare just hours ahead of tonight's race. "Fortunately, we don't suffer many catastrophic events."

Hunter is easy to find in the paddock. As Mercedes F1's Senior Reliability Engineer, she's a regular presence at the side of the garage whenever a car is under the overhead lighting pod. Even now, as the team prepare for the race, she circles studiously around both vehicles, her attention drawn to different points of interest.

"When I'm at the circuit, I will make sure things look just how

I would expect them to, but there's no way I'm able to do that as effectively as the mechanics responsible for different parts of the car. They build and strip it countless times, and so they're my greatest allies," she says, which prompts a modest smile from Flannel, First Mechanic on George Russell's car. "They're my eyes and ears."

In an ideal world, and by her own admission, Hunter's role would be redundant. "If nobody is talking about reliability, that's a good day," she says, though in reality she's run off her feet throughout a race weekend. Not because the car is falling apart in front of her, but because she aims to be on top of any part at the first sign of wear, tear or even just concerning behavior.

In this uncompromising, high-performance sport, any kind of failure on the car could impact upon a race outcome. It could even cost a championship. Which means Hunter has to be constantly ahead of the curve. Vigilance is key, but that's just a small part of her work. Whether she's taking pictures of suspect components or sending fluids to the lab for analysis, her role demands the skills, cunning, and intuition of a detective. "Just because you find a corpse with a gun in their hand, it doesn't mean that they shot themselves," she observes.

In this light, it's not hard to appreciate why Hunter is a big fan of crime podcasts. In both worlds, all is not always what it seems. "Sometimes a faulty part can set off a chain reaction," she explains. "Last season, after a year of really good reliability, we had a DNF in the final race when Lewis was forced to retire the car with a mechanical issue. In the immediate aftermath, we looked at a part that had been causing us problems. We'd always picked up on it, and done a great deal of work to fix, and at first it seemed to have finally caught us out. It was only when we looked into it back at the factory that we found the failing part was actually the result of another fault that had worked its way through the car."

Being able to differentiate between symptom and cause goes some way to explaining Hunter's original plan to train as a vet. "Obviously I went for the super-easy career option," she jokes. "Although cars aren't that different from animals because neither can tell you what's wrong. You have to feel your way around and work it out for yourself."

When Hunter does make her diagnosis, and finds it to be terminal, she has the responsibility for breaking the bad news back at the factory. "I have to be mindful that someone has put a lot of work into it," she says. "Often I'm able to provide data for analysis, and this can be helpful, but sometimes there could be other contributing factors. We go through lots of background processes in finding a solution."

Back at the factory, in between races and throughout the winter, Hunter's work can often intensify. In her drive to minimize faults, and working with her colleagues in reliability, she plays an important role when it comes to the concept, design, manufacture, and testing of components. "People are focused on what performance a part can bring," she says, referring not just to her work on the current car but the development of the W15. "We're looking at issues like temperature and loads, or how it will look after being assembled and taken apart twenty times over."

In discussing her work, it's clear that Emma Hunter goes far beyond just catching faults before the car blows up. She works with intricate monitoring and evaluation processes to understand the behavior of every component down to the last bolt. She cheerfully describes herself as being more paranoid than cautious, "because I don't want to say something is fine and then find it ruins the next race," but stresses that her decisions must always be informed.

Hunter is wholeheartedly driven in her pursuit of reliability, and this extends beyond the car to her wider work within the team. "As well as our dependency on mechanical components, we have a massive dependency on the reliability of people," she says. She's an active member of the team's Women's Network, a group set up in 2022 by Hunter and three female colleagues who had all made the same observation. "When I first started in 2014, it really didn't take me very long to get to know all the women on the technical side of the team or in the design office," she says. "Since then, I'm happy to say that the male-to-female ratio is closing within the factory, just as the range of diversity has accelerated. But while it's been great to see more women coming in, there are still some departments where they're few and far between. So we decided to create a network to allow women to get to know each other across the factory, and it's just grown over time."

Hunter is actively involved in organizing events aimed at empowering women in the team, regularly inviting key speakers to talk about their experiences. "We often approach women in senior positions, the leads and higher-ups, to address an all-female audience. Susie Wolff came to talk about her career, but she also weaved in stories about family life," she says, underlining the aim of showing those women at the start of their careers just what is possible.

When it comes to creating a welcoming environment for women in Formula 1, Emma Hunter's enthusiasm is evident. Recently, the group she helped to found grew big enough to consult on company policy surrounding equality, diversity, and inclusion. In some ways she's one of the sport's female trailblazers, and hopeful that future generations will bring higher expectations as they follow in her footsteps. "When I went into engineering, my fellow students were mostly men," she says, and it's not lost on her that she's currently observing a group of exclusively male mechanics preparing the cars for their installation laps. "I just had to learn to live with it, but that doesn't mean it should stay that way forever."

*

Shaq . . . Rhianna . . . Kylie . . . the celebrities on the grid occupy such a lofty platform of fame that they've elevated themselves beyond their own surnames. After Thursday's stalled start, the Las Vegas Grand Prix has finally delivered on its promise, through qualifying and the buildup to the race, to put on a spellbinding show. The Sphere has spun into overdrive and delighted everyone from the fans in the grandstands to the TV commentators. Despite the sheer scale of glitz and glamour, however, the cars remain the true superstars. And when the lights finally go out, regardless of the debate about entertainment stepping on sport, it's all about the race.

"This is going to be a long night," sighs Ron Meadows over the team's race channel as Lewis Hamilton gets snagged by a Ferrari going into the first turn.

The Mercedes F1 driver recovers, but the marauding pack won't wait. "I lost so many places when I got hit," he radios in from P14.

It's deeply frustrating for Hamilton, but he's also one of the few drivers who opted to start on hard tires instead of mediums. With the virtual safety car allowing him to catch up, and the ability to run longer than much of the competition—including his teammate, who has held on to third place despite the first-corner carnage—he still has a hand to play.

For a street circuit layout that has been unkindly compared to an upside-down pig, the racing action is a runaway success. If graining had been a concern, ultimately it's drama that dictates the outcome. For Mercedes F1, that's embodied by a dogged comeback by Hamilton, even after suffering a puncture on lap sixteen having made wheel-to-wheel contact with Oscar Piastri. Across the field, the overtakes come thick and fast, particularly into the turns out of the Strip. The sight of late brakers knifing down this iconic boulevard never gets tired throughout the race. There is also drama at the corner into this iconic boulevard, when George

Russell fails to register a stubborn Max Verstappen on his inside. Both cars recover from a collision that provokes howls of outrage from the Mercedes F1 garage. For the damage has been done to Russell's race.

"No!" Caught up in the heat of battle, and echoing an infamous moment in Saudi Arabia in 2021 when Toto Wolff angrily hurled his headphones to the floor, Adam McDaid smashes his phone against a garage worktop. It's a measure of the passion running through the team's collective veins, even if it means things must get broken. A moment later, quite possibly remembering his mobile contract, the Senior Media Manager checks the screen is intact. It's good news for McDaid, but that does little for his sense of disappointment when Russell is found to be at fault and handed a five-second time penalty. To soften the blow, he needs to chase and then pass several cars, including Lance Stroll in the Aston Martin and Alpine's Pierre Gasly. "Hunt them down, George," Wolff urges the driver over the radio.

Like all the big shows in town, this is a race that keeps the audience spellbound from start to finish. It's refreshing to watch Verstappen forced to fight for the victory, denying Leclerc the top step of the podium late in the day and taking with it a golden opportunity for Ferrari to steal the advantage in their second-place fight with Mercedes F1. When the checkered flag falls, courtesy of Justin Bieber, it leaves the two teams with just four points between them and everything to play for. With his penalty applied, Russell drops from a hard-fought P4 finish to P8 while Hamilton benefits from the drop to claim P7. Having found himself way back in P17 after the puncture, however, there are positives to be taken to Abu Dhabi and the final grand prix of 2023. For Mercedes F1, Las Vegas is just one of those races in which the results aren't a true reflection of their efforts. Both drivers suffered setbacks, but neither gave up the fight.

Throughout the frustrations of the season Hamilton and Russell have fought doggedly with an uncooperative car to maximize points at every race weekend. It might not be the reward they set their sights upon after facing a previously unthinkable reality way back in Bahrain, but in a week from now Mercedes F1 will close their campaign by securing second place in the World Constructors' Championship.

Inevitably, the headline writers will focus on Red Bull's continued dominance. That Max Verstappen claimed a record nineteen wins out of twenty-two races this season deserves respect and admiration. Nevertheless, it's the story of the battle between the teams behind the front-runner that sums up the spirit of F1. From the front to the back of the grid, the sport demands absolute commitment. Regardless of performance, there's no room for complacency when things are going well or any sense of resignation should a team fall off the pace. It's a continual race to keep up with the pack in readiness to strike for the front when the opportunity arises.

From this moment on, a spirit of humility, resilience, and a hunger to win is the fuel that must drive the Silver Arrows. It's all about forward motion, trusting in a learning process to keep motoring at full tilt no matter what the future brings. Even if the low moments exceed the highs for some time to come, the only way to reach those crests is by working through the challenges while keeping the pedal to the metal.

As George Russell says over the radio, on crossing the finish line at the final race: "That's the Formula 1 roller coaster for you."

CHAPTER TWELVE

DOING SOMETHING DIFFICULT

Mercedes-AMG PETRONAS Formula One Team HQ
Brackley, Northamptonshire
December 5, 2023

"The people here can be quite competitive by nature."

Chief Operating Officer Rob Thomas is reflecting on how a season on the racetrack plays out back at base. He smiles on making the observation, as if to signal it's also a huge understatement. "Even if you hadn't watched the race you can come into work on Monday and know what happened. You just feel it. So ending up with second in the Constructors' Championship, after all the emotional swings, means everything."

For over 2,000 personnel divided across the factories at Brackley and Brixworth, the outcome to what has been a taxing season is a source of immense pride. It also adds a decent bonus to their pay packets, pegged as it is to the finishing position and providing a tangible reward for the contribution made by every single member of the Mercedes F1 team.

The winter shutdown is just weeks away. Christmas is coming and now good cheer is in the air. Nevertheless, Formula 1 is all about winning. It means the team's joy at securing the runners-up prize is weighted by a sense of where their efforts fell short. "I had a similar feeling last year that we shouldn't have been there in the first place," admits James Allison, referring to the opening season under the new regulation changes in which the W13 was plagued by porpoising. "But it's a good feeling to have progressed the W14 through the year."

For the Mercedes F1 Technical Director, as much as the wider team, any chance to reflect on the battle they've been through is limited by the fact that a new front is about to open up. The last checkered flag has fallen for 2023, but in just three months from now the lights will go out on the first race of the 2024 season.

Long before the W14 retired from the track, an energy has been building within these white-walled workspaces, drawing offices, testing labs, and machine rooms to create a successor capable of improving the team's fortunes. For James Allison, Rob Thomas, and the legion of men and women involved in designing, testing, refining, manufacturing, and delivering the W15, a new race is well under way. "There's a part of you worried just about whether you will physically deliver it," says Allison. "Is the factory smoothly working through the tasks necessary to deliver the gleaming thing at the end? Does it feel like the place is humming with activity, or are departments looking like they might break because we're asking too much?"

From the summer onward, the Mercedes F1 factory steadily cranked up the campaign to bring the new car together on time. By December, the operation is running at full throttle. What started as conceptual designs and then technical drawings has evolved to become a drive to manufacture components, ensure they meet rigorous safety and performance demands and ultimately bring lap time to the car. Away from the main headquarters, in a building across the campus boulevard, one specialist group have been working tirelessly to sculpt every surface of the W15 to maximize downforce and air-flow efficiency. When it comes to making an F1 car go faster, aerodynamics is the master key.

Filling an open-plan office floor, close to 100 engineers and designers in the team's aero group are busy manipulating shapes on their computers. We're in a world of computer-aided design (CAD), with ultrawide curved screens at each workstation for an increased sense of depth and dimension. Here, car components such as bodywork items are rendered digitally and then ceaselessly probed and sculpted.

"The car is split into four groups," explains Aerodynamics Director Jarrod Murphy, a critical cog in the Mercedes F1 machine since joining the team in 2013. "You've got the front group, mid group, and rear group," he says, pointing in turn across the space before settling his attention on a dozen or so people at the far end. "They're focused on the future." A moment passes before Murphy clarifies that they're concerned with the concept phase of the W16 and beyond. The majority, he stresses, are responsible for carving out the specifications of every surface of the W15 from the nose to the rear wing for optimal performance.

"It all starts in here," says Murphy, speaking quietly so as not to disturb the atmosphere of intense concentration. "The aerodynamicist has an idea to bring extra performance that they think might be worth a go. So they scheme it in CAD and then run it through a virtual wind tunnel."

By way of an example, Murphy opens up a software suite on his desktop. Known as computational fluid dynamics (CFD), it presents him with a rendering of the W15-in-progress, which he can turn and rotate to view from any angle. Having settled on a front-facing vantage point, Murphy fires up the virtual tunnel. At once, a series of digital vortices cloak the car, as if it's moving at speed through a colored gas representing air pressure, temperature, and turbulence. Clasping the mouse, Murphy floats the camera forward so it passes through the car. In response, the vortices around the edges swirl, change color, shrink, and grow.

"We're always trying to find more downforce for grip," he says, highlighting the clean flow of air under the floor. The aim, he explains, is to create a pocket of low pressure so the car is effectively pressed to the track by the high pressure created elsewhere. "And less drag to go faster on straights," adds Murphy, as he circles the cursor around the controlled-looking maelstrom in the wake of the front wheels.

Working with CFD as a simulation tool, the aerodynamicists have the ability to closely examine the impact of airflow on every last component and item of bodywork on the car. "It's not perfect," he cautions about this virtual tool. "But we'll use it to make a judgment call about whether it'll find its way downstairs."

Jarrod Murphy is referring to the central feature of this building, which is a cavernous hall containing the team's wind tunnel. Like the simulator, it's a highly advanced and closely guarded facility. The tunnel comprises a giant fan facing a conveyor belt that turns at the same speed as the generated wind. Using a model of the car (mounted from an overhead strut, bristling with sensors and scaled to 60 percent, which is the maximum allowed by the FIA) the team are able to build a detailed picture of the aerodynamic forces at work. If a test part graduates from CFD, it's quickly manufactured from a rapid prototype material and added to the model. The number of wind tunnel "runs" a team can make throughout the season is also restricted—as is time working with CFD—which means Murphy and his colleagues aim to make each one count. In simple terms, if a test component is found to increase overall performance, it'll continue along the production chain as a candidate to feature on the real car. "The tunnel is very accurate in measuring downforce, while the CFD provides a better picture of what the airflow is doing," says Murphy. "They complement each other very well."

*

236

Building a Formula 1 car is by no means a linear process. The campaign from concept to delivery is relentless, but in the quest for performance it's a puzzle in which pieces can often change throughout the build. "The chassis was ready in November as we need time for it to go through a raft of crash tests," explains Rob Thomas. "Then come the engine, gearbox, and hydraulics. Everything goes through a process of testing and development. So if you were to film the build with a stop-frame camera from now until January, you'd see the car constantly going through a cycle of coming together in places and then being stripped back down again."

With a massive array of components in the mix, the team don't just evaluate and refine parts in isolation. It's a holistic exercise that considers interactions across the car. Ultimately, the outcome is measured by lap time.

"There are always trade-offs," says Mercedes F1 Performance Director David Nelson, whose group works with engineers in divisions from aerodynamics to tires, suspension and the power unit to optimize the vehicle for the track as well as the drivers. "We could develop a power unit that has more crank power, for example, but that requires more cooling and brings extra drag. It means we have to make a guided decision about where the balance lies," he says, which is where the virtual tools at the team's disposal come into play.

Like Jarrod Murphy, the Australian-born performance head is aware that off-track technology such as the wind tunnel or CFD can be illuminating in evaluating vehicle performance but also comes with limitations. "They all have their strengths and weaknesses in creating that message," says Nelson, referring also to the team's simulator resources. "Our aim is to make the right engineering judgment based on the data."

Nelson's work is complex and extensive, not just in priming

237

and sharpening the W15 but also in acting on feedback from the track once the season is under way. In a sport that gives rise to advantages from engineering and technological innovation, Nelson's group rely heavily on a "capability race." No team can stand still when it comes to their virtual resources. In a bid to close the gap between "representation and interpretation," as he calls it, Nelson's group are on the cutting edge of ensuring everything correlates as closely as possible with reality. It's a constant quest, he observes, in a competition with rivals to produce the fastest car. "We can do a great job," he says, "but others might do a better job. So either we win or we learn, although there's even lessons to be had from crossing the finish line first."

Before David Nelson and his group can assess the W15 in action, they must work with the team back at the factory to bring it to the track. Across the campus, since autumn and now into winter, there is no rest for anyone. "It ramps up until it's absolutely crazy," says Engineering Director Giacomo Tortora. "It really brings home the fact that we are designing and making a new car every year. The level of effort is really impressive."

A former head of Ferrari's simulator program, Tortora has found himself at the heart of car builds at Mercedes F1 since joining the team in 2021. Working under James Allison, the Italian engineer is closely involved in every stage from the concept group to car launch. "For me, the best time is January," he says, speaking of the period after the winter shutdown when the mid-February deadline is fast approaching. "It's dark outside and really horrible, but we've fired up the engine for the first time and the car is beginning to look complete."

Like so many of his colleagues, Tortora finds himself pulled in different directions in the collective bid to get the W15 to the grid on time. It becomes "like a baby" to him throughout this constant cycle of assembly, strip down, refinement, and reconstruction. The bodywork might be one of the last phases of the build, but it originates from a group in the team working tirelessly to manufacture both the flesh and bones of the car. From the chassis to the front and rear wing endplates, the brake ducts, diffuser elements, and everything in between, approximately 80 percent of a modern F1 car relies on the same material for being both stiff and light: carbon fiber. Which starts life, under the watch of Composite Manufacturing & Quality Director Gordon Kelly, as rolls stored in a freezer.

"Think of it as filo pastry," says the bespectacled, sable-haired Scotsman in the white lab coat. He peels away a sheet from a batch that has just been cut into lengths. "If you leave it out too long it goes crispy. So we're on a timer now." Dark, shiny, and paper-thin, the sheet is made from braided strands of carbon and looks like seaweed wrap for sushi. "It's preimpregnated with epoxy resin so it's tacky," Kelly explains. "By applying heat and pressure, it liquefies and then solidifies. So we can mold it into shapes."

Crossing the broad walkway from the loading bay that cuts through his domain, Kelly stops in front of a window into a workspace populated with technicians in team polo tops, lab coats, surgical gloves, and hats. With a 3D rendering of a part laser-cut into a 2D shape, this is where the material is draped and molded. It's called the Clean Room. "Contamination can interfere with the bonding and compromise the material," Kelly explains. "It could be anything from dust to greasy fingers. There was once a case at a facility in the USA where deodorant aerosol from a changing room found its way into the air conditioning system." As a precaution, he says, his Clean Room is a closed environment fitted with air handling units that introduce a little positive pressure. "It means when the doors open air blows out, which reduces the risk of particles getting in."

Carbon fiber crept into the fabric of Formula 1 cars in the early eighties, steadily replacing the use of fiberglass that was common-place at the time but heavier and lacking the same tensile strength. Other materials can be added, making it a composite, such as the resin used for bonding, aluminium or Kevlar for increased durabil-ity and impact resistance. Cutting, layering, and draping carbon fiber sheets around molds to determine the shape and strength of the item required is an art form in itself.

Different weaves provide different qualities, as Kelly demon-strates on a tour of his area in the belly of the Mercedes F1 factory. "Fiber strands woven in two directions produce a material that is strong and stiff all over," he says, stopping at a display rack. Kelly hands me a ducting pipe. It's the length of a crowbar, as solid as steel but light as a feather, which comes as quite a surprise. "The fibers can also be laid in parallel for parts that only need to have strength in one axis, which all saves weight," he adds, setting the pipe back on the rack like a proud curator.

Here, Gordon Kelly has had to raise his voice over the hum emanating from the next stage in the process. Behind us stand five huge steel cylinders. These are the autoclaves, inside which parts are cured into their final shapes under carefully controlled temperatures and pressure. All of them are the size of dumpsters, but two of the five could each literally accommodate a car.

"That's for the floor," says Kelly. "It's the biggest single part of the vehicle. The reason we have two autoclaves this size is in case one dies. In the middle of a build, we just don't have the time for repairs."

Often operating twenty-four hours a day to meet the demands across the team in creating the new car, replacement parts, or updates, the Mercedes F1 composites department is the furnace for the operation. This is where so much of the new car and the streams of updates to follow are forged. Once a finished part has progressed through testing and inspection, it's no coincidence that the walkway connects with the hangar-like space where the W15 will reach a state of final assembly on the eve of the next campaign.

For Kelly, his composites group and the wider workforce across the factory, the build is an extraordinary time. In order to deliver, every member of the team must operate like the high-performance machine they're building, but then these aren't components. They're people.

"It can be extremely demanding," says Giacomo Tortora, who is responsible for more than 200 personnel, "and extremely caring. As a team, that's when we're at our best."

"The pleasure of this job is that it's not a normal job," adds Technical Director James Allison. "The satisfaction comes from succeeding in doing something difficult. The corollary is that it's miserable when you don't succeed. It can't be pleasurable when you're failing, but there's no sense of defeatism. We just have to work hard to fix it."

With the last two seasons in mind, and an organization to helm, Rob Thomas remains forward-thinking but also realistic. "I'm convinced that as a team we will come through this period and be stronger for it. But we'll also be different," he offers. "A lot of new people have joined since our championship run. They bring ideas, a different dynamic, and new ways of thinking, and that's where the excitement lies."

CHAPTER THIRTEEN

FINDING TOTO

Mercedes-AMG PETRONAS Formula 1 Team HQ
Brackley, Northamptonshire
February 7, 2024

On a gray and seemingly unexceptional morning on the last day of January, Lewis Hamilton visited Toto Wolff at his Oxford home. In the short meeting that followed, the seven-times winner of the World Drivers' Championship broke the news that would shake the foundations of Formula 1.

Lewis Hamilton had just signed with Ferrari.

Having activated an early release clause in his contract, the driver who had been at the heart of the Silver Arrows for over a decade was set to leave the team at the end of the upcoming season. From 2025, Hamilton would be driving in the red car.

To place the sense of shock in context, less than five months had passed since the ink dried on a two-year contract extension between the driver and Mercedes F1. As one of the most successful pairings in the history of the sport, it seemed as if nothing could come between them.

"Our story isn't finished," Hamilton had said back in August to mark the renewal, which only strengthened the enigma

242

surrounding his subsequent decision. "We are determined to achieve more together and we won't stop until we do."

One week later, I sit across from the man who must prepare for a new chapter without the character who has charged the team's narrative for so long. It would be understandable to find Toto Wolff still reeling. Instead, from his glass-walled office inside the team's headquarters, the Mercedes F1 boss presents an air of calm assurance.

"I always see opportunity in change," he says of his response to Hamilton's notice. "For a minute, I was in disbelief at the timing of it. The next we talked about what it meant for the team."

The Austrian-born Team Principal speaks fluent English, as well as German, French, Italian, and Polish (his mother's nationality). Nevertheless, Wolff still searches for the precise vocabulary on occasion. In discussing the ramifications of Hamilton's impending departure, it reinforces the impression of a man who chooses his words carefully.

"I *like* the situation," he insists. "It helps us because it avoids the moment where we need to tell the sport's most iconic driver that we want to stop."

It's a statement that lands abruptly. Hamilton turns forty shortly before he climbs into the Ferrari cockpit. While no other driver would underestimate his combination of skill and experience, the Briton is in the autumn of his career. Hamilton freely acknowledges this, as does Fernando Alonso, who is three years his senior and the eldest on the grid. Both drivers show no sign of slowing, but it's here that Wolff expands on his statement. He also does so from the standpoint of a Team Principal who considers his longstanding friendship with the British driver to be ring-fenced from the brutal reality of motor racing.

"There's a reason why we only signed a one-plus-one-year contract," he says of the deal that secured Hamilton for two seasons while also equipping him with the escape clause that he has just deployed. "We're in a sport where cognitive sharpness is extremely important, and I believe everyone has a shelf life. So I need to look at the next generation," he drops in pointedly, though it's as far as he'll be drawn on his thoughts about who will fill the seat. "It's the same in soccer. Managers like Sir Alex Ferguson or Pep Guardiola. They anticipated it in the performance of their top stars and brought in junior players that drove the team for the next years." In the same breath, Wolff acknowledges that the cautious nature of the deal he offered Hamilton in the summer inevitably had some bearing on his decision to accept a multiyear commitment from Maranello (the Italian home of Ferrari).

"I absolutely had it on my radar that Lewis would go," he states. "I just couldn't understand why he'd change to another team before we knew if we were going to be competitive. It also didn't give me any time to react," he continues. "I had to emergency call our partners, and I possibly missed out on negotiating with other drivers who had signed contracts a few weeks earlier like Charles Leclerc and Lando Norris. It put us on the back foot, and that had a commercial impact. But do I take that personally?" Wolff brushes away his own question with one hand. "This was a business decision. We've enjoyed such a successful journey together, and now we have our own objectives. This didn't even move the needle for me," he insists, and then offers that inscrutable smile. "I'm thick-skinned, you know? I've had some pretty tough moments in my life, and this doesn't compare."

Toto Wolff is dressed casually in a shirt open at the throat, light suit, and loafers. His office is the epitome of business elegance: an expansive and meticulously organized desk, fine art on the walls, and an impressive display of team-issued race winner's medals.

Settled into a designer chair in the meeting area, in a moment of calm before the storm of the new season, Wolff occupies a lair that combines simplicity with success. Having recently made an appearance in *Forbes* magazine's Billionaires List for the first time, the former investor and one of three equal shareholders in Mercedes F1 doesn't come across as someone who has known hardship. It's only when he opens up about his "fucked-up upbringing" that it becomes apparent how the experience chiseled his character and ultimately shaped the values of the team.

Torger "Toto" Wolff was born in Vienna in 1972. His Polish mother, Joanna, was a hospital anesthetist, while his Romanian father, Sven, founded a successful transport business. Coming from a relatively affluent family, Wolff and his younger sister were educated privately at a prestigious French school in the Austrian capital. With the children at an age when security and comfort were part of the fabric of their lives, everything changed for the family in 1980 when Sven was diagnosed with a brain tumor.

"My father was ill for almost ten years before he died," says Wolff, reflecting on a traumatic time in which his parents separated, Sven's business collapsed, and financial hardship resulted in the children being marched out of class and sent home for nonpayment of school fees.

"I just wanted to be independent," he continues. Talking about the loss of his father and disintegration of his family life, Wolff articulates the sense of helplessness he experienced with an intensity that frequently heats subjects close to his heart. In his strong Austrian accent—melding crisp consonants with stretched vowels—choice words often boil with emotion. "I couldn't bear the *suffering* and the *illness*, the *humiliation* and the *failure*. At fifteen, I decided to be a grown-up. I would take care of my own life. I felt like a child that had been put onto the street. I needed to *survive*."

Listening to Wolff's origin story explains his fierce determination and drive (though he tells me that his young son, Jack, shares the same qualities, which has led him to question if character is down to nature and not nurture). Having watched a friend race at the iconic Nürburgring in Germany, the seventeen-year-old Toto witnessed drivers attempt to "control the uncontrollable" and duly discovered his calling.

From 1992 to 1994, Wolff started his motorsport career racing in the Austrian and German Formula Ford Championship. When sponsorship issues put the brakes on his ambitions Wolff applied the same focus and attention to his life in the world of finance, in part to fund a return to racing. With a focus on growing tech start-ups, at a time in the early 2000s when smartly run ventures could go stratospheric, the young Austrian investor experienced enormous success.

In 2003, as a reflection of his enduring fascination with the sport, Wolff returned to race in the Italian GT Championship. Off the track, he would go on to mine commercial opportunities in driver management by acquiring a substantial stake in a Formula 3 engine manufacturer. Wolff even enjoyed a stint as a rally driver before a serious crash in 2009 at the Nürburgring, during a lap-record attempt in a Porsche. Heavily concussed, with a torn olfactory nerve and a broken vertebra, the 37-year-old underwent a long period of rehabilitation and reflection on his goals in life. During this time, he started a relationship with the Scottish racing driver Susie Stoddart, whom he would marry in 2011, while electing to hang up his own crash helmet and devote his attention to the business of motorsport. In that same year, with an interest in the hustle and bustle of the paddock, Wolff had become a 15 percent shareholder in Williams Racing. It would be his entry into the world of Formula 1, bringing with him a reputation for strategic wisdom and clarity of purpose that ultimately led to his appointment as Executive Director.

"The competition," he says in explaining what it is about this level of racing that would become the central focus of his professional life. "But actually, you're fighting yourself and you want to win."

After a strong 2012 season, in which Williams Racing won their last grand prix to date, Wolff was invited by the owners of a rival team in the paddock to assess how it could improve its fortunes. Mercedes-Benz had returned to the sport in 2010 after the purchase of the previous season's champions, Brawn GP. They had even drawn Michael Schumacher out of retirement to pair with fellow German driver Nico Rosberg. Since then, however, the newly formed Mercedes GP had struggled to gain traction.

"It came down to resources," says Wolff. "They had the same budget as Williams, once you'd accounted for the difference in driver salaries, but I was targeting fifth in the Constructors' and Mercedes expected to be world champions."

Wolff presented his findings to the board of Mercedes-Benz in Stuttgart. In suggesting they had underestimated the investment required, by assuming they could replicate Brawn's single-season success—a feat largely attributed to engineering ingenuity that subsequently other teams caught up with—he expected a hostile response. Instead, the German car manufacturer made an offer he couldn't refuse.

"They asked me to run the team," he says, outlining a package that would make Wolff the Team Principal and a shareholder with Mercedes-Benz and Niki Lauda.* "This was the moment in which everything was absolutely clear to me. Mercedes

---

* In 2021, two years after the death of Niki Lauda at the age of 70, his estate returned his shareholding in the Mercedes F1 team as part of a wider ownership restructuring. This facilitated an agreement that allowed Mercedes-Benz, Toto Wolff, and principal partner INEOS to become owners in three equal parts.

247

motorsport doesn't go any higher, and I was prepared to go through *any* wall to make it a success." Wolff reinforces his point by punching a fist into the palm of his hand. "Ultimate force."

In 2013, with investment and restructuring in place and having stepped away from Williams, Wolff set about placing what had become the Mercedes-AMG PETRONAS F1 Team on a championship footing. His first season at the helm coincided with the arrival of Lewis Hamilton, who had been recruited from McLaren by Wolff's predecessor, Ross Brawn, along with Lauda, the three-times world champion who would remain as non-executive chairman and a close adviser. In replacing Michael Schumacher following his second retirement from the sport, Hamilton, the 2008 world champion, was considered to be a coup for the Silver Arrows. From that moment Wolff's vision, along with his conviction that Mercedes F1 would deliver a competitive car, gave rise to a partnership that made motorsport history. From 2014 to 2020, Hamilton would come to match Schumacher's record of seven World Drivers' Championship crowns. Only in a thrilling 2016 season was he outraced to the top spot—by his teammate Rosberg. To complete this dominant era, Mercedes F1 went on an unprecedented run to claim eight World Constructors' Championship titles in succession. Their last came in 2021, when Max Verstappen denied Hamilton—in extraordinarily controversial circumstances—the chance to seal his reputation as the greatest driver of all time with an eighth championship win.

For someone who has strived for perfection throughout his adult life, seemingly in response to the fault lines that cracked throughout his childhood, Wolff has found the team's recent struggles hard to bear. Trackside, the Mercedes F1 boss has even sometimes seemed visibly strained by the reality of the situation. A knee operation toward the end of the 2023 season had left me wondering whether what I had often seen in his knotted, frowning expression was down to physical discomfort.

"I don't feel pain on a race weekend," insists Wolff. "It goes completely into the background. What I'm facing is an absolute failure to meet my own expectations. I'm letting myself down."

Wolff is not a high-performance engineer. Nor is he an aerodynamicist, a race strategist, a brake, hydraulics, engine, or tire technician. In leading the team, he makes it his mission to rely on those at the top of their game and effectively unite them under one aim. Throughout the season, he attends almost every engineering meeting and demonstrates a broad comprehension of the complexities at play in summarizing the action points from each session. In his view, just what is the problem that has plagued the team in the last two years?

"Formula One racing is about physics not mystics," Wolff offers. "If you get the physics right, because you've taken the right management and technical decisions, you win races."

While openly acknowledging that the team have yet to mine the full potential from the ground effect that is baked into the technical regulations for the current cars, the Team Principal carefully accepts responsibility for the situation. At the same time, Wolff goes on to admit that toward the end of last season his team had reached breaking point.

"It all started with me," he begins. "I put far too much pressure on myself, and that pressure was felt by others. That exploded after Brazil when I said in the press that we had a car that didn't deserve to win. Some in the organization felt attacked by this. There was a lot of discontent."

It feels like a confession of sorts, and one that Wolff is prepared to own after what he describes as a winter of soul-searching.

"I needed to change," he says. "And that meant becoming a better leader. In January, after the first technical meeting, I asked if I could say something and began with an apology. I told the team that I recognized my shortcomings and had let my frustrations spill over. It hadn't been helpful and I wanted to make a positive contribution." Wolff pauses to reflect on what he's just said, though his candor speaks for him. "That's when we got the feeling back," he adds, "and it really makes me happy."

If Wolff makes it sound like he flicked an internal switch, the longer-term shift in perspective he goes on to describe sheds further light on the fact that he's a different character compared to the previous season. The catalyst, it seems, is a change in perspective.

"We have won eight of the last ten championships, and then we finished third and second. That's not a failure," he declares, as if stress-testing his own statement. Wolff cites Manchester City as an example of a team that had to rebuild to become a powerhouse in top-flight soccer. In Formula 1, the greatest challenge in motorsport, the Mercedes F1 Team Principal signals that he's prepared to go the distance. "We are fighting against formidable competition. And I just needed to accept that if regulation changes are designed to shake up the pecking order then eventually we would be caught out. So now we just have to work our way back to being competitive. I'm still frustrated by the lack of performance," he points out, "but I just needed to see this as a journey and accept that the bad years are part of the normality of being a sports team."

Throughout the last two seasons, Wolff has been vocal in his belief that a cycle in any team's fortunes can be broken. From one race weekend to the next, and one update to another, his hope was that the team would find a way to bring the car alive. It's a view not universally shared across the team, with George Russell and James Allison both inclined toward the view that development takes time and is also relative to improvements by rivals.

Today, Wolff adopts a more philosophical outlook. He acknowledges that Mercedes F1 might have to wait for the grid to reset with the 2026 regulation changes, and yet it's hardwired in his DNA to be the one who dares to believe.

"There's something that we missed," he says, speaking of what must seem a mythical quest at times. "If we can find out what that is, we can have a real go. It would be difficult, and the odds are against us, but I think it's possible."

Mercedes F1 certainly have the resources. Thanks to Wolff's early drive for investment, and the steady growth that came with success, the team possess everything from the equipment to the personnel and the experience to produce a race-winning car. The Team Principal won't give up the search for that missing piece of the physics puzzle, even if legacy carries more weight for him now than pursuing an instant fix to restore order. Wolff can be assured that he's not alone in the bid to *chase every millisecond* as proclaimed by the framed print in a corridor outside his office. From the moment he set out his vision for Mercedes F1 as championship contenders, the 52-year-old has always been recognized within the team for his qualities as a leader.

Justin Hazell knows exactly what this means. At every grand prix weekend, he'll be found hosting guests in the pit garage and paddock. Hazell is passionate about Mercedes F1. His enthusiasm shines through as he provides insight into how the team functions at the racetrack. Hazell is used to fielding questions. His F1 knowledge is deeply impressive. He's there to provide facts, not opinion, and always strives to place the team first in his answers. At the Italian Grand Prix in 2022, however, a guest put Hazell on the spot about which driver was better suited to the Monza racetrack. Was it Lewis Hamilton or George Russell? Unwilling to be evasive, and pressed to give an honest response in his personal view, Hazell suggested that Hamilton would have an edge on account of his vast experience. He thought nothing of it. All in a day's work.

Until the same guest cropped up at a motor home press conference with Toto Wolff that evening, having found a seat among the journalists, and asked the Team Principal to respond to Justin Hazell's assertion that Hamilton was a better driver than Russell.

Standing at the back of the seated area, Hazell was mortified. To make matters worse, the guy had even mispronounced his surname. He watched Wolff absorb the question before turning to his press officer to clarify who had made the statement. As weaponized moments go, this one was certainly dangerous, but the Mercedes F1 team boss effortlessly defused it with an answer praising the individual qualities of both drivers. While the press conference moved on to other matters, Hazell kept his gaze on his shoes and hoped the moment would be quickly forgotten.

It wasn't.

As soon as he arrived in the paddock the next morning, Hazell found himself the subject of a low-level joke in the motor home and pit garage.

"Who is Justin?" his colleagues asked him, often in their best Austrian accent to mimic Wolff. "Does anyone know?"

It was just office banter transferred to the circuit, and Hazell took it in his stride. At the same time, he couldn't help but feel a little wounded. *Who am I?* he brooded to himself. *Just someone who lives and breathes for this team like everyone else.*

Inevitably, the joke slowly burned itself out. As Sunday's race approached, people focused on more important matters. It was only afterward, however, that Hazell discovered the incident hadn't been entirely forgotten. In a confined environment like the motor home, it was only a matter of time before he ran into Wolff himself. Hazell nodded and smiled as he always did in passing, while still dying a little inside, only for the team boss to stop and take him to one side.

"I heard what they've been saying," he said before Hazell could apologize for what had happened. "And it's bullshit!"

"Oh."

Now Hazell looked up at the tall, imposing Team Principal. This was not what he expected to hear. In response, Wolff raised his forefinger.

"I don't know who that guy in the press conference was talking about," he said, and then jabbed him squarely in the chest. "But I know who *you* are."

Hazell's story is just one of many within the team that paint a revealing portrait of the values Wolff embodies. Once again, it all comes down to his formative years. "I want to create a space where nobody feels inadequate or humiliated," says Wolff. "Not everyone has experienced suffering, but respect for each other is something we share as a highly visible sports team. It's a core priority, just like winning races, because only when we do both are we credible. As long as it's not a distraction or a dilution of our performance efforts, then we do it."

Toto Wolff believes in doing the right thing. After the controversy that engulfed the final race of the 2021 season, denying Hamilton his eighth title, he chose not to fight the outcome in court but on the racetrack. While Mercedes F1 have yet to find redemption on that front, it was a response that took the team to higher ground and encouraged racing fans around the world to get behind them. At the same time, and frequently in the face of strong criticism, Formula 1 visits countries on the race calendar with autocratic regimes and problematic human rights records. How does this sit with the values that Wolff has just outlined?

"The spotlight is on them," he says of the host nations in question, "and when I meet ministers from their governments I remind them of that. I tell them that they have to go in the right direction because the world will tear them apart if they don't." Wolff is forthright in his belief that the sport can be a force for change, while also conceding that racing in places where liberties are curbed can be open to some manipulation.

"Is everything right?" Wolff shakes his head. "Are they buying too many sports assets, or offering 'bread and games' to make their population happy? Absolutely. But change is happening," he maintains. "Behind every conservative, traditionalist establishment there is now a younger, educated generation. They're proud of their culture but want to take the establishment on a journey to push their country forward. I'd rather be there than stay away because I think we can contribute to that positive development."

Wolff's moral compass means he's unafraid to venture into sensitive territory populated by strong opinions. Just like the challenge faced by his team, what matters to him is the path and the process even if the destination is some distance away. When it comes to the environmental impact of Formula 1, and my misgivings about the efforts by the sport to reduce its carbon footprint, Wolff speaks for his team.

"We have to be trailblazing," he says, acknowledging the apparent disconnect between environmental concerns and what is effectively a globe-trotting entertainment industry. "We're flying cargo and people around the world, and then racing cars in circles. With a billion and a half people watching us, we have a lot of exposure, and with that comes responsibility."

In Mercedes F1's most recent annual Sustainability Report, Wolff is quoted as saying that performance at any cost is no longer acceptable. With ambitions to become one of the world's most sustainable global professional sports teams, it's a statement that requires some demonstration of action.

"Last year we spent multimillions on initiatives to leave the smallest carbon footprint," says Wolff. He maintains that eradicating it is "not realistic for the majority of people," while firmly believing that innovation is key to living responsibly. "We run our trucks, generators, and planes on sustainable fuel from renewable resources, and also our car from 2026 onward. Mercedes F1 can be role models," he insists. "If we can tell the world that we have made this commitment as a Formula 1 team then other organizations can only follow."

Wolff talks about activities and initiatives that bring "goodness" as if it can be extracted from the team like an essence. Having witnessed the outreach efforts made by the Silver Arrows during race weekends it can certainly be measured by smiles, but there is also a unifying quality in "wanting to be good people." Within a team environment, one seeking to lead the field in bringing positive change and development at different levels, it fosters a sense of connection and pride. In a sport like Formula 1—as Wolff is well aware—it can also drive the will to win.

"Being good as a person and a fierce combatant is the recipe for success," he concludes, before stressing that humility is a quality that he's pleased to see in his team. When I suggest that in Mercedes F1 he's created the family that fell apart for him as a boy, united no matter what the road ahead has in store, Wolff invites me to consider the team in a different light.

"I have a family," says the father of two adult children and a young son from his second marriage, to Susie. "Instead, what we have here are a group of individuals on the same journey. We share the same values and objectives. When everyone is aligned, and playing in their best positions, we're an invincible force. That's not a family." With an intensity in his gaze that hasn't once dimmed since we finally sat down to talk, Toto Wolff leans back in his chair. "That's a *tribe*."

CHAPTER FOURTEEN

TRUST THE PROCESS

Demonstration Day
Silverstone Circuit, Silverstone
February 14, 2024

"The beard doesn't come off until the last day of testing."

On this Valentine's Day morning, Evan Short has done a great job of looking like a dream date. A white beard, grown and thickened over the winter, has transformed his image from genius inventor to grizzled lumberjack. It's only a temporary measure, but one that makes an appearance before each new season when Short's superstitious nature comes to the fore.

Mercedes F1's Trackside Electronics Leader is not alone in hoping luck will shine on this day. The efforts by factory personnel in Brackley and Brixworth to deliver a Formula 1 car in time for the new season are on a par with a small country going on a war footing. As this monumental project gathers pace from early summer into the new year, the next championship challenger only fully comes together in the final phase. It's a complex twenty-four-hour operation, working under huge pressure and fierce deadlines, that demands everyone pull together as one.

And in accordance with FIA regulations, as Mercedes F1 prepare to unveil the W15 to the world, it won't have a single kilometer on the clock. It's only today, at the official launch, that what is essentially a two-of-a-kind prototype vehicle will be driven for the very first time. In this view it's only natural for people like Evan Short to feel a little nervous. Along with the rest of the team, he just hopes to establish that it doesn't just look like a Formula 1 car, it must also act like one.

We're gathered in a big section of Silverstone's 390-meter-long pit complex building, defined by roof slopes that rise and fall to embody the changing velocity of a car around the track. At any race weekend, the Wing accommodates a parade of garages in front of the pit lane. Today, only one is in operation; just big enough for the mechanics to work on a single car. The cavernous space adjacent is filled with rows of benches and chairs. Here, race support team members are gathered along with a lucky few invited from the factory for a rare chance to see their car in action. The time is approaching 10:15 a.m. From this moment on, there's no turning back.

"As soon as I hit go, you hit go."

Daniel Paddock, Creative Social Lead, is preparing to flick the switch. This is effectively a virtual launch on Mercedes F1's official website, which amounts to a prerecorded video introduction by Toto Wolff, George Russell, and Lewis Hamilton. It's backed up by a suite of images that capture the car as if it were a supermodel, though a purposely more muted presentation than previous years. After the difficulties presented by the W15's two predecessors, the team are hoping to let the new car do all the talking. Sharing the table with Paddock, along with responsibility for uploading launch content to the team's digital platforms, his colleagues Tom Dodd and Scott Gay are poised at their keyboards.

"We're up," confirms Paddock as the posts go live, and then he sits back as legions of fans around the world appraise the new W15. Immediately, the first comments begin to roll in. "Please like it," he adds with some anxiety.

Visually, the main headline is the return of the team's classic silver color into the livery mix. It's most notable at the nose and then blends progressively toward the now familiar black bodywork toward the rear of the car. As the feedback continues to flood in, stacking up in different languages but bound together by hearts, fire, and rocket ship emojis, the Instagram post alone attracts 150,000 likes in the first eight minutes. These are hardcore followers, of course, but they bring a welcome energy. At the same time, Paddock scrolls down with another lens in place. Since Lewis Hamilton announced that this will be his final year with Mercedes F1 the team have had to consider what impact this might have on the Silver Arrows' fan base. Stopping briefly to sample the responses, Paddock finally sits back and breathes. "We're good!" He slaps his hand on the tabletop. "People still give a shit."

As part of the launch, the team plan to use one of the two demonstration days allocated each season by the FIA to show off the new car on the track. This is a chance for the team to capture content, not just for their own use but also in their commitments to partner sponsors. It's also an opportunity to run the car, but there is a catch. A demonstration day is limited to no more than fifteen kilometers. That's a handful of laps of Silverstone's short National Circuit configuration, which will provide very little useful data ahead of next week's three-day test in Bahrain. According to Sporting Director Ron Meadows, as the garage begins to fill with as many engineers as mechanics preparing the W15 to face daylight, it's just enough "to check there's no silliness." Do the wheels go round? Are the brakes working? Could the car come to an ugly halt in the pit lane? In spite of rigorous stress-testing in the factory, this is a baby step that needs to go well.

"You have to start positive," says Marcus Dudley, one of several engineers to quietly carry some confidence with him. Just like many of his colleagues, George Russell's voice from the pit garage over the car radio seems refreshed by the winter break. Ready to go again. Some, however, seem more guarded than others.

In his new, crisp white shirt for the season, and hands clasped behind his back, James Allison contemplates the new car as if it were an art show exhibit. Somehow, it looks more compact than its predecessor. The flanks seem tighter, the nose blunted by a degree, as if the mystical wave that broke over this one to carve it into existence carried greater energy. When pressed, the Technical Director admits his main hope is that they've installed some behavioral discipline into this year's car.

"We know we've put loads of downforce on it, but I just want to know that the rear end behaves," he says. "We don't want the drivers to be scared of it as they were last season. It wasn't a question of asking them to 'man up.' They just need to feel connected to it, but we won't know if we've got it right until they drive the car." As for the bigger picture, Allison is circumspect. "Today's running won't tell us if we have a winner," he offers. "But it can show us if we've made a monster."

According to George Russell, who has arrived in the garage alongside Toto Wolff to inspect the car, it doesn't take long as a driver to make that initial assessment. "There's always so much anticipation when you head into a first test with a new car," he says. "So much hard work has gone into it, so many conversations, and we're all hoping it's going to be a winner. But then you can tell in 300 meters if something doesn't feel right," he cautions. "Like last year."

Half an hour later, with the team's media crews stationed at safe points along the pit lane and a crowd of partner guests lining the raised walkway that overlooks the main straight, it falls to Russell to take the W15 for its first spin around the block. He is allotted a grand total of two laps, with a significant break in between each one for the team to assess the car. Down in the garage, engineers can be seen gravitating toward data screens, awaiting the first signs of life.

"Fire up . . ."

At this empty circuit, following the call to arms over team comms by Marcus Dudley, the blast from the engine seems to carry far and wide. Collectively, everyone up on the walkway peers into the mouth of the only occupied cave as if some primal beast has just been summoned.

"OK, go!"

With Russell behind the wheel in his atoll-blue helmet, the W15 lurches into view by a meter. Even on this overcast day, the side vents gleam like shark gills.

And then . . . nothing.

The engine continues to growl, but the car doesn't move. For a heartbeat it looks like there's a problem, only for Russell to quash any such misgivings and launch the car. So assertively does he swing out into the pit lane, having just paused to prepare for this moment, that the back end of the W15 snaps dangerously close to the wall. At the pit exit, ready to capture the charger's first few moments of life on the track, a performance road car with a camera crane mounted on the back accelerates to get ahead. The filming vehicle is no match, however, for the W15, which seems to menace and harangue it up the slope and onto the track itself. Only the drone makes a clean getaway, an eye in the sky as the Mercedes F1 driver takes his new car around a 2.6-kilometer loop. Russell completes it so quickly that the car seems to rematerialize at the opposite end of the pit lane just as soon as the guests have remembered to blink, and then face the other way.

Back in the garage, judging by Russell's body language as he springs out of the car, it seems like the W15 has passed the 300-meter test.

After lunch, the car has been prepared for the Mercedes F1 driver who made headlines around the world just twelve days earlier. For many personnel present today, this is the first time they have seen Lewis Hamilton since his shock announcement that he would be leaving the team for Ferrari at the end of 2024. He's in the garage, chatting to mechanics and engineers while scrutinizing different aspects of the car with intense interest.

"Motivated and focused," the #44 driver says when asked how he's feeling about what will now be his final season with the team. "And we're going to finish on a high."

On the surface, nothing has changed. It's just inevitable that from here on in everyone views this driver so closely intertwined with Mercedes F1 through a red-tinted lens. Even his mother, Carmen Larbalestier, is among Hamilton's guests today to mark what will be his last car launch with the team.

After completing just two laps around today's circuit, the W15 seems to sit in a warmer light back in the garage. The expectations from the team for today may seem low, but at least the first driver to get behind the wheel didn't complete his session like a harbinger of doom. Later, as Hamilton prepares for his demonstration run, Shov is reassured by what he's seen so far. "At testing last year, we wasted a lot of time trying to understand why the W14 wasn't delivering the performance we expected," says the Trackside Engineering Director, "rather than just learning to understand the car that we had."

In one week's time at the Bahrain International Circuit, and with three days of exploration available, Mercedes F1 will set about putting the W15 through its paces. For now, it falls to Hamilton to experience the same preview as his teammate with a couple of clicks around the track. Given that this will be the last time the legendary #44 driver debuts a Mercedes F1 car, plenty of personnel have left the hangar workspaces to watch. Many are young enough to have missed out on the team's dominant run. Inevitably, they can't help but hope that maybe this will be the year Mercedes F1 return to the throne.

Ron Meadows stands among them. A seasoned racing veteran, he knows exactly what that takes. "I enjoy being on the back foot," he confesses. "It means we have to work hard to get where we want to be."

Like everyone else, Meadows joins the exodus from the garage just as soon as Hamilton roars off. With two laps to run consecutively this time, everyone is keen to cross the pit lane and climb the steps to the walkway overlooking the home straight. We don't have long to get into position, however, as Russell is keenly aware, having been in the driving seat that morning. "He'll be round in ten seconds," he says with some urgency, inviting people to join him at a narrow gap in the debris fencing that provides a decent vantage point. The Mercedes F1 driver is still in a cheerful mood after his introduction to the car. Hamilton will also report positively on his initial impression, but for now it's on Russell to express that with a playful glance over his shoulder at the small group massing behind him. "Unless he's not that quick."

Preseason Testing
Bahrain International Circuit, Sakhir
February 21–23, 2024

As the pit lane clock counts down to the opening session, a solitary cloud drifts in front of the sun. Rather than tone down the brightness, which is intense in this Gulf state, it can do little to screen the powerful orb. The light just fans out over the circuit in celestial beams. With the chance for all ten teams to assess their new cars over the course of three days, there can be little hiding here. Every driver on the 2024 grid will be in action, with only one car per team allowed on track at a time.

At the same circuit that hosts the first grand prix of the season in a week from now, Mercedes F1 will seek to whisper to this year's wild horse. It's an exercise in understanding, and a bid to forge a bond that has proved so challenging for the last two years. Through relentless investigation, modification, and refinement, the engineers, technicians, and mechanics will prod and probe their new creation, test experimental parts, and run through different setup configurations. From a mechanical and aerodynamic perspective, the aim is to bring this charger into peak condition while it falls to the drivers to explore its character. This is where Lewis Hamilton and George Russell will come into their own, putting in upward of 2,000 kilometers on the track between them under Toto Wolff's gaze at his seat at the helm on the central island. So many factors contribute to the ride, from tire choice and fuel loads, launch and acceleration, to braking from sky-high speeds and maintaining momentum in corners. All of which requires complete trust in machinery that should feel like an extension of their bodies. And if that falters by just a fraction then so too does performance.

As the track goes live, Mercedes F1 are keen to establish whether the successor to the W14 has evolved to behave in a way that both drivers and the engineers expect. Before attempting to climb the ladder back to the top, they need a "stable platform," which means confirming that the W15 is a responsive, predictable, and compliant car.

"Don't get distracted by what everyone else is doing," Shov reminds the race team from the pit wall as the first cars emerge onto the track. "It generally takes at least a couple of days to get a rough idea of performance. So focus on the run plan and doing it well."

Today, over the course of eight hours with a break for lunch, it falls to George Russell to explore the new car. From the garage, the engineers will collect data and information to assess how closely it correlates with simulations while informing any potential changes further into the season. Every team has broadly the same aim. They're also free to pursue their goals as they see fit. From time to time along the length of the pit lane, cars head out coated in flow-vis paint (a white or fluorescent powder mixed with oil) or clad in fine mesh frames supporting sensors, both of which help to build a picture of aerodynamic behavior. In an ideal world, the incoming data would match expectation. In reality, variants are all part of the performance puzzle and the reason why it's so important for the teams to make full use of their time on the track. "Every thirty seconds we lose is a lap at the end of the day," says Shov by way of illustration.

This season, the changes to the grid are largely cosmetic. For the first time in F1 history, the driver lineup is completely unchanged. Instead, the tinkering comes down to team names and colors. Red Bull's sister team, AlphaTauri, seem to have been rebranded by committee as Visa Cash App RB, while Alfa Romeo's transformation into Stake F1 heralds an electric green and black livery that is impossible to ignore. Appearances count for nothing when it comes to relative performance, however, even if it is hard to discern. With every team following their own plan, the leaderboard on the screens in the garage shouldn't be a focus for attention.

But inevitably it is, not least when Max Verstappen in Red Bull's 2024 F1 car overcomes a sliding start on his opening few laps to punch in a characteristically commanding time.

As sundown marks the end of the first long day, the Mercedes F1 race team regroup on the other side of the paddock for the first debrief of the year. While everyone registers that the Dutch driver looks set to maintain his dominant form, George Russell speaks with cautious optimism about his first proper shakedown in the W15.

"The main headline from me is that the car feels good," he says, echoing his first impressions from Silverstone in a meeting connecting the race team in Bahrain with personnel back in Brackley and Brixworth. "It feels nice to drive and I have substantially more stability from the rear. Corners are much better, whereas last year that's where it felt like I was getting bitten. I feel that I can really lean on the car and push. Braking feels very strong again. I'm rarely locking up the fronts today. I feel confident. But what I don't know," he adds to qualify his remarks, "is if this was a good or a bad thing considering the pace."

And there it is. The fact that nobody can ignore.

Even though the run plan afforded little opportunity for Russell to turn the wheels in anger, there is a rising sense that this may not be the car that comprehensively pulls away from all the problems of the last two years. The leaderboard everyone is supposed to disregard places Mercedes F1 in the middle of the pack. Which is why it must hurt to peek.

"We are all a little bit muted as we just hadn't got the lap time," Toto Wolff remarks later in closing the debrief, "but hearing these comments is so encouraging. We just need to work through the program, and let's see what we can do tomorrow. Red Bull seem very quick at the moment but so be it. If we are half a second off then we will work on it. Even Shov can't make it slower," he quips to finish.

"I wouldn't underestimate that," says the Trackside Engineering Director, as if a touch of humor across the table might keep the sense of optimism afloat.

*

"OK, let's fire up and hold."

With Lewis Hamilton in the cockpit on this second day of testing, it's the turn of his Race Engineer, Bono, to issue instructions to the mechanics to prepare for launch. With the engine snarling and the tires gunned into place, he gives a simple thumbs-up to send the car into the wild. As Hamilton roars down the pit lane and the din drops away, Emma Hunter, Senior Reliability Engineer, watches him go from the edge of the garage. "I'd rather see everything break now if it's going to break at all," she says, but reports nothing unexpected at this stage of testing.

In the same way, during the lunch break, Bono confirms that his driver is broadly positive in his early feedback about the car's handling characteristics. Overnight work in the sim back in Brackley has helped to iron out some handling issues identified during the first day of testing, though the W15 remains a work in progress. "No unhappy faces," Bono reports, having weighed up my question as to whether it's all smiles. "Bottom lips haven't come out."

As for the question of pace, after the team switch from long runs to single-lap performance that afternoon, Hamilton uncovers a telling trait. With the ride height lowered for the "golden hour," as the setting sun burnishes the circuit before the session ends for the day, the driver radios in that bouncing is back. The shower of sparks might look spectacular as he spars playfully with several other cars who also run their planks low to the ground to explore downforce limits, but it's a physically uncomfortable ride. "I've got such a headache," he reports over the umbilical once the car is back in the garage. "It feels like my brain has detached from my skull."

Later in the debrief, with 123 laps of the circuit under his belt, Hamilton takes a deep dive into how the car feels on his watch. "A pretty solid day," he observes, with his microphone so close to

266

his mouth we hear every breath behind his choice of words. "Everyone is working so hard and the car is definitely an improvement. It's a lot more stable than last year, but the bottoming is brutal. I wasn't gaining a lot of performance for each millimeter," he says, referring to the drop in ride height that had left the car looking more like an angle grinder in the closing laps.

Without spelling out the problem, because that's for the engineers to interpret, Hamilton returns to the central issue. The W15 has overcome a great deal of the problems that dogged its predecessor. Broadly speaking, it handles just as the drivers hoped. As a platform, the team has delivered a car that meets expectation. It's just the overall package currently lacks the raw speed that would put it into contention with Red Bull and even Ferrari in a distant second. It's not a power problem but one rooted in the same challenges the team have endured since the technical regulations changed in 2022 to encourage ground effect cars.

"This is a car that needs optimizing," concludes Toto Wolff, who has a deft way of crystallizing a long debrief into a simple call to arms, "and we are pretty good at optimizing."

By their own projections, Mercedes F1 need to find at least three-tenths of a second per lap to contend at the top. Even with all the usual caveats thrown into the mix, it's not the outcome that the team had been holding out for. Equally, there is hope here, compared to the disbelief at the gap to the front of more than half a second that marked the opening of the previous season. Unlike the W14, the new car is a team player. It responds predictably to different setups, so none of that frustration is there. The cause for concern is that it's yet to shine consistently. The engineers and mechanics can prime the car to put in a decent hot lap, or settle it down for long stints without chewing up the tires. What evades them for now is a balance between the two that delivers pace, which is critical given that setup changes cannot be made between qualifying and a race without incurring a penalty.

"It's like trying to stay warm under a duvet that's too small," says Shov in explaining the issue. "If we go too low and too stiff our neck gets cold as a result of bouncing. Too high and soft and our legs freeze because the downforce disappears."

While this testing period is not a competition, and has produced vital data to help the team find a solution, it's increasingly difficult to view the W15 in isolation from the rest of the field. With Shov's initial warnings about comparison long forgotten, any jump up the timing board inevitably invites approving nods in the garage, while a drop down is met by sighs and the odd head shake.

That evening, James Allison sums up the mood with a joke graph. It charts the flip-flopping emotions experienced by the team over a test session that ranges from *We're so back!* to *It's so over.* No doubt Allison would have preferred to deliver only good news in his update to the personnel back at the factory, who worked so hard to create this car. Even so, it serves to bring a small moment of levity to a sobering situation while reminding the team of his conviction that their continued hard work in further refining this year's challenger will deliver a positive outcome. Everyone is on the same page. Even if they need to process the reality of the situation.

Arriving at the circuit the next morning, Communications Manager Charlotte Davies accidentally walks into the toilet adjacent to the office space behind the garage. "That's an apt metaphor," quips a colleague as she backtracks to much laughter. Once everyone has settled at their desks, however, it prompts a conversation about the exacting standards this team have set for themselves. "We clawed our way from nowhere to finish second in the constructors' last year," says Adam McDaid. "The W15 is off the pace but the handling is there. That's progress, but because it's Mercedes and we're not at the front it's perceived as the end of the world."

As the third and final day of testing plays out, with driving duties split between Hamilton and Russell, it seems that Mercedes F1 aren't just gaining insight into the W15. Entering a third season since the new technical regulations came into force, this is a team assessing *themselves*. For what might have seemed like an uncharacteristic falter is now threatening to extend into a slump. No matter what the 2024 season holds in store for Mercedes F1, the team must trust the process. Empires rise and fall, but with leadership, humility, and sheer determination they can also rise again. The great unknown is in the length of time that cycle will take.

"I've been in Formula 1 for long enough to know that miracles don't happen," says George Russell on the subject of overnight comebacks. Unsurprisingly for a driver, Russell is in a hurry. He's just stopped by on the terrace outside the hospitality suite to wolf down a specially prepared meal of chicken, salad, and quinoa—the child's-sized serving being part of a weight optimization program before the season starts. On the walkway in front of us, the palm trees are strung with twinkling bulbs while the moon and the stars provide a higher illumination. As for Mercedes F1, the last three days at the Bahrain International Circuit have shed light on the path ahead. *The car is definitely a step forward and the opportunities to improve it further are very clear,* concludes James Allison in a final report to the factory that also addressed the issues they faced in frank terms. *I am looking forward massively to the fight that is ahead of us.* Like the Technical Director and the race team surrounding him, Russell is ready for the charge. The car has empowered the drivers to feel confident behind the wheel once more. The hope is that speed will come with further exploration and understanding.

"There's an optimism," he says, summing up the mood. "But

we're also not naive to the fact that Formula 1 goes in cycles. And unfortunately for us this is not the Mercedes cycle. But I think for the first time in three years, we feel like we have a car that we can build upon. And that's where the excitement lies."

Once again, the race is on in the hunt for performance. Having bolstered his meal with bread dipped in olive oil, Russell leaves well aware that time waits for no team in this sport. He's flying back to the UK this evening. There, trading shifts with Lewis Hamilton, he'll be working in the simulator ahead of next weekend's opening grand prix of the season. Hurrying down the steps to the walkway, the driver acknowledges a tall, restless-looking Canadian, whose fresh face we haven't seen throughout the winter. For Evan Short has fulfilled his annual ritual of only shaving once testing is complete. "Race trim," says the Trackside Electronics Leader, touching his jawline as if for luck before heading with purpose for the engineers' room.

It might be late in the day, but there's still much work to be done.

The Bahrain Grand Prix
Bahrain International Circuit, Sakhir
February 29–March 2, 2024

One week later, under floodlights in the pit lane, George Russell is back and raring to go as he climbs into his race seat. In his signature blue crash helmet, matching race shoes, and black Mercedes F1 overalls, he cuts a formidable, instantly recognizable presence.

"Is my personal best around this track safe?" I ask.

Russell looks up, his eyes sharpening behind the open visor. "What is it?"

"One minute nineteen," I tell him and he laughs, because we both know he'll beat that warming his tires on the out lap.

The Mercedes F1 driver is in high spirits on this eve of the Bahrain Grand Prix weekend. He might be dressed for battle, but the fight he's preparing to enter is pure fun. For George Russell is at the Bahrain International Karting Circuit, which sits in the shadow of the F1 track behind the final turn. As many personnel from across the paddock stayed over after testing it's been a popular draw, and I had joined a party from Mercedes F1 and several other teams for a somewhat ragged session. Right now, Russell is here to film an item for Sky Sports F1 along with McLaren's Lando Norris and Alex Albon from Williams. In 2019, as rookies facing their first season in F1, the trio marked their arrival with a five-lap lark in standard-issue karts. Now they're back to film a follow-up; older, wiser, but no less up for a laugh in a rare moment away from final preparations for the race weekend ahead.

Sure enough, the battle that unfolds between them is notable not just for the tight but graceful racing lines they pursue but the gleeful corner-cutting that also goes on from start to finish. It's like watching three buzzing bees mess about away from the hive, with no clear winner given the brazen rule-breaking but full marks for sheer entertainment.

Away from the track, Norris, Albon, and Russell are good friends. Once the first grand prix weekend of the season sparks into life, however, they are nothing more than rivals. Like every driver on the grid, they'll exploit any opportunity to get ahead, and the same applies to the team.

"Time for a warm-up?"

Over the comms channel from the garage, in between FP1 and FP2 the next day, Chief Mechanic Matt Deane invites his pit crew to prepare for yet another pit-stop practice. Whether it's a tire change, flap adjustment, or a new nose, Deane will rehearse this sequence so it's second nature in the race itself. This year, after the problems they faced with the pawls, the crew have been issued with redesigned wheel guns, but that's not the only reason why the team believe they'll be sharper this season.

Responding to Deane's summons, his mechanics stop working on the cars to head out of the front of the garage and through an adjacent door. The space inside serves as the team's workshop, but it's also useful for a new feature of the drill program for this season.

"Everybody take a resistance band." As they file in, new team physio Jules Stark is waiting with an open box in her hands. "We'll start with stretches."

As wheel gunners and jack operators, including the towering Karl Fanson, assemble in front of Stark in their team shorts and polo tops, it's evident that they've been working out over the winter. They're toned and even ripped in comparison to the previous season, which is down to the fact that Mercedes F1 have brought in a fitness instructor to put the pit crew through their paces back at the factory.

Outside in the sunshine, while Deane and his troops embark upon a series of squats and lunges in the workshop, Evan Short has arrived to oversee the pit-stop timing from the mobile station. He looks quietly amused. "There's a reason why they're inside," he says, indicating toward the mechanics in red who populate the garage next door. "For so long we've been taking the piss out of Ferrari about doing warm-ups in the pit lane that we're all too embarrassed to be seen doing the same thing."

This season, Mercedes F1 are aiming to find marginal gains in every aspect of their pit-stop procedure. In order for the human machine to function effectively that means paying attention to every aspect of its construction and function. As well as improving fitness—which the mechanics have embraced to the extent that they've created their own gym in the garage this weekend—Deane now rehearses the scramble from the garage to get into position. During the race itself, when the pit crew are seated, Stark will hand out caffeinated chews to keep everyone alert for the call that a car is coming in imminently. As for the punishing practice regime, an overhead camera has been deployed to help analyze movement efficiency.

"*1.94 seconds.*"

"Sticky left front."

"*1.75.*"

"Go again."

After the technician on the mobile station shares the timing of the last pit stop over the comms channel, Deane either makes observations or presses on to the next drill. He's meticulous and methodical, barely blinking as the car is rolled out of the pit box in front of him by five meters and then pushed back in. Already, the times have improved on the previous season. It's a matter of a few tenths, but that could be critical in race conditions. Despite the considerable efforts put into this upswing, Mercedes F1 are well aware that pushing too hard when it comes to finding performance in the pits could be counterproductive. Going too quickly with the new guns, for example, risks crossing a wheel nut thread. That could cost precious seconds to correct or even ruin a driver's day.

"Our focus is on consistency rather than speed," explains Jules Stark afterward as the pit crew break away, removing their mandatory helmets to reveal hot, red faces beaded in sweat. "As they become more consistent, so the speed will follow," she says. "It's a critical role and so we're trying to treat them as athletes."

Midway into FP2, the timing board has established itself as the center of attention. Having tested at this same circuit, much of the exploration and learning by the teams that would normally take up this session is over. The cars are still in their infancy, and the season's development and update barrage has barely begun. Nevertheless, an order is emerging.

By any measure, Max Verstappen seems unbeatable. His teammate, Sergio Pérez, appears to have rediscovered his form over the winter break to provide solid support to the reigning world champion. In the wake of Red Bull, Ferrari have certainly made an impressive start, while Mercedes F1 are in the fight with McLaren and Aston Martin when it comes to best of the rest. "The ride is still a limiting factor in high speed," James Allison remarks about his work in progress, "and there's still understeer to be coaxed out of the car in various places."

The Silver Arrows won't be alone on the grid in finding more performance from their new chargers. That race is well under way, and some will enjoy more success than others. With twenty-four grand prix weekends this season, the longest in the history of F1, there is also scope for any team to face a twist or turn in fortune with the potential to shake up the order.

As Red Bull have discovered for themselves in recent days, in the form of allegations of inappropriate behavior toward a female colleague by their Team Principal, Christian Horner. The story, based on allegations he has consistently denied, started swirling in early February. On the eve of this opening race of the year, an internal investigation by Red Bull cleared Horner of all wrongdoing. The team subsequently suspended on full pay the employee who had made the complaint. Midway through this second session, however, leading figures in the sport, including Toto Wolff and all the Team Principals, received an anonymous email containing what were allegedly screenshots of WhatsApp conversations and images between Horner and the complainant. On the basis of timing alone, it was designed to turn the heat up on the Red Bull Racing boss.

From one race weekend to the next, all manner of rumors and

stories emerge from the paddock as fodder for media outlets, though this one will continue to rumble on as the season progresses. At a deeper level, it raises the issue of what message it sends to women working in motorsport. "If you file a complaint," Lewis Hamilton suggests when asked to make a general comment during a press conference, "you'll be fired."

As for Red Bull, under siege by news crews for the rest of the weekend, they come to embody the fact that momentum behind a race team is not exclusively propelled by performance. Everyone within that team has to be aligned. If tensions develop—and there is plenty of talk about a wider power struggle inside the organization—it can take away that winning edge. When suggestions emerge of displeasure in the Verstappen camp about the course of events, and questions about his future with Red Bull, suddenly it seems as if the matter could have a bearing on the track.

No other team wants to see this kind of drama play out on the sidelines. It goes on to cast a shadow over Verstappen's first win of the season in a race that sees George Russell and Lewis Hamilton battle with unforeseen cooling issues to secure P5 and P7 respectively (from a P3 and P9 start). Even so, this is Formula 1. When a leading team encounters turbulence of any kind then its rivals must be ready to strike. For Mercedes F1, that means redoubling their efforts to unlock pace from this year's car should the championship leaders struggle with issues of their own making.

CHAPTER FIFTEEN

THE HOT SEAT

The Australian Grand Prix
Albert Park Grand Prix Circuit, Melbourne
March 22–24, 2024

The place card on the table displays the number 44. It's reserved for Lewis Hamilton. Thirty minutes earlier, here in the Mercedes F1 hospitality suite, the legendary driver was wolfing down a quick lunch with Bono and his engineers as they consulted telemetry charts on a laptop. Holding court with a vegan poke bowl in one hand and a fork in the other, Hamilton could have been putting a team spin on a scene from a Renaissance painting.

Now the table is empty. The engineers have dispersed, taking their race preparations with them. The surface has been cleared of everything except the place card and Hamilton's insulated water bottle. We've arranged to meet here so we can discuss his journey with the Silver Arrows, and what it means to find himself in his final season with the team. He's on his way, so I'm told, from a quick catch-up with Toto Wolff.

Mindful of the episode at the Spanish Grand Prix the previous season, in which a guest had inadvertently made himself comfortable in Hamilton's personal station behind the car in the pit garage, I hesitate about which side of the table I should occupy. Given that he had favored the bench side for lunch, I pull out the chair opposite. A moment later, just as I'm consulting my note-book at the table, I feel a hand grasp my shoulder.

"Hey man, you're in my seat."

With a start, I look up and around. The seven-times world champion is standing over me. For a split second, I'm mortified. Then I register a winning grin before he drops onto the bench opposite. Lewis Hamilton has arrived, and he's in high spirits.

"I'm just messing with you," he says on settling in to talk.

The Australian Grand Prix is staged in a breezy pocket of green-ery in what is rated as one of the world's "most livable" cities. Melbourne's Albert Park has hosted the race since 1996; long enough for the organizers to establish a temporary circuit every year that feels permanent in character. Stretching 5.2 kilometers in length, with the park's vast lake as a centerpiece, the track boasts a backdrop of tightly packed skyscrapers and the azure blue water of Port Phillip Bay. The fast-flowing fourteen-turn layout is popular with drivers, but close walls demand the utmost con-centration. Mercedes F1 have won four races at this circuit, with Valtteri Bottas last taking the checkered flag in 2019. The Finn-ish driver's successor, George Russell, also won his first podium for the team here in 2022.

Albert Park also has a reputation for staging entertaining races. There were plenty of incidents in the 2023 edition, including one riotous restart that took out four cars in the first three turns. This weekend, a record-breaking crowd fills the grandstands and spreads across grassland that is fading after a long, hot summer Down Under. The fans were in attendance long before the sup-port races started, as was Mercedes F1's reserve driver, Fred Vesti. The 22-year-old Dane is a quiet, mild-mannered young man, but a commanding presence behind the wheel of a racing car. Like so many of his peers, he's also a circuit enthusiast.

"It's special because it feels like a normal track," he had told me earlier. "The run-off, gravel, and grass creates a sense of space, which encourages the drivers to push really hard." Finishing second in the 2023 Formula 2 Championship, Vesti is a graduate of Mercedes F1's prestigious junior program. This season he shares stand-in duties with Mick Schumacher, who is away preparing for his second race with Alpine's hypercar team in the 2024 World Endurance Championship.

Having painted a picture of the Albert Park track as a fun and forgiving place to race, however, he had raised a finger of caution before revealing its true nature. "In reality, it's narrow in places with a lot of walls. That makes it very similar to street circuits such as Monaco and Singapore. The slightest mistake," he warned, and illustrated what can be calamitous consequences with a flick of his hand. "So, drivers can go in with a lot of confidence, but as soon as they go beyond the limit they're just . . . out."

A parade of broad-leafed trees spans one side of the paddock, providing welcome shade. Each team suite is fronted by a garden terrace and architectural planting. Personnel and guests occupy the tables, with so many wearing shades they could be mandatory. When an engine fires up from the garages opposite, its sustained, jagged intensity reminds everyone that beyond the laid-back vibes of this race weekend a track battle is looming. For Lewis Hamilton, Albert Park has played a significant role in his long career on the front line of F1. Making his debut here in 2007 for McLaren, the #44 driver has gone on to accumulate eight pole positions at this circuit.* Last year, in a race interrupted by three red flags, Hamilton deftly negotiated the chaos

---

* A record for the number of pole positions by a driver at the same circuit—one shared by Michael Schumacher and Ayrton Senna—until Lewis Hamilton added a ninth to his tally at the Hungarian Grand Prix.

to finish second. It's a place that he clearly enjoys, and that's evident in his upbeat manner this race weekend. At what is the third grand prix of 2024, Mercedes F1 are still in a period of discovery with the W15. After Bahrain, where the car proved to be stable on the track but lacking a performance edge, the team have focused their efforts on a schedule of forthcoming upgrades to unlock consistent pace. It meant the long straights and high-speed turns that made up the seafront track at the last race in Jeddah, Saudi Arabia, would be especially challenging for Lewis Hamilton and George Russell, who finished ninth and sixth respectively.

The team are still far from where they want to be, but compared to last year this season feels like a reset. Mercedes F1 have come to terms with the fact that despite their unprecedented run of success coming to a close, the only way is forward. What's more, the road to victory in this highly competitive sport might well be long and winding. If anything, the W15 in its current form exemplifies the complex engineering and aerodynamic challenges of building a championship winner. While the team hope to find performance in the car, right now their outlook is the driving force. There is hard work ahead, through this season and beyond, but the self-belief that it will be worthwhile is evident. As Team Principal, Toto Wolff leads the way, and yet he must count on his drivers to be in lockstep behind him.

On paper, the shock announcement by Lewis Hamilton that he would be racing for Ferrari from 2025 should have seen that onward march in disarray. In reality, Wolff has come to consider the impending seat vacancy as an integral part of the rebuild. He also continues to insist it's too soon to talk about the drivers under consideration to become George Russell's teammate. While the seventeen-year-old Kimi Antonelli, who is often described as the next Max Verstappen, is in the running, Wolff remains "in no rush at all" to fill the seat, and is content to let the season develop before reaching a decision. At the same time, the outgoing driver has acquired a new veil of mystique by pledging his ongoing commitment to the team. Nothing has changed, so Hamilton has been at pains to say, which continues to confound many in view of his decision to leave.

"I feel like I'm ending a relationship that's perfectly fine," he offers at the outset of our conversation. "We're still in love. I haven't lost faith in the team. I'm just leaving for myself."

Sir Lewis Hamilton, knighted in the 2021 New Year Honours list for his outstanding achievement and contribution to motorsport, is a man of many contradictions. Assertive on the track but humble in person, he's also an environmental advocate with plenty of air miles and a multimillionaire social equity activist. The 39-year-old Briton is certainly one of a kind, which goes some way to explaining why he's such a compelling figure in the public eye. At the heart of this enduring fascination is his hard-fought journey to becoming the most successful driver in Formula 1 history.

Resilience defines Hamilton's upbringing. Born in 1985 to a white British mother and black British father of Grenadian descent, who separated when he was two years old, the Stevenage boy's mixed-race heritage singled him out for racist abuse growing up. His modest family means also presented an initial barrier to entering a sport that had captured his imagination from an early age. Having showed determination and even prize-winning precision with a radio-controlled car, the young Hamilton forged a passion for racing go-karts. On the track, his talent set him apart from his peers. Aged ten, he became the youngest driver to win the British Cadet Kart Championship. Recognizing his son's potential, and in order to support his fledgling career in motorsport, Hamilton's father, Anthony, would take on supplementary jobs and ultimately became his manager for many years.

Rising through the ranks, from Formula Renault to Formula 3 and GP2, Hamilton earned his first seat in Formula 1 with the Mercedes-powered McLaren team in 2007. In his rookie season, the 22-year-old shone like a comet. Hamilton missed out on winning the World Drivers' Championship by a single point while narrowly beating his established teammate, Fernando Alonso, to take second place. The crown would come one season later, securing his reputation as an F1 name with a golden future. In joining Mercedes F1 in 2013, Hamilton would go on to become an unstoppable force together with his new team, earning six more drivers' titles and contributing to eight World Constructors' Championship wins. He is widely considered to be a living legend in the sport and his popular appeal has led to global recognition. When asked to define how that feels, Hamilton's response reveals an all-important grounding.

"I still think of myself as the kid from Stevenage," he says. "What's changed is people's perception of me."

In articulating how this plays out in everyday life, Hamilton calls upon a small observation that must have implications for his sense of self. "Whenever I meet someone, no matter where I am in the world, I often hear a noise from them after I turn around and walk away. That response is always different. Some people are cool and others lose their shit, but it's as if they can't show me everything face-to-face."

In conversation, Hamilton is modest by nature, which is some feat in view of his megastar status. There are few people in the world, I suggest, whose presence has the same impact. Is there anyone, I ask, who has ever had the same effect on him?

"Nelson Mandela was the real deal," he says, nodding appreciatively. Then, with a growing smile, Hamilton offers another name that he knows can't match the gravity of the late South African statesman but which clearly means a great deal to him. "And I've met Mel Gibson."

For a moment I think this Formula 1 icon, who is courted by leading figures from sport, industry, and popular culture most race weekends, is playing with me again. Instead, he shares an account of a relatively unremarkable introduction to the face of a host of nineties action movies that Hamilton grew up watching. "It blew me away," he says of the encounter, and then pauses to reflect on what that means. "Yeah, it was a nice feeling."

In observing how fans respond to Lewis Hamilton from the paddock to public appearances, it's evident that he's a hero to many people. Kids are particularly drawn into his orbit, often rendered starstruck, and the driver is adept at engaging with them. At a young age, I wonder, who did he look up to?

"My dad was my superhero," he says, without hesitation. "At school, I was bullied a lot. I'd come home and suppress my feelings about it, but he was just that strong leader who encouraged me to never give up. Dad took me boxing when I was about seven or eight," he continues. "I found myself in the ring with this kid who was the same size as me but about two years older, and proper rough. In the first round, he beat the living shit out of me. I came out crying and with a bloody nose. I told my dad I didn't want to go back in for another round. I was scared, and that was the first time he enforced the belief in me to keep pushing. So, I went into the ring for the next round with his words in mind, and that kid never landed another punch."

On the track, Hamilton is a fighter in every sense. Raw talent will only get a driver so far at this level of motorsport. It takes a combination of discipline, determination, racecraft, technical understanding, team collaboration, and an unrelenting will to win. Throughout his long F1 career, and especially with the Silver

Arrows, Hamilton has earned his reputation as the driver to watch. He's a captivating act, ferocious but fair and never shy of braking late or making bold moves stick. Combined with a back-story that contrasts sharply with the advantaged and often wealthy upbringing of so many of his peers on the track, he's the hero of his own F1 fairy tale. Over the years, Hamilton has worked hard to harness that box-office interest in him as a driver to draw attention to issues close to his heart. When asked what first motivated him to speak up on topics such as racial inequality, social justice, and environmental sustainability, Hamilton reaches for his phone on the table.

"We all use social media," he says, speaking as someone with more than 35 million followers on Instagram alone. "I just had to ask myself what I was going to do to make an impact with it? For a long time I was living the dream, winning all these world championships. Of course, I was really grateful, but it wasn't helping people." Hamilton sets his phone back on the table, an immensely powerful tool in his hands. "That's something I've always wanted to do."

The driver's efforts to make a difference off the track aren't limited to purposeful posts. In 2021, backed by an initial personal pledge of £20 million, Hamilton launched the Mission 44 foundation. Setting out to empower young people from underserved and underrepresented backgrounds, the foundation works to encourage inclusive opportunities in education and employment. It has a particular focus on STEM subjects (science, technology, engineering, and mathematics) that essentially open doors into motorsport. By extension, as the only Black driver in the history of the category, Hamilton has pledged to change the face of F1.

"I was born to race, but that isn't my purpose in life," he says, commenting on his commitment to making tangible change on issues surrounding diversity. "My purpose is to utilize the power

I've been given from winning seven world titles. I don't always get it right, but it's the thing I love to do."

For someone who has transformed a driver's paddock arrival into a high-fashion catwalk (regularly selecting clothing by under-represented and emerging designers), Hamilton is in fact quite shy at heart. He's a thinker, with a close circle of friends, heartfelt in his beliefs but forthright in expressing them in his determination to use his platform to make a difference. In finding his voice, Hamilton is quick to acknowledge the support and encouragement he's received from the team throughout his time as a Mercedes F1 driver.

"They've been incredible," says Hamilton. "When I joined from McLaren [where he felt he had to conform], I told them I was different from other drivers. I look different, and I liked to do things differently, and they just let me be who I am."

Such personal freedom off the track runs parallel with Lewis Hamilton's professional achievements behind the wheel with Mercedes F1. From 2013 onward, he seemed to grow into himself as an individual as much as a driver. Then came the unparalleled run that earned him six more drivers' crowns and contributed to eight consecutive constructors' wins. Hamilton and Mercedes F1 became a formidable force, one bonded at its core by the late Niki Lauda and Toto Wolff, whom Hamilton holds in the highest regard. For a driver with a record 103 race victories to his name as at this weekend (82 with the Silver Arrows), he surprises by nominating a moment offtrack that sums up his proudest moment with the team.

"Before the pandemic, whenever I visited the factory I came across very few people of color," he says. While lockdown curtailed operations, and caused disruption to the racing calendar that season, Mercedes F1 continued with a recruitment focus that had already been established—with encouragement from

Hamilton—to build diversity into the team. On his return to the Brackley campus, after months away, the #44 driver was struck by the transformation.

"All of a sudden I saw people from different backgrounds," he says. "That was so important to me. There's still not enough diversity in the sport, and unless that's challenged it'll stay that way, but the team are leading the change and that's just such a cool thing." Hamilton credits Toto Wolff for sharing in his values and enabling the drive, which was most visibly represented by the livery switch in 2020 from a predominance of silver to black in support of the fight against racism. In the same year, at an organizational level, Mercedes F1 launched the Accelerate 25 program, which aims to ensure at least a quarter of new starters come from underrepresented backgrounds in each year up to and including 2025. This is the purpose that Lewis Hamilton finds most fulfilling, though he's well aware that his ability to push for such a transformation comes from track success.

"They've gone above and beyond," he says of the team that now collaborates with the Mulberry Schools Trust to run a STEM academy and provide young people from underrepresented backgrounds with mentoring and work experience opportunities. "There's always more work to be done, but they're on course."

That Hamilton has nothing but praise for Mercedes F1 makes his decision to end their record-breaking relationship so intriguing. After eleven years, this season will be his last as a Silver Arrows driver. Inevitably, the driver's announcement was interpreted by many as a reflection of his faith in Mercedes F1 to return to the front of the grid once more. It's no secret that an eighth drivers' title would complete a career that Hamilton aims to look back upon as his "masterpiece." Quick to extinguish the suggestion, Hamilton presents what he considers to be one simple reason.

"It's been a childhood dream," he says of the move to Ferrari. "I think it's probably the same for every kid who loves motorsport. You know? Driving the red car. The fact is I'm moving toward the end of my career," he continues frankly. "I've only got a few years left, and so I started thinking how I'd feel looking back on it all. I asked myself if I'd be truly happy if I just stayed with the team rather than experiencing something different. I thought about it long and hard over the winter. It was a heavy time. I have this amazing thing going on here, after all. It's been a huge privilege, and I genuinely love working with everyone. I also know moving is a big risk," he concedes, "but then I *love* risk. In the end, I just couldn't get it out of my head." With a shrug and the spark of a smile, Hamilton signals that he has no further explanation. "I gotta try!"

For a driver who it was widely believed would play out his days with Mercedes F1, Hamilton knew that his decision to leave would be as painful to digest by some as it was for him to share. His priority, he says, was in breaking the news to the Team Principal, Toto Wolff, before a rumored leak made headlines.

"It was the hardest meeting I've ever had," he says of the visit to Wolff's home ahead of the new season. "I needed to do it in person because that's what integrity is all about, but I knew it would be difficult. Ultimately, as humans we're hurt when things end. But I also know that our friendship goes beyond business. That's how I view it and I hope Toto does, too."

Hamilton goes on to describe the challenge he faced the next day, shortly before news broke, having arranged to go paintballing with the Mercedes F1 race team. In view of events, what should have been a traditional preseason get together with the likes of Bono, Michael Sansoni, Evan Short, Marcus Dudley and Mad Dog took on a new complexion for the driver. "It's always been a chance for everyone to have some fun," he says. "So, I arrived in the car park and saw my team waiting to go in. They all looked so relaxed and ready to have a good time. I was just so nervous about what I had to say that for a couple of minutes I couldn't bring myself to get out of the car."

When he did summon the courage, Hamilton addressed his team after they had suited up for the session. "Everyone was so kind, so understanding, and so positive," he says, sounding as relieved now by their response as he must have been at the time, and laughs when I ask if he found himself particularly targeted when the paintballing got under way. "I'm committed to giving my all to this season," he insists, "but later this year I know there's a realization that will hit me hard. I'm not going to be visiting the factory any more, or seeing my teammates, whom I adore."

Lewis Hamilton has made a career decision that will inevitably change the F1 landscape. By his own admission, he's leaving the security of a team that has evolved around him over the years for one that may require some adaptation from both sides for him to thrive. For Mercedes F1 and their departing star, it's a chance to reinvent themselves to a certain degree. What's important to Hamilton is that he can continue to express himself freely as the Silver Arrows have enabled him to do since joining from McLaren in 2013.

"I was thirteen when I signed with them," he says of his former team, known at the time for tightly controlling driver activities and image. "Eventually it felt like I was turning into an adult but still living at home with the family. I needed to move out to my own place and experience new things. I just wanted to pay my own bills!" he adds, laughing. "I still love that team, but I'm way closer to this one. We've been together longer, and gone through so much emotionally."

Behind closed doors, without minders at his side, that majestic status conferred upon Hamilton disappears. Instead, the racer emerges, one who is entirely uncompromising in his preparations.

Throughout my time with the team, I have been present at engineering meetings where Hamilton will quiz individuals about car setup details in a way that leaves no margin for anything but the highest standards. Then again, this is Formula 1. In the pursuit of performance, anything less is just not good enough. In the rare time away from that zone, when not rushing to fulfill commercial or media engagements—often plugged into his earbuds with a fixed gaze ahead that screams "do not disturb"—the driver can afford to downshift a gear. Among the team he's an equal, and this is evident from both Hamilton and Russell when they make time to thank everyone for their hard work over the race weekend. Regardless of the outcome on the track, fist bumps are a courtesy they both extend to everyone from mechanics to marketing personnel. As the pair show their appreciation for the individual efforts across the team, it's often here that a lighter side emerges from the #44 driver. He can be quick to joke and laugh before heading for the exit. On the other side, as his security detail pick him up, fans will be waiting. As will the aura they have conjured for him.

Given his background and rise to the hallowed halls of the sport, joining racing gods like Juan Manuel Fangio, Ayrton Senna, and Michael Schumacher, the interest in Lewis Hamilton is likely to intensify with his move to Ferrari. Whatever the future holds, however, nothing can take away from his achievements with a team that means so much to him. At the same time, Hamilton is well aware that in activating a clause in his contract giving one year's notice he's also set himself a trap.

When it comes to demonstrating his ongoing allegiance to Mercedes F1 as the season plays out, his actions on the track will always speak louder than words. With the team working day and night to draw performance from the W15, currently the opportunities for him to prove it are challenging. Indeed, this weekend's race will deny him that chance when his car suffers a rare power unit failure. Despite his early retirement, and George Russell's bid for a decent points haul ending with a crash while chasing Fernando Alonso in the closing laps—just as Fred Vesti had described—the team remain focused on making progress. There are updates in the pipeline that look promising, and a growing confidence in the direction of travel. Even if those gains are incremental, they all build toward a cycle of renewal, while contributing to an F1 outfit that must back themselves at all times. And if anyone questions whether a driver preparing to race for another team might lack that loyalty and commitment, Lewis Hamilton proves otherwise on screeching out of his bay and into the pit lane during one of the weekend's practice sessions.

"That Ferrari mechanic needs to step back," he warns over the team radio, referring to a casual incursion over demarcation lines between the Mercedes F1 garage and their Italian rivals. "Next time I swear he won't be so lucky."

CHAPTER SIXTEEN

FIRE UP AND GO

The Monaco Grand Prix
Circuit de Monaco, Monaco
May 24–26, 2024

In the pit lane above the harbor, during a moment of relative peace and calm before the first practice session of the weekend, Team Physiotherapist Jules Stark faces the Mercedes F1 garage.

"Are we doing this, or what?"

A moment passes before the first figure in a black team polo shirt and shorts emerges into the sunshine. He does so with some trepidation, taking a resistance band from a box as instructed, but as more follow a collective confidence seems to build. For a pit crew who previously couldn't quite bring themselves to warm up in public before rolling out the car, this is progress.

"Some still prefer to hang back in the garage," Stark concedes afterward, but stresses that it's all about small steps. "This is new for a lot of these guys. They're comfortable around cars, but they also see that our pit stop times are improving. They recognize the reward."

This weekend, at the jewel in the racing calendar, Stark's contribution goes far beyond preparing the pit crew for the physical demands of their role. Taking into account psychological and ergonomic considerations, she's working closely with the Chief

290

Mechanic, Matt Deane, to fully realize the team's maxim: "Chase every millisecond." At the last race in Imola, Mercedes F1 topped the fastest pit-stop standings. Red Bull might have been dominant in the pit box for some time, but this is Formula 1. Every team is in hot pursuit.

Staged in Monte Carlo, a prestigious district in the tiny principality hemmed into the French Riviera, the Monaco Grand Prix takes place on a tight, narrow street circuit more suited to mopeds than today's monstrous cars.

"You can't afford to hurry preparations here." Mick Schumacher is on reserve driver duties this weekend. Having raced this unforgiving track in different classes, he is well aware that the close walls are constantly just a minor lapse in concentration away. "If you rush things," he says, looking out from the harborside paddock at the cosmopolitan enclave that hosts the race, "it doesn't end well."

Every turn at this track is a landmark, from the opening right-hander of Sainte Dévote, up the hill to the highest point at Casino Square. From there, the cars spill down to the Grand Hotel Hairpin, one of the tightest turns on the calendar, demanding special suspension components and full steering lock from the drivers in order to haul the car around. Racing along the lower section of the circuit, Portier, Tunnel, Tabac, the famous Swimming Pool chicane and La Rascasse arrive in quick succession for the drivers and provide no margin for error. With a pit lane on the inside and no gravel traps from start to finish, this short 3.3-kilometer track is punchy and potentially punishing. At best, it encourages a risk-and-reward approach to racing. With sparse overtaking opportunities available, however, the outcome can be all but determined by the qualifying grid.

So when Lewis Hamilton starts the weekend by topping the

time sheets in FP1, and with a very strong showing from both Mercedes F1 drivers in FP2 and FP3, by rights the team should be elated. It's certainly considered to be a positive development—and that's reflected in the smiles and mood inside the motor home—but not a giant leap. Realistically, according to Technical Director James Allison, "Ferrari will have their noses in front and then McLaren," come qualifying and the race. Red Bull lead the championship and remain the team to beat, but also seem to be showing recent signs of vulnerability. In Miami at the beginning of the month, much to the delight of fans sensing fractures in the established order, Max Verstappen notably failed to hold on to McLaren's Lando Norris, who took his maiden F1 win.

The pack at the front is tightening, with Ferrari also hounding Red Bull alongside McLaren, and Mercedes F1 are closing in. Right now, thanks to a herculean effort at the factory to provide updates to the W15 that are having a positive effect on the car, it comes down to improvements by a few tenths of a second. In a sport with such fine margins, this is something that a well-organized team can build upon. What might not seem like much right now can soon roll into something significant.

The Silver Arrows aren't just making small steps on the track or in the pit box. In the garage, one mechanic in particular has come to represent another modest advance that brings the team closer to their goals. Last season, way back at the Spanish Grand Prix, Spares Coordinator Georgia Parslow had traveled out to Barcelona to cover for a colleague. Having previously shadowed him at a clutch of races, and following his departure at the end of the 2023 season, the 25-year-old joined the race team to become the first full-time female mechanic for Mercedes F1.

"I feel like I've gained twenty-six big brothers," says Parslow on summing up how it feels to be working in such a male-dominated environment at the track. "I'm here on merit and everyone recognizes that. We work, eat, travel, and socialize together. I just had to find my place in the puzzle."

While Parslow's priority is to make sure all the parts required for the car are requested, tracked, and delivered on time, she is well aware of the significance of her presence in such a high-visibility environment. During pit-stop practices, she stands out among several mechanics who volunteer to push the car into the box. "I'm only five foot high, so that attracts attention," she laughs. "But it's also really nice when little girls visiting the pit lane notice me. I see their eyes follow me around, and imagine they're wondering about the possibilities."

Parslow first found her calling during work experience as a 16-year-old, when she chose to join her father at a Mercedes road car dealership. Such was her enthusiasm and proficiency that she earned the opportunity to spend a week with Mercedes F1. "On my first morning at the Brackley factory, just walking from the stores to race base, literally everyone said hello. I knew straight-away that I could belong here."

Working with vehicle parts for close to nine years has left Parslow "looking at a car and picturing it broken down into components like flat-pack furniture." She's also developed a pio-neering attitude as a woman in this field, taking great pride in overcoming obstacles. On discovering that clothing for garage personnel only catered for men, Parslow was pleased that Mer-cedes F1 rectified the oversight. "Team gear for female mechanics is coming through now," she says, and suddenly seems to grow in stature on the strength of her smile alone. "If that makes life a little easier for the next generation of women, then I've made a difference."

As the qualifying hour approaches, it feels as if expensive yachts from nautical miles around have been drawn into the harbor by the magnetic pull of this millionaires' haven. Serving as a theater auditorium for the race weekend, everything from luxury hotels and grand apartment blocks to historic buildings rises up in tiers behind the waterfront track. Even the clouds peeping over the steep hills behind the principality could be gathered to witness the session. As for the box seats in the house, they can be found on a vessel dedicated to Mercedes F1 that's so commanding it's moored outside the harbor walls.

Part of the Ritz-Carlton Yacht Collection, *Evrima* is a flagship in every sense.

At 190 meters long, and boasting 149 luxury terraced suites, it's more of a sky-high-end cruise ship. This weekend it's host to the team's partners and guests. They'll enjoy appearances from Toto Wolff, George Russell, and Lewis Hamilton along with a special concert—on deck and under the stars—by singer-songwriter John Legend. With tenders zipping back and forth between the ship and the jetties in the harbor, Mercedes F1 have extended their reach at this Monaco Grand Prix in the most visible way. It builds on the success of the Miami and Vegas Clubs, as well as more recent headline spectacles. Just a few weeks earlier, Hamilton brought New York's Fifth Avenue to a standstill with a showcase run and several donuts in the W12 to celebrate a new partnership with WhatsApp. The previous evening, in collaboration with the team, the instant messaging giant had lit up the Empire State Building with an animated light show to introduce the new Mercedes F1 racing car emoji.

The scale and ambition of such events speaks to the enduring popularity of the Silver Arrows. What's most striking, perhaps, is the fact that Mercedes F1 have gone without a race win since Brazil in 2022, when George Russell claimed his first F1 victory. Confounding conventional thinking when it comes to commercial interests in motorsport, the recent challenges faced by the team do not seem to have diminished the strength of their part-nerships. Even as one of the most recognizable brands in sport, with a 2023 turnover exceeding £500 million (an increase of just over £70 million compared to the previous year), Mercedes F1 know that ultimately performance is the lifeblood. This weekend in Monaco, there is a strong sense that the team is entering a new phase. Nobody expects Hamilton or Russell to top the time sheets in qualifying. Even so, there is a growing confidence in the stream of car updates now arriving at each race weekend. In briefings, press conferences, and interviews, drivers talk of the team having found its north star at last.

For any team in this sport with a target in mind, a confidence in the direction of travel is more important than the distance it faces. When George Russell secures P5 on the grid for the Monaco Grand Prix, just 0.001 seconds behind McLaren's Lando Norris, it's a measure of just how tightly contested the fight at the front is becoming. That Verstappen's Red Bull sits behind Russell in P6, sandwiched by Hamilton, is one more encouraging sign.

Since the wake-up call of the opening race of last season, Mer-cedes F1 have come a long way. The 2023 season wasn't the comeback the team had envisaged: a quick return to their championship-winning ways after a single-season blip. Instead, it became an exercise in fighting for every available point with a challenging car to finish second in the World Constructors' Championship. Toto Wolff has often talked about resilience as a winning quality, but it's only when a team are in a chasing posture that it's truly put to the test.

Inevitably, as such a trying season progressed, attention turned to the next car in the making. Could the W15 transform the team's fortunes? In this sport, only the stopwatch can provide the definitive answer, which meant waiting for the new season to begin. While the car started the season lacking ultimate pace, it succeeded in providing the stable platform that had been lacking in the W14. After the disappointment of a double DNF in Melbourne (a race weekend that demonstrated how sheer bad luck can be a contributing factor for any team when the wheels start spinning), Mercedes F1 have begun to build on solid foundations at last. From Japan to China, and Miami to Imola, and with a huge push from the factory to fast-track updates, the team stabilized in terms of position while steadily gaining traction on their rivals. It's all relative, of course, as Technical Director James Allison is keenly aware.

"The playing field is continually in motion," he says, which means any progress on the track can only be measured against the competition. By this metric, eight races into the season, Mercedes F1 are pulling away from the pack behind and closing in on a tightening fight at the front. It's not a question of a comeback but a turning point, and one that has been a long time in the making.

The team today is very different from the tight but tense outfit I joined eighteen months earlier. In that pit garage, as the timing board determined the grid order for the opening race of the 2023 season, Mercedes F1 carried their previous success like a yoke around their shoulders. "There was definitely an anxiety that with eight consecutive Constructors' Championships we couldn't afford to have another off year," reflects the Trackside Electronics Leader, Evan Short. "We felt we were out of position. In reality, it was exactly where we should have been. Once we came to terms with that we could focus on the fight."

This weekend, three months into the 2024 season, Mercedes F1 are in a better place. The hunger to win is just as fierce. It's the only way to survive in this sport, but now the team are entirely forward-facing. If anything, they're emerging from the pain and frustration of recent years with a sense of liberation. Even

Hamilton's surprise announcement that he would be leaving feeds into the belief that a reset is under way. Mercedes F1 made motor racing history with their reign from 2014 to 2021, but it doesn't determine their future. It's a view that's expressed in different ways across the team, but one perhaps best summed up for me on a recent visit to the factory. Back at base, Engineering Director Giacomo Tortora told me he had learned from a long career in the sport that there's only one way a team with multiple championships can stage a successful tilt toward contention. By way of illustration, he called upon his experience working at Maranello for eight years until joining Mercedes F1 in 2021.

"At Ferrari, people used to say *quando vincevamo*, which means 'when we used to win.' Every time I heard that expression," he said of moments when the Italian team attempted to resurrect their constructors' victories from 1999 to 2004, "I knew that bad decisions were going to be taken. Why? Because the sport has moved on, and new people have joined the team with fresh ideas. So, if you try to get back to ways that put you first on the grid, you're going to be dead last. Being good again isn't doing what you used to do. It's something you have to reinvent." There, Giacomo Tortora had taken a breath as if to consider outlining what that involves, before choosing instead to just smile. "And I *love* it!"

Formula 1 is an infernally challenging sport and by extension exquisitely rewarding. On a technical level, it comes down to a quest for mechanical and aerodynamic mastery. The manufacture and production demands to deliver and develop two cars each season are relentless, and wrapped up in a complex operation on a par with a military campaign. From a driver's perspective, making every moment on track count requires outstanding levels of precision, consistency, communication, and bravery. Combined with the tactical considerations in competition to reach the finish line first, the commercial pressures to fuel the undertaking, as well as fan engagement to drive marketability and even morale, the orchestration required from every team to bring it all together is immense. Unlike the NFL, NBA, or the Premier League, the players on this field aren't exclusively responsible for the final result. The majority are in position behind the scenes and number into the thousands. It means if Mercedes F1 are to excel, every member of the race team and the workforce back at the factories in Brackley and Brixworth must work as one.

In essence, performance begins with the *people*.

Increasingly over the last eighteen months, I've come to recognize that individual commitment from every level of the team isn't just an expectation but a reality. More immediately, in everyone I've got to know and observed in action, it comes from the heart. I've been at circuits, shortly before a race, when a mechanic hurries into a back-room workspace in search of spare chairs for the pit crew. Each time, nobody pretends to tune out and stare a little harder at their laptop screens. Everyone gives up their seats without hesitation, volunteers to carry them across to the pit garage, and then finds a way to continue working on their feet. Then there's the standing ovation that the engineers give a driver on arriving at a debrief after a notable achievement, or the fact that the factory operates in a state of near constant mobilization. There, I found everyone from student interns onward recognized their contribution to be as essential to the overall effort as an overtaking move on the track. Two drivers and a team boss might represent the face of Mercedes F1. Behind it, there is a collective that must operate at the same high level as the car itself. The work is intense, and both recognized and rewarded, but it's not the binding element at the heart of Toto's tribe.

That comes down to values.

Most significantly, they're not simply buzzwords on an office wall. They form the soul of the team. From passion to innovation, teamwork, commitment, and even kindness, these are qualities that personnel embody as much as a competitive spirit that's central to the sport. It's the right thing to represent, as many will say. It also feels good to make such a contribution in a collective environment.

In line with Wolff's vision for Mercedes F1, this is how championships should be won.

In writing this book, it could be said that I joined the team at the worst possible time. Instead of the promised comeback, Mercedes F1 effectively wrote off their hopes of being championship contenders for the 2023 season after qualifying for the first race. In doing so, however, I witnessed a team undergo a period of soul-searching and then rebuilding that said more about the character of the Silver Arrows than a cabinet full of trophies. Eighteen months later, as the lights go out on my final grand prix weekend without having witnessed either driver lay claim to a win, the team must feel I'm leaving at the worst time, too. I view things differently.

Here in Monaco, the race finishes with the top ten in the same grid order in which it started. Despite the absence of overtaking, Mercedes F1 still make meaningful progress. George Russell does a fine job of preserving worn tires to keep Max Verstappen at bay while Lewis Hamilton claims an extra point for the fastest lap. In doing so, he becomes the first F1 driver to achieve one in seventeen different seasons.* This year, Monaco belongs to its native son and Ferrari driver Charles Leclerc, but Mercedes F1 leave with something they've been working to gain for so long. I register it for myself in a team boss whose

---

* A record previously held by Michael Schumacher, who registered a fastest lap in sixteen seasons.

office door is open, the excited talk in the motor home surrounding potential drivers to partner Russell moving forward,
the bearing of the race engineers as they file from a debrief,
updates that deliver on track as the simulations predicted, and
the telemetry charts that prove the Silver Arrows are quietly
gaining ground.

As my time embedded with Mercedes F1 comes to an end, I
leave a team beginning to build a force that can be pivotal in
this sport: momentum. It starts with incremental improvements,
which can still make a difference in this highly competitive
sport, but as everything aligns—and that forward motion gathers
ground—performance can be exponential.

"The trajectory is going in the right direction," says Toto Wolff
quite simply in the scrum out in the pit lane after the Monaco
race, and he knows the value in that. In Formula 1, a sport that
demands so much from so many, that growing sense of propulsion
isn't about grabbing the occasional podium but creating the right
environment within the team to mount a sustainable championship campaign.

Breaking a cycle in F1 might well be possible, but nothing can
replicate the energy that comes from embarking upon a new one.

Every team has the potential to push toward the front of the
grid, of course, and in recent years that all-important momentum
has belonged to Red Bull. In a competition in which each team is
already traveling at full throttle, Mercedes F1 have had to meta-
phorically pit and then return to the track with a renewed sense
of purpose, improved traction, and more efficient racing lines.
They have some catching up to do, but both on and off the track
I see a team locking into place what it takes to return to the front
in time. And should that lead to another reign, as can happen in
this sport, the Silver Arrows will have achieved it by cutting
themselves loose from a glorious past and growing from the

experience. As Toto Wolff sees it, having come through a reckoning of his own over the winter period, Formula 1 is a race without end. Until the checkered flag falls on his active career, as it will for everyone within the sport, what matters is the journey.

"I want to look back when I'm eighty and say to myself that I was successful in my own benchmarking," he had remarked to me on considering what Mercedes F1 will mean to him when all is said and done. "There is no sports team in the world that has won every single championship they entered on a sustainable basis. We have won eight of the last ten championships, and then finished third and second. That's not a failure. This is Formula 1. We are fighting against formidable teams, and I want to put more Mercedes stars on our famous wall," he added, referring to a giant grid on display in the Brackley factory accounting for every constructors' win since the championship began in 1958. Each square contains a team badge and represents a battle fought across a season. Lotus loom large in the early days, as do Williams throughout the eighties and nineties. McLaren also become a winning force throughout this time while Ferrari pepper the grid across five decades. Among others, Cooper, Brabham, and Renault are in the mix, along with the great outlier in the form of Brawn's single-season win. Then there's Mercedes F1, the longest unbroken line of badges on the grid. It might be bookended by Red Bull, but the most telling standout is all the empty squares that follow. The wall is impressive, but there's only one way to truly appreciate the intensely competitive story it represents, and that's where Toto Wolff now stands. "I'm looking at the bigger picture," he had said to finish.

That evening, as the mechanics strip down the cars in the pit garage and the sun settles over another race weekend, I head out of the paddock for the final time. Along the way, I say goodbye to

Mercedes F1 personnel who have allowed me to be part of their tribe for so long.

"You don't have to be writing a book about the team to be welcome here anytime," says Shov as we shake hands, though of course plenty of his colleagues quip that perhaps I'd like to return for a sequel when they're winning.

When people who work in F1 choose to move on from this relentless, all-consuming sport, they say it takes some adjusting to get used to the slowing in pace. As I take my pass in hand to swipe out through the gates, I know how they must feel. As does Mercedes F1's veteran Chief Mechanic, Matt Deane, I think, who catches me before I go.

"I'll never leave," he jokes, having said that I'll know where to find him. "This sport gets into your blood. It becomes a way of life."

EPILOGUE

Shortly after the start of the 2024 season, on a sheet of paper torn from my notebook, Technical Director James Allison sketched a drawing of the W15 to illustrate what he believed to be holding back performance. With the car in side profile, and the understanding that the detail of what followed was for my eyes only, he proceeded to add lines between anchor points, arrows, and figures. What had struck me more than the technicalities that Allison unpacked in layman's terms was his conviction that the issue could be overcome.

"It was a difficult birth, and that's been quite distressing for all of us because we should have seen it coming," he said candidly of the car and his responsibilities. "But although the problem is complicated, it's not *infinitely* complicated. We're getting a handle on it, and soon we'll reach a point where we move from the back to the front foot."

The exchange took place at the factory in Brackley. There, the workforce were in high gear producing a stream of updates for the W15. With a succession of subtle aerodynamic and mechanical fixes, adaptations and evolutions ahead, scheduled across race weekends through the first half of the season, the Mercedes F1 Technical Director came across like someone whose faith in the team was matched by his appreciation of physics as an objective force. As Allison completed the calculations to support his drawing, it seemed that in his mind there could be only one outcome.

If that transition to the front foot commenced at the 2024 Monaco Grand Prix, the process would soon gather pace. A fortnight after closing the gap to the front of the pack on the streets of Monte Carlo, Mercedes F1 command attention—and bring jubilant scenes to the pit garage—when George Russell claims pole position at the Canadian Grand Prix. In a demonstration of just how fine the margins have become in this sport, Russell and Verstappen match each other to the millisecond as they cross the line in qualifying, with the #63 driver set to start at the front having chalked up his lap time first. Finishing an eventful race in P3, with his teammate advancing through the field from P7 to P4, both Russell and Hamilton echo Allison's gratitude to the personnel back at Brackley and Brixworth for their extraordinary spirit through a challenging time. *We have been pushing so hard, and it is completely undeniable that these efforts are starting to bring us what we are seeking,* the Technical Director writes in his update from the Montreal paddock to the factories. *There is more to come . . . and the days ahead should be exciting.*

A fortnight later at the Spanish Grand Prix, a P3 and P4 finish for Hamilton and Russell respectively serves to strengthen the belief that the team are on a positive trajectory at last. It's not quite enough to catch the Red Bull–to–beat, Max Verstappen, though Lando Norris fills the Dutchman's mirrors. As an engine supplier to McLaren, that's enough for Mercedes to believe it can be done. The momentum is undoubtedly growing, and yet nobody can foresee how the next two races will play out. In Austria, George Russell is in position to capitalize on a late tangle between

Norris and Verstappen to claim the team's first victory since his sole F1 win in Brazil back in 2022.

"Yabba Dabba Doo!" he yells over the team radio on taking the checkered flag, an impromptu victory cry and a gift for the Mercedes F1 social media team. It's a win by a driver at the top of his game that Toto Wolff has longed to see, and though the upswing in performance played a part, so too did the fate of the team's rivals on track. *Yes, it was a result of their misfortune,* concedes Shov in his turn to deliver the trackside dispatch, *but more than that, it was a result of our collective hard work. This team exists to win championships and if we can continue to work like we have done then we will achieve that goal in the not-too-distant future.*

Just one week later, in front of a record-breaking crowd at Silverstone, there can be no doubt that the Silver Arrows have returned to contention. With George Russell in fine form to qualify in pole position, and Lewis Hamilton in P2, the front row lockout brings a sense of validation. This is a team, a whole organization, emerging from a long, humbling and challenging period. Yes, there's a sense of excitement as well as rising hope after all the effort that has gone into providing the drivers with a competitive car. As the lights go out for the start of the 2024 British Grand Prix, however, it's tempered by the fact that Mercedes F1 have been through so much to get here. With false dawns on that journey, Wolff and his race team must not depart from the process that has advanced them to this moment.

In a race marked by rain, sunshine, and high drama, both George Russell and Lewis Hamilton discover something that has been so hard for the team to deliver sustainably for several seasons: pace. The cars punch through the circuit's high-speed straights and corners, and swing like pendulums through the counterturns of Maggots and Becketts. Both Norris and Verstappen challenge, with the McLaren driver taking the lead in damp conditions, but ultimately the result belongs to Mercedes F1. The handling is there, as are the speed and assured strategic calls. Heartbreakingly for Russell, so too is a critical cooling problem that forces an early retirement after a stellar drive. It leaves his teammate leading the charge for the line, and a thrilling closing stint in which the roar of the fans on their feet in the stands exceeds the thunder of the cars on track.

On taking the checkered flag, Lewis Hamilton claims his first grand prix win since the penultimate race of 2021. It's a momentous achievement on many levels. For an elated Toto Wolff, this is "a fairy tale" for the team and for the #44 driver, marking their final British Grand Prix together, and their 150th podium as a driver–team partnership. For Hamilton, it marks his 104th career victory and a record-breaking ninth win for an F1 driver at the same circuit. The significance is not lost on him, moved to tears over the team radio as he brings the car home. "Thank you so much, guys. It means a lot to get this one. A big thank you to all the fans. Love you guys . . . I love you, Bono."

For Hamilton's Race Engineer, who will be invited onto the podium to accept the constructor's trophy on behalf of the team, the win ranks as one of the most emotional in his long-standing partnership with the driver. "It's been 945 days since his last win," says Peter "Bono" Bonnington. "As time passed, that doubt crept in for Lewis as much as me. In our minds, we started to ask if we were still capable. Without a championship-smashing car, could we still rise to the occasion when we had the chance to make a difference?" He pauses there and grins. "Well, it turns out that we can."

During the final stint of the race, with Verstappen giving chase, Hamilton's Race Engineer admits that it was a struggle to stay focused. "Silverstone is a magical place because you can hear the sound of the crowd following the cars around the circuit. It's like a wave of noise, and that's all I could hear each time Lewis came out of the final corner. I started getting ahead of myself, thinking we could win this, and had to pull myself back into the moment so I could do my job. It was only on the final lap that I knew it was done. Lewis just had to bring it home, and when he crossed the line the pit garage erupted like we'd won the championship."

The joyous scenes that closed the 2024 British Grand Prix will come to be one of the defining moments for Mercedes F1. From George Russell waiting in parc fermé to be the first to congratulate Hamilton, to Toto Wolff celebrating with team veterans and relative newcomers for whom this is a new experience, it's a victory several seasons in the making. "Lewis and I have never received so many messages of congratulations," Bono tells me later, though admits that the pair had slightly different experiences from each other. "He had messages from the likes of the other Bono and Barack Obama. Mine were mostly from my neighbors."

As for James Allison, who sketched out the issue with the W15 and led the unrelenting efforts by the men and women at the factory to engineer a solution, it's a win earned by every member of the team. "There's something irreplaceably precious about doing a job that serves up such strong emotions," says the Mercedes F1 Technical Director, reflecting on this turning point as much as the experience of recent years. "When it hurts, it really hurts. But when it's good, there's nothing like it. And today was really, really good."

ACKNOWLEDGMENTS

Like most things in motor sport, this book represents the efforts of a committed team behind the scenes. I'd like to extend my heartfelt thanks to my editors, Ben Brusey at Penguin Random House and Aubrey Martinson at Crown Publishing. I am also very grateful to Joanna Taylor, David Edwards, Daniel Balado-Lopez, Jessica Fletcher, Cameron Watson, Ania Gordon, and Hana Sparkes for their invaluable contributions. For the cover design, my thanks go to Peter Routh, Claire Lythgoe, James Laing, May Glen, and Dan Simpkins. Then there's Philippa Milnes-Smith and Eleanor Lawler at The Soho Agency for keeping it all on track.

At home, a big thank-you goes to my wife, Emma, and my family for understanding the nature of life in Formula 1. For eighteen months, it took me away in every sense, but the checkered flag has finally fallen. I am also grateful to Paul and Joanne Sinton-Hewitt for taking such good care of Sprint during the final stint.

Finally, a heartfelt thanks to Toto Wolff and everyone at Mercedes F1 for allowing me to join the team with my notebook and pen for such an extended period. Your welcome, transparency, helpfulness, hospitality, and good humor went above and beyond all expectation. It's been quite a ride.

INDEX

ABOUT THE AUTHOR

Matt Whyman is an award-winning novelist and writer of non-fiction. Whyman has co-written books with some of the world's leading figures in sport, high performance, and popular culture, including Gareth Southgate, Matthew Syed, Billy Connolly, and Sir David Attenborough.